THE Baseball ◇25◇ Research JOURNAL

Editor: Mark Alvarez
Designated Reader: Dick Thompson
Copy Editor: A.D. Suehsdorf

THE BASEBALL RESEARCH JOURNAL (ISSN 0734-6891, ISBN 0-910137-66-8), Number 25. Published by The Society for American Baseball Research, Inc. P.O. Box 93183, Cleveland, OH, 44101. Postage paid at Birmingham, AL. Copyright The Society for American Baseball Research, Inc. All rights reserved. Reproduction in whole or in part ... prohibited. Printed by EBSCO Media, Bir...

SABR PUBLICATIONS ORDER FORM

BASEBALL RESEARCH JOURNAL

The *Baseball Research Journal* is the annual publication of the society featuring some of the best research done by members. Articles range from statistical in nature to biographical sketches, plus nearly every other topic in baseball.

____	1975 (112 pp)	........................$3.00
____	1976 (128 pp)	........................$4.00
____	1977 (144 pp)	........................$4.00
____	1978 (160 pp)	........................$4.00
____	1979 (160 pp)	........................$5.00
____	1980 (180 pp)	........................$5.00
____	1981 (180 pp)	........................$5.00
*	1982 (184 pp)	
*	1983 (188 pp)	

larger format

____	1984 (88 pp)	........................$6.00
____	1985 (88 pp)	........................$6.00
____	1986 (88 pp)	........................$6.00
____	1987 (88 pp)	........................$6.00
____	1988 (88 pp)	........................$7.00
____	1989 (88 pp)	........................$8.00
____	1990 (88 pp)	........................$8.00
____	1991 (88 pp)	........................$8.00
____	1992 (96 pp)	........................$7.95
____	1993 (112 pp)	........................$9.95
____	1994 (112 pp)	........................$9.95
____	1995 (144 pp)	........................$9.95

BASEBALL HISTORICAL REVIEW
____ 1981; Best of the '72-'74 BRJs $6.00

INDEX TO SABR PUBLICATIONS
____ 1987 (58 pp) $3.00
TNP, BRJ & SABR Review of Bks, V. I

BASEBALL RECORDS UPDATE 1993
____ 1993 ....$4.95
Changes to the Statistical Record found by the SABR Baseball Records Committee

HOME RUNS IN THE OLD BALLPARKS
____ 1995 ....$9.95
.....member price, $5.95
Listings of top 5 HR hitters in parks no longer in use.

AWARD VOTING
____ 1988 (72 pp) $7.00
History & listing of MVP, Rookie of the Year & Cy Young Awards

THE NATIONAL PASTIME

The National Pastime features articles by members more general in nature, although some volumes are arranged around a theme, as noted below.

____	#1 Fall, 1982 (88 pp)	........$5.00
*	#2 Fall, 1983 (88 pp)	
____	#3 Spring 1984 (88 pp)	
	19th Century Pictorial	$7.00
____	#4 Spring 1985 (88 pp)	........$6.00
____	#5 Winter, 1985 (88 pp)	........$6.00
____	#6 Spring, 1986 (88 pp)	
	Dead Ball Era Pictorial	$8.00
____	#7 Winter, 1987 (88 pp)	........$6.00
____	#8 Spring, 1988 (80 pp)	
	Nap Lajoie Biography	$8.00
*	#9 1989 (88 pp)	
____	#10 Fall, 1990 (88 pp)	........$8.00
____	#11 Fall, 1991 (88 pp)	........$7.95
____	#12 Summer, 1992 (96 pp)	
	The International Pastime	$7.95
____	#13 Summer, 1993 (96 pp)	........$7.95
____	#14 Summer, 1994 (112 pp)	........$9.95
____	#15 Spring, 1995 (156 pp)	........$9.95
____	#16 Spring, 1996 (144 pp.)	........$9.95

THE FEDERAL LEAGUE OF 1914-15
____ 1989 (64 pp) $12.00
Baseball's Third Major League

THE NEGRO LEAGUES BOOK
____	1994 (382 pp, softcover)	........$29.95
____	1994 (382 pp, hardcover)	........$49.95
____	1994 (382 pp, limited edit.)	......$149.95
	(Leather bound, slipcase, autographed)	

COOPERSTOWN CORNER
Columns From The Sporting News *by Lee Allen*
____ 1990 (181 pp) $10.00

RUN, RABBIT, RUN
Tales of Walter "Rabbit" Maranville
____ 1991 (96 pp) $9.95

SABR REVIEW OF BOOKS
Articles of Baseball Literary Criticism
____	Volume 1, 1986	........$6.00
____	Volume 2, 1987	........$6.00
____	Volume 3, 1988	........$6.00
____	Volume 4, 1989	........$7.00
*	Volume 5, 1990	

* - out of print

SABR's Books on the Minors

MINOR LEAGUE BASEBALL STARS
____ Volume I, 1978 (132 pp)
over 160 player records $5.00
____ Volume II, 1984 (158 pp)
175 players + managers $5.00
____ Volume III, 1992 (184 pp)
250 players $9.95

MINOR LEAGUE HISTORY JOURNAL
a publication of SABR's Minor League Committee
____	Volume 1 (40 pp)	..........$6.00
____	Volume 2 (54 pp)	..........$6.00
____	Volume 3 (72 pp)	..........$7.00

SABR's Books on the 19th Century

NINETEENTH CENTURY STARS
____ 1988 (144 pp) $10.00
Bios of America's First Heroes (Non-Hall of Famers)

BASE BALL: HOW TO BECOME A PLAYER
by John Montgomery Ward *(reprint of 1888)*
____ 1993 (149 pp) $9.95

Baseball's Regional Flavor

SAINT LOUIS'S FAVORITE SPORT
____ 1992 Convention Publication (64 pp) $7.50

A HISTORY OF SAN DIEGO BASEBALL
____ 1993 Convention Publication (40 pp) $7.50

TEXAS IS BASEBALL COUNTRY
____ 1994 Convention Publication (48 pp) $5.00

BASEBALL IN PITTSBURGH
____ 1995 Convention Publication (64 pp) $7.50

UNIONS TO ROYALS:
THE STORY OF PROFESSIONAL BASEBALL IN KANSAS CITY
____ 1996 Convention Publication (64 pp) $7.50

Book Shipping Costs
1 book	$1.50
2-3 books	$2.50
4-5 books	$5.00
6-10 books	$7.50
11+ books	$9.00

Book delivery is usually 3-6 weeks.

Membership Dues _____

Book Total _____

Shipping _____

TOTAL _____

Discover, Master Card & Visa Accepted

SABR members receive *Baseball Research Journal, The National Pastime*, one or more special publications, a membership directory, and *The SABR Bulletin*, SABR's newsletter. Additional membership benefits include access to a National Convention and regional meetings, research exchange and research paper collection, the SABR lending library, occasional discounts on baseball trade publications and 6,000 other baseball enthusiasts like yourself around the country and the world.

To join SABR, send check, money order, Visa, Master or Discover Card in US funds or equivalent (dues are $35 US, $45 Canada, Mexico; $50 Overseas) to SABR, PO Box 93183, Cleveland OH 44101.

Name: _____

Address: _____

City, State, ZIP: _____

8/8/96

Card # _____

Exp Date _____

Signature _____

Lowest Season ERA? Ferdie Schupp.

He meets the criteria

Daniel R. Levitt

Last summer while on vacation I picked up an interesting book from 1947 by Frank Menke titled *The Encyclopedia of Sports*. The baseball section contained a table listing "Least Earned Runs," i.e. the lowest single-season ERAs. I was surprised to see that the lowest single season earned run average was credited to Ferdie Schupp of the New York Giants for his 1916 ERA of 0.90 in 140 innings pitched. The current encyclopedias and record books award the single season ERA record to the table's second pitcher, Dutch Leonard, for his 1.01 ERA (often shown revised as either 1.00 or 0.96) in 1914 for the Boston Red Sox, and the 1916 NL ERA title to Grover Cleveland Alexander and his ERA of 1.55.

This situation intrigued me, so I looked into it. After investigation I have to conclude that Ferdinand M. Schupp should indeed be recognized as the ERA champion for 1916 and thus the record holder for lowest single-season ERA.

As a brief career note, Ferdie Schupp went on to lead the Giants to the pennant the next year while leading the league in winning percentage with a record of 21-7. Although he played until 1922, Schupp never regained his effectiveness when he returned from the service after the First World War.

I think three tests must be met in order for Schupp to be credited with the ERA record. First, the mark must have been recognized at the time it was recorded. Second, the record must be accepted for a sufficiently long period afterward. Exactly how long "sufficiently long" is can obviously be debated; however in the present case the time frame is nearly forty years. Finally, no new *facts* should appear that call into question the mark itself. When *qualifications* for a particular statistical championship change, previous leaders in these categories do not forfeit a title; only when *facts* are adjusted is any change in a prior designated annual leader contemplated. The following analysis demonstrates that Schupp clearly meets all these criteria.

The single-season Earned Run Average record is typically calculated from one of three years: 1893, when the pitching distance first became 60'6"; 1901, when the so called modern era began; or 1912 (1913 in the American League), when ERA first became an official statistic. Ferdie Schupp's 1916 ERA would be a record under any of these three starting dates.

Recognition—The New York *Times* of November 28, 1916, devotes four paragraphs to National League pitching leaders for the year. The headline for the article is "SCHUPP LEADS PITCHERS." The subtitle to the article reads "LESS THAN ONE RUN PER GAME SCORED OFF YOUTHFUL GIANT," and the first paragraph begins, "Ferdie Schupp, the youthful lefthander of the Giants, was the most effective pitcher in the National League last season, according to the official averages compiled by Secretary John A. Heydler."

In the November 30, 1916, issue, *The Sporting News*

Daniel R. Levitt is a past president of the Halsey Hall Chapter of SABR and recently attended his first national convention outside his home state of Minnesota. He thoroughly enjoyed himself.

reports the final National League pitching averages. The headline for the article is "FERD SCHUPP MAKES REMARKABLE RECORD FOR EFFECTIVENESS IN BOX." The article is subtitled "NATIONAL LEAGUE PITCHING AVERAGES SHOW GIANTS' SOUTHPAW ALLOWED LESS THAN ONE EARNED RUN PER GAME IN 1916—ALEXANDER STEADIEST PITCHER." The introductory paragraph summarizes Schupp's season as follows:

> Ferdinand Schupp, the New York Giants' little southpaw, who didn't get started until after midseason, made a new and remarkable record for pitching effectiveness in the National League in the 1916 season. Pitching 140 innings, Schupp allowed but 14 earned runs (runs for which the pitcher was responsible) or less than one earned run per game. Four of Schupp's eight complete games were shutouts. He allowed but 79 hits in his 140 innings. For effectiveness he therefore stands in a class by himself.

Spalding's Official Base Ball Book for 1917 lists the "official records of National League pitchers who participated in twelve or more games during the season of 1916." The top of the list notes they are "Arranged According to Percentage of Earned Runs per Nine-Inning Game." Schupp and his 0.90 ERA sit at the top of this ranking.

Further evidence that the being atop the pitcher records constituted league leadership can be found in the *next* year's arrangement, when the National League adopted the ten-complete-game qualification standard. The introduction to the National League pitcher records for 1917 in the 1918 *Spalding Guide* notes:

> In arranging the National League pitchers of 1917 in order of their effectiveness, it was found expedient to divide the 83 pitchers into three groups. The first of these embraces all those who bore the brunt of the campaign and pitched at least 10 complete games....

That the above change signaled a new qualification standard is further evidenced by the introduction to the pitcher records in later guides which refer back to this change in 1917. For example the 1923 *Spalding Official Base Ball Record* refers to arranging the pitcher records for 1922 into three groups, "the same arrangement as the past five years." That is, the ten-complete-game standard began five years previously, in 1917.

Clearly, the pitcher placed at the top of the ERA rankings was the accepted leader. When the standard for qualification changed, a different organization for the rankings was devised.

Longevity—Schupp's record was recognized for a sufficiently long period of time. A number of additional examples can be cited indicating Schupp was long credited with the single-season ERA record.

The 1923 *Spalding Base Ball Record* includes "The Little Red Book" which contains "Records Of Previous Years." Under "Major League Record Holders 1876-1922," the "Best Earned Run Average Since 1900" is credited to F. Schupp at 0.90.

The Sporting News Record Book for 1929 contains a paragraph titled "Ferd Schupp's Great Record." The paragraph concludes:

> ...for in 1919 [sic], Ferd Schupp of the New York Giants allowed an average of less than one [earned run] per game. Schupp's average for that year was .90 earned runs a game, a great record.

The Sporting News Baseball Guide and Record Book for 1943 contains a section entitled "Outstanding Major League Records." Ferdie Schupp and his 0.90 ERA is listed under "Lowest Earned-Run Average, Season, Majors."

Official Baseball 1945, published by A.S. Barnes and the authorized guide for that year, includes a single page titled "Major League Topnotchers." The mark for "Lowest earned-run average season (since 1912)" is credited to Ferd. M. Schupp .

Finally, *The Official Encyclopedia of Baseball*, Revised Edition, by Hy Turkin and S.C. Thompson (1956) contains a section listing annual league leaders. The earned run average leader for 1916 in the National League is Schupp at an ERA of 0.90. No pitcher is listed with a lower ERA.

The above examples covering nearly 40 years indicate that Ferdie Schupp was widely held to be the single-season earned run average record holder.

No new facts—No hidden earned runs or twice recorded innings pitched have ever been suspected. *Total Baseball, Fourth Edition*, records Schupp with 140 innings pitched and an ERA of 0.90, as did the official National League records at the time.

Only in the cases of revised facts, such as the discovery that Ty Cobb twice received credit for a 1910 game, is changing the recognition of an annual league leader debated. In the case of evolving playing time qualifications for a particular statistic, league leaders are not adjusted. For example, the current qualification requirement for the ERA title is one inning pitched for each game the team plays. Four pitchers are rightly recognized as single-season leaders despite not meeting this standard. These pitchers all qualified under the previous ten-complete-game standard discussed above: Monte Pearson in 1933 threw 135 innings, Howie Pollet in 1943 recorded only 118 innings pitched, Hank Borowy in 1945 threw only 122 innings, and Jim Hearn was awarded the league ERA title in 1950 despite only 134 innings pitched.

Ferdie Schupp was recognized as the 1916 earned run average leader and as the record holder for a significant period of time thereafter. He should be recognized as such today.

Ever wonder why they called him "Wild Bill"?

Wild Bill Pierson pitched for Connie Mack in 1918, 1919, and 1924. His 31 walks in 32 career innings may have accounted for his nickname, but then again, Bill seemed out of control in more ways than one.

If Bill Pierson, recently reinstated by Commissioner Landis, returns to active duty, either with the Philadelphia Athletics or some other club, he will be seen on the mound wearing spectacles. Pierson, during the time he was out of the game as an ineligible, was the victim of an explosion that impaired his vision and he has had such trouble with his eyes since that he has to wear glasses.

—The Sporting News, *November 29, 1923*

William Pierson, a former major league pitcher, who was with the Giants and Athletics, was shot in the right leg in an Atlantic City cafe last week. The player, who has lately been connected with minor league clubs, refused to discuss the affair.

—The Sporting News, *December 22, 1927*

Bill Pierson, 29, a pitcher, who had brief stays with the Philadelphia Athletics and Pittsburgh Pirates, fell into the meshes of the law in Atlantic City last week. He, with two other men, was held without bail on a charge of robbery. Police claim the trio has been responsible for a number of store holdups.

—The Sporting News, *December 20, 1928*

William (Wild Bill) Pierson, formerly a pitcher for the Philadelphia Athletics and Pittsburgh Pirates, was convicted of grand larceny and carrying concealed weapons at Mays Landing, N.J., last week. He had been arrested in Atlantic City on a charge of robbing stores and faces a sentence of 20 years in prison.

—The Sporting News, *April 25, 1929*

—Dick Thompson

World Series Sweeps

More than you think

Father Gerry Beirne

Everyone knows that George Stallings' Miracle Braves of 1914 were the first team to sweep a World Series—four games straight. Right? Moreover, since 1914, eleven more teams have swept their other league rivals in four-game sweeps (1927, 1928, 1932, 1938, 1950, 1954, 1963, 1966, 1976, 1989 and 1990), with the Yankees naturally as leaders in both Series Swept (five) and Being Swept (two). But are these the only World Series "four-straight-games-won-sweeps?" In the words of Sportin' Life in "Porgy and Bess," "It ain't necessarily so."

Before 1914, two other teams had already won four straight games in a single World Series, and since then eight more clubs have won four straight World Series games—in Series that went more than four games. There are three situations in which one team won four straight World Series games without being credited with a sweep—they are, first, a tie game, second, losing the first game, and third, losing more than the first game. Let's take a closer look.

1903: Boston (AL) 5, Pittsburgh (NL) 3—The 1903 World Series was initiated by Pirates Prexy Barney Dreyfuss, who magnanimously invited the junior circuit upstarts to meet his mighty Pirates in a best five-of-nine playoff. Henry Killilea's Boston Pilgrims were the intended victims. Both teams featured great playing managers—Fred Clarke in left for Pittsburgh and Jimmy Collins at third for Boston. Cy

Young (28-9) opened for Boston but gave up four runs in the very first World Series inning. Jim Sebring hit the first home run and Pittsburgh jumped to a 3-1 lead in games before the pitching-rich Bostons (Bill Dinneen 3-1 plus Young 2-1, 45 strikeouts combined) overcame a weary Pirates staff. Deacon Phillippe completed five games, winning three of them. He was not enough, however, to beat back the Boston tandem which hurled 69 of the 71 Boston innings, to sweep the final four games and capture the inaugural World Series.

1907: Chicago (NL) 4, Detroit (AL) 0, One Tie—This was the first of three consecutive years of Detroit Tiger failure in post season play. The best they could muster was a 3-3 tie in Game One with the vengeful Cubs, who had been upset by the White Sox Hitless Wonders in 1906. The toothless Tigers plated only three more runners in the four remaining games and committed nine errors to help the swoon. Ty Cobb batted .200, Germany Schaefer .143, and Sam Crawford .238 against the Chicago mound quartet of Mordecai Brown, Ed Reulbach, Orval Overall, and Jack Pfiester, whose collective ERA was a snappy 0.75. Only 7,300 Detroit fans turned out for the finale.

1915: Boston (AL) 4, Philadelphia (NL) 1—This is not customarily considered a World Series sweep, but the Red Sox did win four straight over the Phillies

Father Gerry Beirne is the pastor of St. Philip's Church in Greenville, Rhode Island, home of the semi-annual Lajoie-Start Regional meetings.

after Grover Cleveland Alexander's opening game win on a neat eight-hit, six-strikeout affair. This year featured the same two cities as the previous Fall Classic only with the two league representatives flip-flopped, and Braves Field serving as the home field for the Bostonians because of its larger seating capacity. The rival managers, the Phillies' Pat Moran and the Red Sox's Bill Carrigan, were both New Englanders and former catchers. Babe Ruth led the Sox that year with four home runs, while Gavvy Cravath dwarfed the Babe and everyone else with 24 homers and 115 RBIs. In front of Woodrow Wilson, the first United States President ever to see a World Series game, Rube Foster spun a three-hitter and drove in the winning run in the first of four Red Sox wins. Over 40,000 saw Dutch Leonard beat Alexander 2-1, and then Ernie Shore topped George Chalmers, again 2-1. Harry Hooper hit two homers in Game Five, and Foster beat Rixey, 5-4, as Boston won three of the four games in their final at bat.

1920: Cleveland (AL) 5, Brooklyn (NL) 2—Brooklyn had an excellent pitcher in Burleigh Grimes (23-11), but Cleveland had an excellent staff. Stan Coveleski was 24-14, Jim Bagby 31-12, Ray Caldwell 20-10, and late season addition Duster Mails was a perfect 7-0. The first three games were in The Borough, with the home team winning twice, but when the Series went to the city by the lake, it all turned sour for the Robins. Coveleski won Game Four on a five-hitter. Game Five was the famous "Bill Wambsganss triple play-Elmer Smith grand slam-Jim Bagby first homer by a pitcher" contest, Cleveland winning as Bagby gave up 13 hits but only one run. Mails beat Sherry Smith 1-0 on three hits in Game Six and Coveleski made his third start, completed his third game, threw his third five-hitter and got his third win, besting Grimes 3-0. Brooklyn scored just two runs in the final four games, hitting only .205 with nary a home run in the Series.

1922: New York (NL) 4, New York (AL) 0, One Tie—This year saw the World Series revert for good to a seven game set, but it was the same teams, stars and ball park (Polo Grounds) as 1921. Again, it was Meusel against Meusel, McGraw against Ruth and the Giants against the Yankees. Game One went to the National Leaguers 3-2 on a three-run eighth inning, Rosy Ryan getting the win in relief over Bullet Joe Bush (26-7). Game Two was the scandalous tilt which umpires Klem and Hildebrand called after the tenth inning "with 45 minutes of sunshine remaining" and

the clubs tied at 3-3. There was such an ugly outcry that Commissioner Landis ordered that the proceeds ($120,000) be sent to military hospitals. With all games played in New York, there were no days off between games, and the men of McGraw took their last world championship in succeeding days with Jack Scott besting Waite Hoyt, 3-0, Hugh McQuillan over Carl Mays, 4-3 and Art Nehf winning the final game for the second year in a row, 5-3, again over Bush.

1942: St. Louis (NL) 4, New York (AL) 1—In the first of the war years, the Yankees were at the top of the baseball world and, as expected, beat the "Kiddie Kardinals" in Game One 7-4, Red Ruffing over Mort Cooper. But youngsters Stan Musial, Marty Marion, Whitey Kurowski, and Johnny Beazley stunned the New Yorkers by sweeping the next four in a row. Beazley beat Tiny Bonham; Ernie White dealt the Yanks their first World Series shutout in 42 games; Max Lanier bested Atley Donald, both in relief, in Game Four, and Beazley came back to best Ruffing again 4-2, in the finale to surprise the perennial champions as well as the rest of America. Only Jimmy Brown hit .300 (exactly) for the Cards, while the Yanks outhit them 44-39 (Rizzuto walloped .381), the Cards made ten errors to New York's five and left 32 men on base to 34 Yankees. While the Yanks evened the score in 1943, these Cardinals were good enough to be the last National League team to win three consecutive pennants, repeating as World Champions in 1944 and 1946.

1969: New York (NL) 4, Baltimore (AL) 1—The Miracle Mets fell, as expected, to Mike Cuellar (23-11), 4-1, in Game One, even behind their own 25-7 ace, Tom Seaver. Ho-hum, the public mused, will it be Jim Palmer (16-4) and Dave McNally (20-7), or McNally and Palmer the rest of the way to squelch the euphoria of these expansion, upstart wannabes? After all, the Mets were synonymous with losing and the Orioles had won the American League East by 19 games in the first year of divisional play.

In Game Two, Jerry Koosman gave up only two singles and Al Weis drove in the winning run with a ninth-inning single to even the Series. Gary (13-12) Gentry drove in two runs while giving up only three hits before he got relief help from Nolan Ryan, who gave up one more. Tommie Agee added to the Met magic with a leadoff home run and a dazzling catch to nudge the Mets ahead, two games to one. In Game Four, Cuellar again gave up just one run, but so did his bullpen, and so did Seaver, as the Mets won 2-1 in ten innings on Pete Richert's throwing error.

The die seemed cast even though Baltimore took a 3-0 lead in Game Five. But the Long Islanders were not to be denied—all the breaks went their way. A Donn Clendenon homer followed a disputed Cleeon Jones HBP. Al Weis, only .215, two homers, 23 RBIs in the regular season, but .455 in the Series, hit another home run and two Oriole errors gave the championship to the Miracle Mets, four games straight after the opening game loss.

1978: New York (AL) 4, Los Angeles (NL) 2— This season saw a post-season first—a team won the first two games and then lost the next four! It was the third straight Series for this fine late-seventies Yankees club. Billy Martin had been replaced as manager by Dick Howser and then Bob Lemon in midseason. Tom Lasorda was at the Dodger helm. The same two teams had squared off in 1977, the Yanks winning 4-2, with Mike Torrez getting two victories. This, however, was the year of "wait until next year!" LA roared out of the gate with an 11-5 first-game victory, Tommy John over Ed Figueroa. Game Two was also captured by the West Coasters, Burt Hooton over Jim Hunter, as Bob Welch, in high drama, fanned Reggie for the final out with the winning run on base.

Back in Gotham, however, gravy turned to glue as Ron Guidry bested Don Sutton, 5-1, as Graig Nettles turned back several Dodger rallies with sterling third-base play. Game Four saw Jackson beat Welch, this time in ten innings. His controversial "hit-by-shortstop's-throw" broke up a double play and allowed one run to score. In the tenth, his single set up Lou Piniella's game winner to even the Series. Game Five was vintage Yankee—a 12-2 massacre.

In Los Angeles the home team turned to Don Sutton (15-11) to keep them alive. He gave up five runs in five innings, while Catfish Hunter and Goose Gossage yielded but two Dodger tallies as the Yankees became the first team to ever win the World Series in four straight games after losing the first two. Brian Doyle hit .438, Bucky Dent .417, and Reggie Jackson .391, while the touted Dodger mound staff mustered a dismal 5.47 ERA. Davey Lopes' three home runs matched the entire Yankee team, and Bill Russell had

eleven base hits, but the New Yorkers were tough and determined, and victorious.

1981: Los Angeles (NL) 4, New York (AL) 2— "What goes around, comes around" and 1981 was the flip side of 1978. The ten-week strike cancelled 713 games, and the playoff system eliminated the Cardinals and Reds, two teams with better regular season records than teams that made the playoffs. This time the Dodgers spotted the Yankees a two-game lead, only to come back and sweep the next four straight. Poor George Frazier of the Yankees was saddled with three of the losses. Fernando Valenzuela got the first Dodger victory in Game Three. Game Four saw ten pitchers yield 27 base hits, but the Dodgers prevailed 8-7 on shoddy New York outfield play and bullpen work.

Despite three Dodger errors, Jerry Reuss overcame Guidry and Gossage to capture Game Five 2-1 as the National Leaguers edged ahead. Burt Hooton recovered from his 1978 6.48 ERA nightmare to be the winning pitcher in Game Six. Pedro Guerrero drove in five runs and was named Co-MVP with Steve Yeager and Ron Cey. Besides Frazier's 17.18 ERA, other Series "non-illuminaries" were Dave Winfield, sho hit .045, Davey Lopes, who committed six errors, and Bob Welch, who did not retire a single Yankee batter in Game Four.

1983: Baltimore (AL) 4, Philadelphia (NL) 1— Our final four-game-sweep-in-a-more-than-four-game-World-Series is the 1983 fall classic. Just as in 1915, the Phillies won Game One, behind John Denny for their sole victory. The rebuilt Phils were dubbed the "Wheeze Kids" because of their advanced age—Rose, Morgan, Perez, McGraw, and Carlton were all around 40. For the Orioles, Joe Altobelli was trying to win a World Series as well as a pennant in his first year as manager. Baltimore was led by MVP Cal Ripken and near MVP Eddie Murray, but it was light-hitting Rick Dempsey who was voted Series MVP because of his timely and powerful hitting. Garry Maddox, who had hit a Game One home run, became the final out of the Series when winning pitcher Scott McGregor got him on a liner to short.

Maris in '61 vs. Ruth in '27

A comparison of baseball's two greatest homer seasons

Jerry Sulecki

One of the principal reasons the single-season home run record of '61 by Roger Maris has not been broken in recent years has been the curtailing of certain players' schedules due to work stoppages and injuries.

Ken Griffey, Jr. and Matt Williams both had fantastic chances at Maris' record when their seasons ended.

There has once again been talk of a juiced-up baseball and even all-time home run leader Hank Aaron suspects the ball is "wrapped very, very tight" though "some people may deny it."

Aaron thinks someone like Albert Belle with his tremendous power, his unwavering focus, a homer-friendly ball park, and the proper supporting cast will 'hammer' this mark very soon.

Barring the unforeseen, the single-season home run record will almost certainly be broken. It will happen soon because of ballplayers religiously following weight, strength, and diet regimens year-round, pitching talent being diluted due to team expansion, and the strike zone being defined smaller than ever.

This, then, is a good time for a summing-up comparison between Roger Maris' and Babe Ruth's record-setting seasons.

What follows is everything statistically anyone might want to know about Roger Maris in 1961 and Babe Ruth in 1927.

Asterisk or no asterisk.

	G	AB	H	BA	R	RBI	1B	2B	3B	HR	TB	SA	BB	SO
Maris	161	590	159	.269	132	142	78	16	4	61	366	.620	94	67
Ruth	151	540	192	.356	158	164	95	29	8	60	417	.772	138	89
+ or -	-10	-50	+33	+.087	+26	+22	+17	+13	+4	-1	+51	+.152	+44	+22

Home Runs by Team

	Bal	Bos	Chi	Cle	Det	KC	LA	Minn	Phil	ST.L	Wash	Total
Maris	3	7	13	8	8	5	4	4	X	X	9	61
Ruth	X	11	6	9	8	X	X	X	9	9	8	60

Jerry Sulecki umpires softball and officiates high school football in Ohio.

Home Runs by Inning

	1	2	3	4	5	6	7	8	9	10	11	12	Total
Maris	8	2	14	10	3	7	7	7	2	0	0	1	61
Ruth	17	1	4	6	7	7	5	7	4	0	2	0	60

Home Runs with Men on Base

	None	One	Two	Three	HR RBI	Total RBI	HR/RBI Pct.
Maris	31	20	10	0	91	142	64%
Ruth	30	22	7	1	99	164	60%

Home Runs At Home and Away

	Home	Away	Total
Maris	30	31	61
Ruth	28	32	60

Home Runs by Day-Night-In Doubleheaders

	Day	Night	1st Game	2nd Game
Maris	40	21	2	7
Ruth	60	X	10	6

Percentage of League Home Runs

	HR	Pct.		Next Highest
Maris	1,196	5%	46	J. Gentile (BAL)
Ruth	439	14%	17	K. Williams (ST.L)

Percentage of Team Home Runs

	HR	Pct.		Next Highest
Maris	240	25%	54	M. Mantle (NY)
Ruth	158	38%	47	L. Gehrig (NY)

Home Runs by Month

	April	May	June	July	Aug.	Sept.	Oct.	Total
Maris	1	11	15	13	11	9	1	61
Ruth	4	12	9	9	9	17	X	60

Home Runs by Day of Week

	Sun	Mon	Tue	Wed	Thu	Fri	Sat	Total
Maris	14	1	13	11	4	6	12	61
Ruth	15	9	6	7	8	12	3	60

Home Runs by Date—First Half of Month

	1	2	3	4	5	6	7	8	9	10	11	12	13	14	15	Total
Maris	2	5	2	3	1	3	2	0	3	0	3	1	4	1	2	32
Ruth	2	1	1	0	2	3	3	1	2	2	4	2	2	0	1	26

Home Runs by Date - Second Half of Month

	16	17	18	19	20	21	22	23	24	25	26	27	28	29	30	31	Total
Maris	3	3	1	2	4	2	2	0	1	4	3	0	1	0	2	1	29
Ruth	3	2	1	0	1	1	5	2	2	0	2	2	3	4	3	3	34

Home Runs off Various Pitchers and Their Records

	Total Pitchers	LH	RH	Total Wins	Total Losses	Pct.	Mean ERA	> .500	< .500
Maris	47	9	38	385	415	.481	4.32	23	24
Ruth	33	9	24	347	380	.477	3.97	15	18

Indicative Data

	HT	WT	B	T	Bat Inches	Bat Ounces	Hall of Fame?
Maris	6'0"	197	L	R	35	33	NO
Ruth	6'2"	215	L	L	35	44	1936

Age When Breaking Home Run Record

	Years	Month	Days
Maris	27	0	21
Ruth	32	7	24

Years Holding Home Run Record

Maris   1961 to 1996 = 35 Years

Ruth   1927 to 1961 = 34 Years

Sources:

Roger Maris* A Title to Fame by Harvey Rosenfeld, Prairie House, Inc. Fargo, North Dakota (1991)

The Ballplayers, Edited by Mike Shatzkin, William Morrow, New York, New York (1990)

The Life that Ruth Built, by Marshall Smelser, Bison Book, University of Nebraska Press, Lincoln, Nebraska (1993)

Baseball Encyclopedia, Macmillan Publishing Company, New York, New York (1990)

Fleeting Major League Moments

Herb Washington may be the most prolific career pinch runner, scoring 33 runs in 101 appearances as a pinch running specialist with the Oakland Athletics in 1974-75. However, he was just one of two dozen players whose major league careers consisted solely of pinch-running appearances, with no chance at bat or appearance in the field. Eddie Phillips and Jack Cassani are runners-up to Washington as career pinch runners.

Phillips pinch ran nine times for the 1953 St. Louis Cardinals, scoring four runs in his September duty that year, as the Cardinals tried to hold on to third place in the National League. Phillips was successful in scoring the first three times manager Eddie Stanky sent him in to pinch run, all eighth-inning scoring rallies in games the Cardinals went on to win, on September 10, 13, and 16. But he was only successful in scoring one more time in six attempts, a seventh-inning rally in the second game of a September 22 doubleheader as the Cardinals defeated the second-place Braves, 10-7. While Phillips pinch ran for the likes of position players Ray Jablonski, Red Schoendienst, Solly Hemus, and Harry Elliot in pre-ninth-inning situations, Phillips never took the field or got up to bat.

Cassani pinch ran eight times for the 1949 Pittsburgh Pirates, scoring three times. On Opening Day, April 9, at Chicago's Wrigley Field, he pinch ran for Dixie Walker in the top of the ninth inning of a scoreless game, and scored the game's only run on a bases-loaded fielder's choice. Cassani scored twice more in seven pinch-running chances, but like Phillips never saw major league action again.

—Charlie Bevis

A Baseball Rarity

1-0 games won by a steal of home

L. Robert Davids

While there have been 565 1-0 major league games won by a home run since 1876 (Ted Williams did the honors five times), diligent research into the last 100 years has uncovered only sixteen 1-0 games won by a steal of home . Of course, the circumstances are quite different as the long-ball hitter wins the game with one swing of his bat. Most of the drama is tied to that boundary belt in an otherwise scoreless contest. Games won by steals of home have little connection with batting power. They are won by speed, alertness, and aggressiveness. Almost always it is a team effort, and the opposing pitchers are an important part of that package. Here is a brief rundown of each game.

July 25, 1897
Fourth inning
Bill Dahlen, Colts vs Colonels at Chicago

Dahlen returned to the Colts' lineup after a long absence due to injury and was given a spirited ovation. He responded with a special game performance. With light rain falling, he singled to rookie Honus Wagner in right-center. Walter Thornton bunted him to second, and Bill moved to third on a throwing error to first base. Perry Werden returned the ball to pitcher Bert Cunningham, who dropped it, picked it up, and prepared for delivery. Dahlen, who had moved off third, dashed for the plate. Cap Anson, the 45-year-old player-manager, who was batting, welcomed him home. Louisville came back in the sixth, but "a foxy trick of Fred Clarke cost the Colonels a run." The Captain singled and reached second on Tom McCreery's bunt. The second-base bag came loose and Clarke picked it up and ran for third. Pitcher Jim Callahan threw to third-baseman Bill Everett, who tagged Clarke on the basepath. The latter protested, saying he had possession of second base. Umpire Hank O'Day did not let this technicality influence his vigorous out-call. The rain became heavy in the seventh and the game was called.

Aug. 11, 1899
Second inning
Bill Dahlen, Dodgers vs Colonels at Brooklyn

John Anderson led off the second with a bunt single. Bert Cunningham then hit Dahlen with a pitch, and "Doc Casey sacrificed both runners up a peg." Duke Farrell hit back to the box and Cunningham threw out Anderson at home as Dahlen moved to third. Catcher Chief Zimmer then moved forward as Farrell ran for second and threw him out. Dahlen scampered to the plate and scored because Cunningham, who took the return throw from second-baseman Claude Ritchey, failed to touch "Bad Bill." Brickyard Kennedy won for the Dodgers and Cunningham lost his second 1-0 game to Dahlen and Company.

L. Robert Davids *is the founder of SABR and the compiler of* Baseball Briefs.

April 28, 1906
Ninth inning
Frank Chance, Cubs vs Reds at Chicago

In the last of the ninth in a nothing-nothing game, manager Chance, batting cleanup, took matters into his own hands. He singled to right off Jake Weimer and moved to second on a one-base blow by Joe Tinker. Johnny Evers strode to the plate, but Chance signaled him back and called on Pat Moran to pinch hit. Moran rapped a hard one to Jim Delahanty at third, who tried for a double play, and did get Tinker at second, but Joe blocked little Miller Huggins' throw to first. Huggins protested vigorously and demanded that umpire Bill Klem declare Moran out at first because of Tinker's interference. Chance had moved to third on the play and as the quarrel intensified, dashed for home with the game-ending run. Weimer had allowed six hits and Mordecai Brown, the winner, four. There was one double play: Tinker to Evers to Chance.

July 6, 1914
Fourth inning
George McBride, Senators vs Red Sox at Wash.

McBride, captain of the Nats, doubled off Red Sox hurler Rankin Johnson and moved to third when Eddie Ainsmith flied deep to Tris Speaker in center. With Rankin pitching to Walter Johnson, his opposite number, McBride took off from third. The ball pitched was inside, but the Big Train did not budge from the plate until George was almost on top of him. It was a close play, but the split-second timing resulted in a "safe" call from umpire Oliver Chill. Rankin Johnson gave up six hits and Walter four. It was the latter's sixteenth 1-0 win. He would go on to pitch a record thirty-eight 1-0 wins in his career.

May 18, 1915
First inning
Frank Schulte, Cubs vs Giants at New York

Jeff Tesreau of the Giants whiffed Art Phelan and then gave up a double to Bob Fisher. Schulte rapped to Art Fletcher at short and he ran down

Fisher. Heinie Zimmerman singled Frank to third and then the two crafty base stealers engineered a double steal. Schulte's score stood up for the next eight innings. The winning pitcher was Bert Humphries, who had topped the NL in percentage with a 16-4 mark in 1913. He and Big Jeff each allowed only three hits. It was Suffragettes Day at the Polo Grounds and the ladies declared they would donate $5 to each player scoring a run. It was a bargain day for them. When Schulte was given the "fiver" in a brief ceremony at the end of the game, he passed it on to Mrs. Schulte, who "had left the growing peaches in Georgia long enough to attend the Gotham series."

July 27, 1915
First inning
Clyde Milan, Senators vs Indians at Wash.

With teammate Dan Moeller camped on third base, Milan bounced a ball to Jay Kirke at first base. Kirke threw home to catch Moeller, but the elusive runner was able to maneuver back and forth between home and third until the speedy Milan reached the hot corner. Cleveland hurler Rip Hagerman took a long windup against batter Oscar Shanks and Milan, a top base stealer of that era, beat the ball to the plate. In addition to his speed on the bases, Milan saved the game in the field. In the third, Bill Wambsganss (carried as Wamby in the box score) belted a surprisingly long drive to deep center. Running at full throttle,

Clyde Milan on the basepath.

Milan snagged the ball over his shoulder. Clyde had to share the limelight with Washington hurler Bert Gallia, who allowed only one hit while Hagerman gave up two. Joe Jackson hit for Hagerman in the ninth but grounded out in a very close play.

June 5, 1916
Fourth inning
Heinie Zimmerman, Cubs vs Braves at Boston

Zim led off the fourth with a double and trotted to third on a fly by Vic Saier. He stayed there while Jimmy Archer tapped back to Braves' hurler Art Nehf for the second out. With weak-hitting Eddie Mulligan at bat and Nehf winding up, Heinie dashed for the plate. "Nehf pitched the ball on the wrong side just wide enough to let Heinie escape the tag." Four hits were made off winning pitcher Gene Packard and five off Nehf, who was described as "also southpawed." Packard fielded very well, making seven assists and one putout at home plate. The year before, on September 29, 1915, he had won a 1-0 game for Kansas City in the Federal League on his own home run.

August 27, 1917
Fourth inning
Max Carey, Pirates vs Giants at New York

Carey, who would lead the National League in stolen bases ten years, beat out a bunt and reached second on a single by Tony Boeckel. Both attempted to move up on the next pitch by Rube Benton. Max reached third, and when he saw that Boeckel got entangled with Buck Herzog at second, he set off for home and made it. Wilbur Cooper was the winning pitcher, while Benton took the loss. Honus Wagner, in his final season at age 43, played first base where he was credited with fourteen putouts. Jim Thorpe pinch-hit for the Giants in the ninth to no avail. This was Carey's thirteenth steal of home. He attained a career total of thirty-three, a National League record.

June 14, 1919
Third inning
George J. Burns, Giants vs Cubs at Chicago

Burns was undoubtedly the star of the game with two doubles and the SOH in the third stanza. He forced Giants' hurler Fred Toney at first base before Ross Youngs singled him around to third. They then signaled a double steal. Cubs' catcher Bill Killefer made a short throw to second and the ball was returned immediately to the plate—but too late to catch Burns. Toney won the 1-0 game over southpaw Jim Vaughn of the Cubs, a game reminiscent of the famous nine-inning double no-hitter between the Reds and Cubs, which Cincinnati and Toney won 1-0 in the tenth on May 2, 1917.

June 25, 1931
Seventh inning
George Watkins, Cards vs Dodgers at Brooklyn

Dazzy Vance had retired the first twenty-one Cardinals in order until Watkins, who had batted .373 as a rookie in 1930, bunted safely in the seventh. Jim Bottomley singled him to third. "Vance immediately began his well-known routine of lobbing two throws to first before firing a fast one over there." Watkins waited only for the second toss and took off. When first-baseman Del Bissonette received the routine throw, he quickly air-mailed the ball home, but Watkins had already crossed the plate. Bottomley moved to second on the double steal. Rookie Paul Derringer, who allowed six hits, was the winner. Vance gave up three and lost.

May 8, 1939
Sixth inning
Pepper Martin, Cards vs Dodgers at Brooklyn

Pitcher Russell "Red" Evans of the Dodgers was locked in a torrid hurling duel with Lefty Bob Weiland of the Cardinals and made the mistake of not paying attention to veteran Pepper Martin on third base. Martin had singled and moved to third on infield outs by Joe Medwick and Johnny Mize. Pepper decided that if those power hitters were not able to drive him in, he would go on his own. He had the unknowing cooperation of Evans, who let him stray at least fifteen feet off third. Even some fans shouted "pick him off." The Wild Horse of the Osage galloped homeward. "Evans awakened a fraction of a second too late as Martin slid across the plate." Brooklyn manager Leo Durocher tried to pull the game out in the ninth when former Yankee teammate Tony Lazzeri singled. Leo then batted for relief hurler Ira Hutchinson, but rolled weakly to second for the final out. I asked Red Evans, who was a SABR member from Arkansas in the early 1980s if he remembered the Martin steal of home. He said, half-jokingly, "I still have nightmares about it."

August 5, 1942
Fifth inning
Don Kolloway, White Sox vs Tigers at Chicago

Kolloway opened the sixth with his second single of the game off Hal Newhouser. Wally Moses bunt-singled him to second and Don moved to third when

Myril Hoag grounded into a double play. On the first pitch to Luke Appling, he broke for home and nicked the corner of the plate with his left shoe. Detroit catcher Ed Parsons said he had tagged the runner, but, when he argued too long and loud, he was ejected by umpire Bill Summers. Losing hurler Newhouser, who was 8-14 that season, gave up seven hits and fellow southpaw Ed Smith five.

August 25, 1944
Third inning
Joe Hoover, Tigers vs Browns at Detroit

A wartime replacement player for Detroit, the good-fielding shortstop batted eighth. Hoover opened the third with a single off Denny Galehouse. He then stole second and moved to third when pitcher Dizzy Trout grounded to George McQuinn at first base. Joe remained at the hot corner as Roger Cramer flied out to Al Zarilla in short left. Eddie Mayo walked and when Galehouse pitched to Pinky Higgins, Mayo made a belated break for second. When he became temporarily trapped in a rundown, Hoover dashed for the plate. This brought a throw from McQuinn, but Joe "deftly avoided the tag of Brownie catcher Frank Mancuso." Mayo completed the double steal and Rudy York shortly ended the inning by fouling out. Trout allowed only four hits overall. It was his fourth shutout and twenty-first win of the season. Galehouse gave up four hits in seven innings and George Caster one. Although the Browns lost this close contest, they beat out the Bengals by one game to win their first and only pennant.

July 7, 1945(1)
First inning
Wally Moses, White Sox vs A's at Chicago

Moses, who became a prolific base stealer in his thirties, led off the game with a walk, was bunted to second by Roy Schalk and moved to third on an infield out by Kerby Farrell. When Philadelphia hurler Luther Knerr took a leisurely windup, Moses dashed home with the run that stood up for the remainder of the game. Spectacled Bill Dietrich gave up nine hits, but bested Knerr who yielded six. Although this was a "leadoff" steal of home for Moses, he was the only major league player to steal home three times in extra innings in his career. Frank Frisch and Tony Lazzeri had done it twice.

September 21, 1964
Sixth inning
Chico Ruiz, Reds vs Phillies at Philadelphia

The rookie third baseman singled off the Phil's Art Mahaffey and moved to third on another single by Vada Pinson. With one strike on Frank Robinson, pitcher Mahaffey was taken completely by surprise when second-baseman Tony Taylor shouted "there he goes" as the fleet-footed Cuban broke for home. Mahaffey uncorked a high, wide pitch which catcher Clay Dalrymple wasn't able to get his mitt on before Ruiz slid over the plate. Mahaffey allowed six hits before being relieved by Larry Locke in the seventh inning. Bobby Shantz, who was closing out his career, pitched the ninth. The hurling star was the Greek righthander John Tsitouris, who allowed six hits in his only shutout of the season. This was Chico's only career steal of home. He died eight years later in an auto crash at age 33.

July 31, 1972
Fourth inning
Amos Otis, Royals vs Angels at Anaheim

Pitcher Nolan Ryan was not having one of his best days. He walked former Mets teammate Amos Otis and then was charged with two of his three errors while throwing wildly trying to pick him off base. With John Mayberry at bat and the count three-and-two, Otis got a good jump on Ryan, who was planning to throw a curve, but tried to switch to a fast ball. The complication was that neither Bob Lemon, the Royals manager, George Strickland, the third-base coach, nor Mayberry, the batter, was aware of Otis' plan to steal home. A horrified Lemon said: "I didn't tell him to go. His head could have gone over the left-field fence, and I'd get sent up for manslaughter." Mayberry said: "I was the most surprised guy in the ball park. If it had been a strike, I would have struck out." Fortunately, it was a ball and "Famous Amos" scored. Ryan gave up only one hit in the eight frames he worked. He fanned eleven and walked six. Eddie Fisher pitched the ninth. The Royals Roger Nelson allowed three hits in the 1-0 win.

This was the last of the 16 steals of home which won a 1-0 game, and only two of them took place in the last half century. Obviously, there is no number comparison with home runs winning 1-0 games. In summary, however, an appropriate question would be: Did any of these players who "stole" a 1-0 game also win a 1-0 game with a home run? Yes, Frank Schulte did it twice: July 1, 1912 (in the twelfth inning), and Sep. 15, 1915; Max Carey, May 7, 1916; George Burns, June 12, 1918; and Pepper Martin, June 21, 1931.

Postwar Stadiums

Will we miss them when they're gone?

Phil Gruen

Atlanta-Fulton County Stadium is scheduled to meet the wrecker's ball in 1997. After 32 years of major league existence, the destruction of the 1965 stadium will mark a symbolic beginning to the end of the much denigrated "modern," or postwar era, stadiums; a premonitory death-knell for the twelve sports facilities erected between 1960 and 1971.[1] The elimination of Atlanta's Stadium is not likely to be greatly mourned. Like many stadiums of the postwar age, it is routinely vilified for a dull, regularized appearance: too much concrete, too symmetrical, too bland.

Criticism of the postwar stadiums[2] is so widespread today among architectural critics, city planners, public officials, team owners, players, journalists, fans, and baseball historians that it has become difficult to gain any perspective on these facilities as originally constructed. The derision is compounded by the praise heaped upon the new old-fashioned baseball parks in Baltimore, Cleveland, Denver, and Arlington—ballparks hailed for their alleged return to the past and for providing a much needed departure from the prosaic sterility of the postwar stadiums.[3]

The new ballparks incorporate elements common to ballparks of the early twentieth century in their design, thereby providing the illusion that baseball as it was experienced in the past can be experienced today. Moreover, the new ballparks include materials traditional to both older ballparks and architectural

Phil Gruen is working toward a Ph.D. in architecture at the University of California, Berkeley. A three-year SABR veteran, he has been an Oakland A's fan since age five.

history in general, such as rusticated stone, brick, and exposed steel, to complement familiar historic forms, like arches, gables, and keystones. Like the older ballparks, they are often placed into the existing street pattern of the city, even if this necessitates the creation of new streets and blocks to break up an otherwise gigantic architectural footprint. The new ballparks are cheered for this apparent return to tradition, and they are further praised for planners' efforts to link them with the urban context. Support for the new ballparks is often heightened by comparing them to the stadiums of the postwar years. The old-fashioned design of the new parks is seen not as retrogressive, but as liberating, relative to the allegedly insipid, artificial, and destructive design of the postwar stadiums.

The cookie cutters in context—To be sure, many people will cheer a gradual elimination of the postwar stadiums. Critics today commonly lament certain aspects, such as artificial surfaces, standardized outfield dimensions, exterior pedestrian circulation ramps, massive parking lots, domes, huge scale, and enormous seating capacities (particularly in relation to the smaller scale and smaller capacities of the early twentieth century ballparks).[4] In addition, critics decry their overwhelming use of concrete and, for nearly all of them, a multipurpose function (the stadiums serve not only baseball, but also football, concerts, trade shows, religious gatherings, and other events).

Critics contend that the postwar stadiums generally

changed ballpark design and the game of baseball for the worse, and they harp on the stadiums' relative sameness. Their most vehement criticism is directed toward five stadiums which appear today to be cut from the same mold: Atlanta-Fulton County Stadium, St. Louis's Busch Memorial Stadium, Cincinnati's Riverfront Stadium, Pittsburgh's Three Rivers Stadium, and Philadelphia's Veterans Stadium. These stadiums are interchangeably referred to as the "cookie-cutters" or the concrete "ashtrays," "doughnuts," or "ovals."[5] To point up their relative similarities, critics often invoke the now-famous quote by former Philadelphia Phillies third baseman Richie Hebner: "I stand at the plate in Philadelphia," Hebner once said, "and I don't honestly know whether I'm in Pittsburgh, Cincinnati, St. Louis, or Philly. They all look alike."[6]

It is also frequently heard today that baseball should be played in intimate facilities on natural grass under the sun and in the city, and that the postwar stadium—especially the domed ones—create artificial environments, removing the unpredictability that results from grass surfaces, asymmetrical outfields, and unexpected shifts in the weather. Critics argue that these stadiums, like indoor shopping malls, turn inward and away from the city, their circular shapes perhaps useful for their multipurpose function but poor for providing views to the surroundings and conveying a sense of "place." Furthermore, they frequently point out that the stadiums of the postwar era are out of touch with their surrounding context.[7] Some critics, for example, consider these stadiums "suburban" in character even if they are located downtown. They argue that the stadiums are disruptive because they sit on "superblocks" which alter the natural pattern of streets and blocks, and manipulate them to serve other needs, like large parking lots.

Yet the criticism directed against the postwar stadiums employs a contemporary perspective. It is rewarding to take a more detached view; to ground the postwar stadiums in their historical moment, to see them as products of a time when the American city was being built—or *rebuilt*—in a fashion which championed technology and progress. What emerges is a picture of these stadiums at home with their context, blending effectively with the developments of the postwar city. The postwar stadiums are, in many ways, prominent historical markers of a distinctive chapter in American urban history.

Redevelopment—A surge of urban development marked the years following the second world war.

When many industries and businesses moved away from the downtown areas and numerous middle-to-upper class residents headed toward the expanding suburbs, American cities were left without a strong tax base and soon experienced a loss of civic prestige. To help offset the rapidly decentralizing and deteriorating inner cores of larger cities and to attract people, businesses, and money back downtown, American cities from the late 1940s to the early 1970s used available federal funds to rebuild their decaying centers in a new fashion.[8] New sports facilities were often a part of a city's renewal program.

The redevelopment of the center city, however, frequently involved the destruction of its existing environment. Large chunks of the historic city were eliminated during much of the renewal, and numerous residents were forced to abandon homes in the bulldozer's path. But gleaming new office blocks, civic centers, libraries, courthouses, plazas, parking lots, expressways, and stadiums soon rose across American downtowns, providing a new, spiffy look for the center city. Most of the new developments eschewed ornament and historic references, part of an effort to give cities a technologically oriented appearance which looked to the future, not the past.

This postwar renewal is largely castigated by historians and planners today. Many of them argue that the city suffered gaping holes in its fabric; that the new projects—intended to pave the way for a new civic vitality—carved up existing urban patterns and destroyed countless communities and historic buildings in the name of "progress."

At the time of the renewal, however, detractors were few.[9] Many civic officials had viewed the older city as "shabby" and "obsolescent," and they designed their renewal to rid the downtowns of clutter and to "clear" the slums.[10] The unadorned, concrete stadiums of this period, surrounded as they were by acres of parking and well-serviced by expressways in recently cleared areas of the city, meshed formally with the contemporary civic developments. As publicly subsidized endeavors, they also meshed ideologically with the new developments. Just as public officials attempted to upgrade the city's image by granting tax breaks to developers for new office buildings and by employing federal monies for new infrastructure and housing, the officials also imagined the construction of new stadiums as integral to the revitalization of the center city. In 1966, for instance, St. Louis city officials noted that building Busch Memorial Stadium sparked the redevelopment of downtown.[11] Pittsburgh's civic officials conceived the erection of

Three Rivers Stadium in 1970 in much the same fashion, and it too contributed to an improved image of the center city.[12]

Urban renaissance—Envisioned as important pieces of an urban renaissance, many of the postwar stadiums were appropriately situated in, or near, the central business district. Of the twelve major league baseball stadiums built between 1960 and 1971, two are located in or adjacent to the central business district, and three are nearby.[13] In addition, six are within city limits even if they are not in the middle of downtown.[14] Only New York's Shea Stadium is located in what might be considered a suburban area.[15]

Busch Memorial Stadium, for example, is virtually a part of St. Louis's central business district, just east of city hall and southwest of the old courthouse. Skyscrapers and the Gateway Arch loom to the north and northeast, visible from many seats inside the stadium. Cincinnati's Riverfront Stadium sits just on the southern edge of downtown, removed from it only by Interstate 71 and Pete Rose Way. Downtown buildings can be viewed from many right field seats. Pittsburgh's Three Rivers Stadium is separated from the heart of downtown only by the Allegheny River and the short span of the Fort Duquesne Bridge, and the tops of downtown office buildings can also be seen from many seats in the upper deck.

Furthermore, the postwar stadiums can be understood as contextual with their surroundings; their heavy use of concrete, for example, actually blends with their expressway neighbors. This is especially apparent in Atlanta-Fulton County Stadium, where the treatment of the exterior echoes the maze of expressways to its north. The concrete piers intersecting the horizontal ramps on the exterior of Cincinnati's Riverfront Stadium complement the steel framework of the neighboring bridges that span the Ohio River. The undulating exterior pedestrian access ramps in Cincinnati and Pittsburgh recall their waterfront sites. In St. Louis, architect Edward Durrell Stone added a ring of small arches atop Busch Memorial Stadium, making explicit reference to the Gateway Arch to its east. Even the scale of many postwar stadiums appears less extreme in their urban locations, particularly if one considers the nearby skyscrapers.

Enthusiastic acceptance—People also flocked to these new facilities when they opened. In their first seasons, attendance at the new stadiums—in almost all cases—increased by more than 100 percent. Attendance figures leveled off after the initial year, but some stadiums, such as Dodger Stadium and Busch Memorial Stadium, still entertain more than two million fans annually, considerably more than ever attended games in those teams' older, smaller ballparks. (It should be readily acknowledged that older ballparks like Chicago's Wrigley Field and Boston's Fenway Park have consistently garnered high attendance figures despite their age and the inconsistent performance of their teams. But Busch Memorial Stadium has also consistently averaged more than 2.2 million fans per season since its initial year, and over 2.6 million during the past ten seasons.)[16]

At the time, fans, public officials, the press, and the players generally applauded these newer, larger stadiums, often referencing monuments of the past to point up their grandeur. Los Angeles *Times* columnist Jim Murray, for example, eulogized Dodger Stadium as "not just any baseball park but the Taj Mahal, the Parthenon, and the Westminster Abbey of baseball."[17] Richard Nixon hailed San Francisco's Candlestick Park on the day it opened as "the greatest baseball park in America—a magnificent stadium in which to have a World Series."[18] Former commissioner Ford Frick declared Shea Stadium an "excellent plant," former National League president Warren Giles called it a "fantastic" place, and one of two managers who participated in the stadium's inaugural game added that it was a "showplace," and a well-planned, "beautiful stadium."[19] Because it was built on the former site of a garbage dump in a marshy area in Flushing Meadow, Queens, one journalist referred to Shea as the "Taj Mahal of the Marshlands."[20]

The Houston Astrodome, the first major league baseball stadium to feature a dome, artificial turf, and plush luxury skyboxes, merited a tremendous amount of acclaim when it opened. Joseph Durso, a journalist, declared it the "Taj Mahal of the Southwest," and evangelist Billy Graham proclaimed it the "Eighth Wonder of the World." While recognized generally as an engineering marvel, pitcher Jim Bouton described it as "science fiction," and tourists flocked from all over to visit the stadium even on *non*-game days so they could receive guided tours of the structure.[21] In the throes of the Cold War and the space race with the former Soviet Union, the space-age imagery associated with the Astrodome—right down to its very name—seems expressly characteristic of its time.

Other, less futuristic stadiums also received their due. The low-lying appearance of Oakland's Coliseum, designed by Myron Goldsmith of Skidmore, Owings, and Merrill, prompted *Architectural Record* editors to declare it an "elegant" and "remarkable" structure which appeared "intimate" and smaller than most of its contemporaries because the playing field dropped twenty-nine feet below ground level.[22] The design of multipurpose Jack Murphy Stadium for San Diego impressed the American Institute of Architects sufficiently its designers were presented with an annual Honor Award. The AIA cited the stadium's even distribution of vertical and horizontal elements, the "expression" of the circular exterior pedestrian access ramps, and its overall "structurally clear architectural statement of San Diego."[23]

Many people even extolled the "concrete doughnuts" upon completion. *Progressive Architecture,* for example, noted the "rugged charm" of Atlanta's stadium, while the New York *Times* lauded Busch Memorial Stadium as "magnificent," "first class," and a thing of "lasting beauty."[24] Pittsburgh's Three Rivers Stadium, often criticized today as a drab, dismal place to watch a game, was initially declared a "sparkling new stadium" that ranked among the "finest" of recently built stadiums and one that was integral to the transformation of a once heavily industrialized city into one with a sleek, corporate image manifest in a clearly identifiable downtown.[25] In addition, a New York *Times* journalist noted the "splendor" of Philadelphia's Veterans Stadium at its opening, and a Phillies' pitcher called it "beautiful."[26]

Dinasaurs—It is interesting to note that the original acclaim for the postwar stadiums is similar to that which accompanied the opening of Baltimore's Oriole Park at Camden Yards, its contemporaries in Cleveland, Arlington, and Denver. Today's support for these new old-fashioned designs attempts to bury the postwar stadiums once and for all, just as the initial popularity of the postwar stadiums helped many fans forget about the early twentieth century ballparks that they replaced.

With more cities considering the desertion of their postwar stadiums in favor of new old-fashioned ballparks, the postwar stadium may soon become an endangered species; the new ballparks threaten to close the book on an era of stadium construction which may have had its moment but, as many would argue, ultimately failed.[27] Various owners and some city officials in and around San Francisco have been pressing for a new baseball facility for years. Now civic officials in Anaheim, Cincinnati, Philadelphia, Pittsburgh, San Diego, and Seattle are indicating that they, too, would like new old-fashioned, baseball-only ballparks—preferably modeled after Camden Yards. The new old-fashioned ballpark for the Atlanta

Braves, to emerge from the Olympic Stadium, should be ready for play in 1997.

The Tiger Stadium Fan Club fights hard to save Detroit's currently threatened Tiger Stadium, the oldest major league ballpark still standing. Tiger Stadium, like Chicago's Wrigley Field and Boston's Fenway Park, is typical of the first fireproof baseball facilities that were built to fit into existing urban street patterns early on the twentieth century. These early ballparks have storied pasts, and were—some still are—integral, vibrant parts of their communities.

The postwar stadiums, too, were—and are—significant parts of their urban context and monuments to their time. Rising up among the expressways and office towers, or standing alone amid acres of parking on the city's edge, the large, postwar stadiums are emblematic of an era committed to bigger-than-life civic symbols, built at a time when the image of the city was manifested in bold, monumental, and futuristic projects. However destructive to the older city fabric they may have been, the postwar stadiums projected the optimism and confidence that accompanied their construction, a confidence in the advances of their age.

Atlanta-Fulton County Stadium, a particularly characteristic design from the postwar era, however, is nearing its end. Riverfront Stadium may not last into the next century. And what about Houston? With the NFL Oilers moving to Nashville and the baseball Astros looking to other markets, who knows how long the Astrodome will be needed? Will there be any effort to preserve these, and other, postwar stadiums? Today we often regret the loss of many of the early twentieth century ballparks, some of which were destroyed in the wake of postwar stadium construction. History has the tendency to repeat itself. It is only from a historical distance that we begin to gauge what we have lost.

Notes:

1. In addition to Atlanta-Fulton County Stadium, these stadiums include San Francisco's Candlestick Park (1960), Los Angeles' Dodger Stadium (1962), New York City's Shea Stadium (1964), Houston's Astrodome (1965), Anaheim's Stadium (1966), St. Louis' Busch Memorial Stadium (1966), San Diego's Jack Murphy Stadium (1967), Oakland's Alameda County Coliseum (1968), Cincinnati's Riverfront Stadium (1970), Pittsburgh's Three Rivers Stadium (1970), and Philadelphia's Veterans Stadium (1971). Six more stadiums were built between 1973 and 1989, many of which bear elements that are similar to those of the postwar stadiums. These stadiums include Kansas City's Kauffman Stadium (1973), Montreal's Olympic Stadium (1976), Seattle's Kingdome (1977), Minneapolis' Metrodome (1982), Miami's Joe Robbie Stadium (1987), and Toronto's SkyDome (1989). Joe Robbie Stadium was built originally for the Miami Dolphins football

team, but it is possible that Joe Robbie had it designed with baseball use in mind as well. (See David Whitford, *Playing Hardball: The High-Stakes Battle for Baseball's New Franchises* (New York: Doubleday Books, 1993), 159-60.

2. These stadiums are generally referred to as "modern" in much of the literature, and they are often described in such a way as to distinguish them from the "post-modern" or "neoclassic" ballparks that have been built in the 1990s. The use of these terms is problematic, however, because the new ballparks bear many aspects in common with those of the so-called "modern" period (huge scale, luxury skyboxes, large parking lots, expressway access, cantilevered construction, public funding, etc.). My use of the term "postwar," therefore, is to group these ballparks by time period, rather than grouping them under tenuous stylistic umbrellas.

3. For example, when Baltimore's Oriole Park at Camden Yards opened, former Commissioner Fay Vincent said it was exactly what ballparks "should" be. Columnist George Will wrote that it was "bound to generate memories." See Patricia Leigh Brown, "Field of Dreams Comes True in Baltimore," *New York Times* (March 5, 1992), C: 1, and Thomas Boswell, "Now That's the Way to Build a Ballpark," *Washington Post* (April 4, 1992), H: 1.

4. The postwar stadiums featured an average seating capacity of 50,265 when they opened, at least 15,000 greater than the average capacity of the early twentieth century ballparks when they closed. Figures calculated from Philip Lowry, *Green Cathedrals* (Westport, Conn: Addison-Wesley Publishing Co., 1992).

5. For the use of these terms and criticism of the postwar stadiums along these lines, see, for example, Michael Benson, *Ballparks of North America: A Comprehensive Historical Reference to Baseball Grounds, Yards, and Stadiums, 1845 to Present* (Jefferson, North Carolina: McFarland and Company, 1989), xxviii; Philip Bess, *City Baseball Magic: Plain Talk and Uncommon Sense About Cities and Baseball Parks* (Minneapolis: The Minneapolis Review of Baseball, 1989), 5-15; Lowry, *Green Cathedrals*, 2-11; Lawrence S. Ritter, *Lost Ballparks: A Celebration of Baseball's Legendary Fields* (London: Viking Studio Books, 1992), 1-7; Michael Gershman, *Diamonds: The Evolution of the Ballpark* (Boston: Houghton Mifflin Company, 1993), 191-211; Paul Goldberger, "At Home in the City, Baseball's Newest Parks Succeed," *New York Times* (April 17, 1994), 8: 9; Blair Kamin, "Context Sport: For New Ballparks, Questions of Place Come With Territory," *Chicago Tribune* (May 8, 1994), 13: 20; John Pastier, "The Houses That Baseball Built," *Humanities* 15, no. 4 (July-August 1994): 19-22.

6. See, for example, Bess, *City Baseball Magic*, 5.

7. Jack Diamond and Sarah Pearce, "The Domed Stadium, Toronto," *The Canadian Architect* 32, no. 5 (May, 1987): 30-34; Bess, *City Baseball Magic*, 18-20; John Pastier, "The Business of Baseball: Creative Proposals Can't Save Comiskey Park," *Inland Architect* 33, no. 1 (January-February, 1989), 57; Ritter, *Lost Ballparks*, 4.

8. It should be noted that the revitalization of the urban core is a constant process, dating as far back as ancient Rome. Even the postwar urban renewal practices have their immediate forebears: from 1933 to 1940, for instance, $4 million of federal funding was put into WPA efforts to improve roads and streets.

9. Some of the notable exceptions include Jane Jacobs, *The Death and Life of Great American Cities* (New York: Random House, 1961), and Lewis Mumford, *The City in History: Its Origins, Its Transformations, And Its Prospects* (New York: Harcourt, Brace and World, 1961).

10. See, for example, Will Lissner, "Urban Renewal Reviving Center of Nation's Cities," *New York Times* (April 6, 1964), A: 1. Lissner notes that urban renewal is "beginning to transform the slum-ridden downtown sections of the

nation's larger cities into sleek new inner cores of rejuvenated urban areas." Also see Bernard J. Freiden and Lynne B. Sagalyn, *Downtown, Inc.: How America Rebuilds Cities* (Cambridge, Mass: The MIT Press, 1989), 15-17.

11. *Progressive Architecture*, "Several Significant Southern Stadia," *Progressive Architecture* 45 (May 1964): 64; Terry Boers, "New Park, History on Sox Side," Chicago *Sun-Times* (April 17, 1991): 7.

12. See, for example, Douglas E. Kneeland, "Pittsburgh: A Brawny City Puts on a Silk Shirt," *New York Times* (October 3, 1970): 33+, and William H. Whyte, *City: Rediscovering the Center* (New York: Doubleday Books, 1988), 313.

13. Stadiums in St. Louis and Cincinnati are either part of or attached to the downtown core, and those in Los Angeles, Atlanta, and Pittsburgh are nearby.

14. These include stadiums in San Francisco, Anaheim, Houston, Oakland, San Diego, and Philadelphia.

15. If one includes the six stadiums built from 1973 to 1989 in this general "postwar" group, Kauffman Stadium in Kansas City and Joe Robbie Stadium in Miami must also be considered facilities in suburban locations. But the stadiums in Montreal, Seattle, Minneapolis, and Toronto are all located either next to the central business district or within the limits of their respective cities.

16. These figures tabulated from Craig Carter, ed., *The Sporting News Complete Baseball Record Book* (St. Louis: The Sporting News, 1993). My totals do not include the strike-shortened or strike-affected seasons of 1981, 1994, and 1995.

17. From the Los Angeles *Times*, (April 10, 1962), as quoted in Neil J. Sullivan, *The Dodgers Move West* (New York: Oxford University Press, 1987), 197.

18. Lawrence E. Davies, "Giants Beat Cards in Opener; Record 67,550 Watch Dodgers Nip Cubs in 11th," *New York Times* (April 13, 1960): 47.

19. Leonard Koppett, "Shea Stadium Opens With Big Traffic Jam," *New York Times* (April 18, 1964): 1.

20. Robert Lipsyte, "'Fabulous' Stadium Delights Fans: Gleaming Ball Park Widely Acclaimed as Out of this World," *New York Times* (April 18, 1964): 20.

21. See Joseph Durso, "Astros Down Yanks, 2-1, in First Major League Game Played Under Roof," *New York Times* (April 10, 1965): 23, and Howard Taubman, "Show Biz: The Big Dome," *New York Times* (June 6, 1965), 5: 3.

22. Architectural Record, "An Elegant Sports and Recreation Center," *Architectural Record* 143 (June, 1968): 121-28.

23. AIA Journal, "The 1969 Honor Awards: Frank L. Hope & Associates: San Diego Stadium, San Diego, California," *AIA Journal* 51 (June 1969): 103.

24. See New York Times, "U.S. Business: Atlanta's New Stadium Expected to Be Boon to City," *New York Times* (March 28, 1965), 3: 15; Progressive Architecture, "Home of the Braves?", *Progressive Architecture* 47 (March 1966): 199; and William N. Wallace, "Cards Win as St. Louis Stadium Opens," *New York Times* (May 13, 1966): 46.

25. Leonard Koppett, "Pirates Open Their New Park, But Reds Celebrate 3-2 Victory," *New York Times* (July 17, 1970): 23, and Kneeland, "Brawny City Puts on a Silk Shirt," 33+.

26. United Press International, "35,000 Attend Dedication of $5 Million 'Hitter's Park' in Philadelphia," *New York Times* (April 5, 1971): 40, and Dave Anderson, "Philadelphia Stadium Has High Winds, Hot Pants and, They Hope, Few Boos," *New York Times* (April 4, 1971), 5: 3.

27. In Cincinnati, both the Bengals and the Reds have indicated that they want new facilities. The Angels, too, desire a new stadium. Atlanta's new ballpark is being built first for the 1996 Summer Olympics, after which it will be converted into a baseball-only, natural grass, open-air, asymmetrical ballpark for the Braves.

Who Won the Game Today? No One!

Once fairly common, tie games are increasingly rare

Al Yellon

As you look at the annual standings through the history of baseball, or at the year-by-year records of your favorite team, one statistic is invariably left out—the ties.

Ties, you say? You think ties belong in hockey games. Why, you could paraphrase Tom Hanks' famous line from *A League of Their Own*: "There's no ties in baseball!"

I am here to tell you that there *are* ties in baseball. These games are commonly ignored, since according to the peculiar rules by which baseball is governed, they must be replayed in their entirety, rather than from the point at which they are stopped, even though all the individual statistics accumulated in them count if they go more than five innings.

You have probably never attended, or even seen on television, a tie game. To give you an idea just how rare ties are, consider this comparison of other infrequent, but notable, occurrences in baseball from 1969 through 1995:

Tie games	38
Hitting for cycle	65
No-hitters	75
Three or four HR in game	149

In this article, I will first provide a brief perspective on the history of ties since 1900, and then a brief

Al Yellon is a television director in Chicago who is proud to have attended three tie games.

summary of all tie games played since 1969. I've chosen the arbitrary dividing line of 1969, when divisional play came in, for the summary portion of this article because since then the number of tie games has diminished dramatically. Here are the ties played, by decade, between 1900 and 1968:

	NL	AL	Total
1900-1909	98	104	202
1910-1919	95	92	187
1920-1929	30	36	66
1930-1939	43	49	92
1940-1949	56	43	99
1950-1959	27	32	59
1960-1968	19	16	35
1900-1968	**368**	**372**	**740**

From 1900 till 1919, much of which is commonly, if inaccurately, known as the Dead Ball Era, scores were low and long extra-inning games were frequent. Combine that with slower trains, which meant longer travel times between cities, and the absence of night games, meaning more games called for darkness, and you can clearly see ties were more frequent.

Then came the high-scoring 1920s and a precipitous decline in the number of ties. This can be almost wholly attributed to the increase in offense during the period, lowering the number of long pitching duels and reducing the number of extra-inning games.

In the 1930s and 1940s, when the number of ties blipped upward, several factors were at work. Part of it certainly has to do with the Depression and less money available for changing travel plans, thus necessitating ties when train schedules had to be met. In fact, some games were ended at a certain hour by prior agreement between the clubs. Similarly, local curfews were common in many cities, notably in Boston, which for years had a 6:30 PM curfew. Also, day games commonly started at 3:00 PM or later, local time, in order to attract the 7 AM–3 PM, or so-called "first shift," factory workers to the ballparks, in an era when attendance was low.

It almost certainly has nothing to do with the game itself, since if anything the 1930s were higher-scoring years than the prior decade. The 1940s increase can perhaps be explained by the inferior teams that took the field during the war years, with the resulting decreases in scoring, including a 24-inning, 1-1 tie between Detroit and Philadelphia on July 21, 1945, as well as wartime travel restrictions.

After World War II, and especially since 1950, the primary reason for the decline is the advent of night baseball. Lights in baseball parks allowed owners and umpires to wait out longer rain delays. Games no longer needed to be called for darkness. And, of course, the increase in the amount of air travel, especially after teams were established in California, meant that clubs could wait longer before leaving one city for the next one.

In the current divisional-play era, economic factors are paramount. Clubs don't want to reschedule games for open dates, having to pay their nonplaying employees more money for extra days' work. Also, the Players' Association now has the right to approve rescheduling of postponed games, with the result that most clubs will go to any length to finish, especially if the alternative is to play a doubleheader, something no one does any more unless forced to by a rain-out.

Here is a list by club of all ties since divisional play began through the 1995 season:

NL		AL	
Atlanta	5	Baltimore	1
Cincinnati	4	Boston	1
Chicago	8	California	2
Colorado	0	Chicago	7
Florida	0	Cleveland	2
Houston	1	Detroit	1
Los Angeles	3	Kansas City	2
Montreal	4	Milwaukee	3*
New York	3	Minnesota	2
Philadelphia	4	New York	3
Pittsburgh	3	Oakland	0
St. Louis	7	Seattle	2
San Diego	2	Texas	4
San Francisco	0	Toronto	2

(* includes one as Seattle Pilots in 1969)

With that as background, here is a brief summary of each of the thirty-eight tie games played since divisional play began:

May 31, 1969, Kansas City 2, N.Y. Yankees 2, 7-1/2 innings, at Kansas City:

The game began in windy, 80-degree, threatening conditions, and there was a delay of over an hour before the third inning. The Royals scored single runs in the first and fourth innings, including a 415-foot home run by Mike Fiore in the fourth. The tying run scored on a missed DP opportunity. After an apparent inning-ending DP grounder hit by Horace Clarke in the top of the seventh, the relay throw to first baseman Fiore was a little wide and he couldn't hold it, allowing Jim Lyttle to score the tying run. After a second rain delay with one out in the top of the eighth, the grounds were ruled unplayable and the game was called.

June 7, 1969, Cincinnati 5, Chicago Cubs 5, 8-1/2 innings, at Chicago:

On a cloudy, unseasonably cool day, Ernie Banks' two-run homer helped give the Cubs a 5-2 lead entering the eighth. But the Cub bullpen blew the lead, and Woody Woodward scored the tying run just ahead of a diving tag by Randy Hundley in the top of the eighth. A drizzle became a downpour soon after, and the game was called at 4:40 PM, after a fifty-minute delay. (It stopped raining twenty minutes later. League rules now require at least a seventy-five-minute wait after the first rain delay.) This tie may have played a role in the famous Cub collapse. It was common then, as now, to replay such games the following day, if at all possible. But this tie was not replayed until what was to have been an open date, August 25, when the Cubs were beginning to get fatigued, and their lead was slipping away. Could that unscheduled game (which the Cubs lost, 9-8, despite a furious four-run rally in the bottom of the ninth), with its strain both on the pitching staff and the starting lineup, have added to this?

Sept. 12, 1969, California 1, Seattle 1, 9-1/2 innings, second game, at Seattle:

Only 5,085 saw one of the last games involving the Seattle Pilots before they became the Milwaukee Brewers the following year. There were nineteen hits:

fifteen singles, three doubles and a triple by the Angels' Jay Johnstone in the sixth (though he failed to score from third with only one out). Johnstone did single home Jim Fregosi in the Angels' eighth after he had doubled. The Seattle run scored in the bottom of that inning on a walk, sacrifice, and single.

May 11, 1970, N.Y. Yankees 5, Milwaukee 5, 9 innings, at Milwaukee:

The Pilots had barely moved to Milwaukee when they were involved in the majors' next tie the following spring. The game included a combination of strange circumstances involving several seldom-used players. The Brewers had taken a 3-0 lead, all on unearned runs scored in the third. They managed to nurse a 5-2 lead into the ninth, when 21-year-old Frank Tepedino, playing in one of only sixteen games he got into that year, led off with a single. After a fielder's choice, Jerry Kenney, who hit only .193 for the season, also singled. Then the tying runs scored on errors by Tommy Harper, in only his first season as a third baseman, and second baseman John Kennedy, who played only eighteen games at that position in 1970 and was sold to the Red Sox on June 26. The Brewers did get the winning run into scoring position in the bottom of the ninth, but didn't score.

May 1, 1971, Montreal 2, St. Louis 2, 7 innings, at St. Louis:

Dal Maxvill, of all people, drove in both Cardinal runs (one-twelfth of his season total of 24 RBI) in the second with his only triple of the season, which would have been wiped off the books had the game not gone more than five innings. There was a rain delay of 35 minutes after the top of the fifth, with St. Louis then leading, 2-1. They would have been declared the winner had it not stopped raining. Instead, the Expos tied it in the top of the sixth.

July 4, 1972, Chicago Cubs 3, Atlanta 3, 7-1/2 innings, second game, at Atlanta:

Back in the days when holiday doubleheaders were common, the fourth-largest crowd to that time in Atlanta history—50,597 (the largest crowd to see any of these divisional-playera ties)—saw Denny McLain make his Atlanta debut. The Cubs had tied the game in the top of the seventh on a misplayed hit by Ron Santo which wound up being scored a triple, and were threatening in the eighth with runners on first and third when the rain came. McLain pitched all seven-plus innings for one of only two complete games he pitched in 1972, his last season in the majors.

May 19, 1973, Los Angeles 7, Atlanta 7, 13 innings, at Atlanta:

This wild game began in a heavy drizzle, with water collecting in the outfield. Tommy John took a 6-1 lead into the bottom of the eighth, but Dick Dietz' three-run double tied it, the biggest lead blown in any of these ties. The Dodgers again took the lead in the top of the twelfth, but Dave Johnson was hit by Charlie Hough and Mike Lum's double into the outfield puddles brought him in, the first of only two of these games in which the tie was broken, then remade, in an extra inning. In the top of the thirteenth LA had a runner in scoring position when a sudden torrential downpour brought rain and hail so quickly that the ground crew couldn't even get the tarp down.

April 7, 1974, California 4, Chicago White Sox 4, 10 innings, at Chicago:

The teams both entered the game winless at 0-2 and finished it the same way in a game played in 39-degree temperatures with a biting 23-mph wind blowing off Lake Michigan. A crowd of 8,383 paid to see Ron Santo, in only his third game for the Sox, drive in the tying run with two out in the bottom of the ninth. So, instead of a 4-3 loss, White Sox fans were treated to the sight of a scoreless tenth inning, with batters fighting a driving snowstorm.

April 11, 1974, Chicago White Sox 4, Minnesota 4, 6 innings, at Minnesota:

The following Thursday, only 2,138 hardy souls, the smallest crowd among the post-1969 ties, came to watch the White Sox and Twins battle to a stirring six-inning tie that was called after only a 40-minute wait, because the grounds were unplayable. The White Sox *still* hadn't won a game (and neither had the 0-4 Twins), and once again they left the same way. Another thing these two ties had in common: the tying run was scored in the last inning, Santo involved again, this time scoring after a walk on a Ken Henderson double.

September 12, 1974, Texas 2, Chi. White Sox 2, 6 innings, at Chicago:

A clean sweep of sorts for the White Sox in 1974 as they were involved in all three of the tie games played that year. Once again, a tiny crowd of 3,821 (for a total of only 14,342 to see all three of the 1974 ties) watched the proceedings on a soggy night, with Ken Henderson hitting a game-tying home run in the bottom of the sixth inning, after which a 45-minute rain delay forced the postponement. This was the final appearance of the Rangers in Chicago in 1974, so the make-up of this tie was scheduled as part of a twi-night doubleheader in Arlington on September 24. That date was rained out as well, as was *another* make-up doubleheader planned for the next night. That would have been a three-game series if played, and had occurred the 1974 White Sox would have established, and would still hold, the major league record for most games played in a season at 166. (That record is 165, held by the 1962 Dodgers and Giants, who played three extra games in a pennant playoff.) They did wind up playing 163, with the three ties, and their won-loss record? What else: 80-80!

August 25, 1975, Houston 3, St. Louis 3, 10 innings, at St. Louis:

On this night in St. Louis, the Astros were only one out away from an eleven-inning win. Cliff Johnson had homered in the top of the eleventh to give the Astros the lead; and in fact this homer had given him six in six consecutive games. But a thunderstorm hit, and more than two hours later, the game was called. If the lead in a game has changed and an inning has not been completed, the score reverts to the last completed inning. So for Houston, it was just a frustrating 3-3, ten-inning tie. And for Cliff Johnson, that home run was washed off the books. Johnson does, however, still hold the Astros' club record with five homers in five consecutive games.

April 8, 1979, Philadelphia 2, St. Louis 2, 5 innings, at St. Louis:

It was more than three years before the next tie game in the majors. On an unusually warm early April Sunday, the Cards spotted the Phils a 2-0 lead before tying the game in the bottom of the fifth on a two-run double by Keith Hernandez following walks to pitcher Bob Forsch and Lou Brock. The Phillies came right back in the top of the sixth with a run on doubles by Larry Bowa and Mike Schmidt. Rain prevented the bottom of the sixth from being played, and just as before, the score reverted to the 2-2 tie after five.

June 25, 1979, Pittsburgh 3, N.Y. Mets 3, 11 innings, at New York:

This game could have been a simple 3-1 Pirate victory on their way to the "We are Family" championship year. But Buc reliever Grant Jackson gave up two runs in the bottom of the ninth, thus providing the 6,611 fans with one of the stranger moments of the season. Thick fog descended over Shea Stadium, with visibility becoming increasingly difficult. After the eleventh inning outfielders complained they couldn't see the batter, so coaches went out and tried hitting fungoes to the fielders, none of which were caught. The game was then called.

June 2, 1980, Texas 1, Chicago White Sox 1, 6 innings, at Chicago:

Once again the tie was established in the last completed inning played. Doubles by Lamar Johnson and Jim Morrison in the fifth tied the game at 1; the teams did manage to get to one out in the bottom of the sixth before the game had to be postponed. And the rainy, cool (68 degrees) weather in Chicago extended to the Detroit area, making this one of two dates since 1969 on which two ties were played.

June 2, 1980, Seattle 3, Detroit 3, 13 innings, at Detroit:

In this game, no runs were scored after the sixth inning despite Shane Rawley walking five batters (two intentionally) in the tenth through thirteenth innings. In the ninth, former Tiger Willie Horton, ending his career as a Mariner, came out to pinch hit with a man on and two out, to a standing ovation. But this potential drama ended when he hit a comebacker to Jack Morris. The game plodded on till the thirteenth, when a thunderstorm hit at midnight. When it was still raining at 1:00 AM (the AL curfew time; the NL has no such curfew—see the next game) the game was called.

June 9, 1980, San Diego 6, Cincinnati 6, 10-1/2 innings, at Cincinnati:

This game saw the greatest comeback to tie in the bottom of the ninth of any of the post-1969 ties. The Pads had taken a 6-2 lead into the bottom of the ninth, thanks mainly to a two-run homer by Jerry Turner. There had already been three rain delays by this time: prior to the game, before the bottom of the second inning, and an hour and 39 minutes in the middle of the eighth. In the bottom of the ninth Ray Knight grounded out, but then Johnny Bench singled. Junior Kennedy walked, and Rick Auerbach flied to left, so only one out remained for a San Diego win. But Dave Collins walked to load the bases. Dave Concepcion had the big blow next—a bases-clearing double. Still, San Diego led 6-5. Ken Griffey singled in Concepcion with the tying run. Only then did manager Jerry Coleman make a pitching change, bringing in John D'Acquisto, who got George Foster to fly out. In the eleventh, it began to rain again, and after another hour and 21 minute rain delay the game was called at 2:30 AM.

July 26, 1980, Texas 1, Chicago White Sox 1, 5-1/2 innings, second game, at Chicago:

The Texas-Chicago combination accounts for three of the thirty-eight divisional play era ties, more than any other. Mickey Rivers scored the only run for the Rangers in both of the 1980 ties. The White Sox had a 70-90 record in 1980 and played 162 games despite making up both of these ties (ordinarily you would then expect them to have played 164 games). The reason: two games scheduled against the Red Sox in August were rained out and not made up. The White Sox wound up playing Texas fourteen times that year, and, of course, wound up splitting the games 6-6, plus the two ties.

April 22, 1981, N.Y. Mets 2, Pittsburgh 2, 8-1/2 innings, at Pittsburgh:

The 1981 strike year produced the largest number of ties (five) for any year since 1969. That is pure coincidence, though as we shall see below the strike did play a role. The Pirates played only fourteen games that April, including this tie, and had six other games rained out, including an exhibition they were to have played against their top farm club in Portland. This particular tie was uneventful. It was the only game of a scheduled three-game series that managed to be played at all.

April 29, 1981, St. Louis 2, Chicago Cubs 2, 11 innings, at Chicago:

It was a very chilly 50 degrees, windy, cloudy and off and on rainy the day the Cubs and Cardinals attempted to play a doubleheader in front of 4,067. The Cubs won the first game to snap a twelve-game losing streak, and tied up the second game in the bottom of the seventh when Leon Durham homered off the man for whom he was traded the previous off-season, Bruce Sutter. At 5:50 PM on this gloomy Wednesday, the game was suspended, under the special rule for then-lightless Wrigley Field. It was scheduled to be resumed on July 3, before the next St. Louis appearance in Chicago. That date was cancelled by the strike. The Cardinals made one more trip to Chicago in 1981, on September 21 and 22, but on September 8 the National League cancelled the resumption of this game, due to disagreement over which half of the split season the result would count in, and the game was declared a tie.

April 29, 1981, Seattle 7, Minnesota 7, 8 innings, at Minnesota:

For the second time in the post-1969 era two ties were played on the same day. In Minnesota, it was 61 degrees and raining. And in the final season the Twins played outdoors, the two teams combined for six walks and twenty-eight hits despite playing in a steady rain. And the Twins had to come from a 7-4 deficit to tie it up in (of course) the bottom of the eighth, with the final out coming at the plate as Dave Engle attempted to stretch his RBI triple into an inside-the-park home run.

May 10, 1981, Chicago Cubs 2, Atlanta 2, 14 innings, at Atlanta:

This is the longest of all the ties played since 1969. The wet weather in Atlanta caused Brave reliever Rick Camp to slip on the rubber while delivering a pitch to Cub pinch hitter Hector Cruz. Cruz delivered a two-out, ninth-inning, game-tying home run, the only baserunner Camp allowed in a three-inning relief appearance. After five more fruitless innings and 91 minutes of rain delays, the game was called. It was to have been made up July 21 as part of a doubleheader, but that date was also cancelled by the strike.

October 1, 1981, Chicago Cubs 2, N.Y. Mets 2, 8-1/2 innings, at New York:

The 1981 Cubs tie the 1974 White Sox for most ties in any single season since 1969 (3). This meaningless game between the two worst teams in the National League was played in 47-degree weather before 3,553 diehards. Nothing of note happened and as it was the final meeting of the teams for the season, the game was not made up.

June 1, 1982, Milwaukee 2, Baltimore 2, 9 innings, at Baltimore:

A couple of notable things happened here: in the third, Ted Simmons flipped the ball on the ground after John Lowenstein struck out. Problem: only two were out! A run scored. Later, Gary Roenicke made a great catch to rob Cecil Cooper of a home run. There were three rain delays, and as the teams took the field for the top of the tenth, Sammy Stewart was announced as a new pitcher. Rain then stopped play before a Milwaukee hitter stepped in, resulting in an appearance credited to Stewart with no batters faced.

May 24, 1983, Texas 2, Kansas City 2, 5 innings, at Kansas City:

Both teams scored in the fifth inning, the Rangers on a home run by Larry Parrish, the Royals coming back to tie on a single by George Brett and triple by Hal McRae, in a game that took one hour and forty-five minutes, which sounds quick, until you remember that they only played five innings!

June 28, 1983, Montreal 5, Philadelphia 5, 11 innings, at Philadelphia:

This game featured another late-inning comeback that forced the tie. In this case it was a two-run bottom-of-the-ninth rally by the Phils after Montreal had taken the lead, 5-3, in the top of that inning. With one out, Ivan DeJesus singled, scored on a triple by Joe Lefebvre, who then scored the tying run on a Pete Rose single.

September 28, 1983, Los Angeles 4, San Diego 4, 13 innings, at San Diego:

This late-season game between the Dodgers and Padres slogged on for 4:01 before finally being called. The game almost ended in the tenth after a home run by LA's Derrel Thomas. The Padres, though, came back with a run in their half of the tenth, on a walk to Kevin McReynolds, who advanced on a sacrifice, and was singled in by Garry Templeton. It was only the second time the tie was broken in the top of an extra inning, only to be re-established in the bottom. The only tie game played in California since 1969 was seen by 23,588.

May 13, 1984, Toronto 4, Cleveland 4, 7-1/2 innings, at Cleveland:

The Indians scored four runs in the first inning off Jim Clancy, then proceeded to slowly bleed the lead away, a run at a time. Toronto scored one each in the second, third, fourth, and sixth, all off Rick Sutcliffe, in one of the last starts he made for the Tribe before being traded to the Cubs and having his Cy Young 16-1 year for them. Clancy, meanwhile, survived the first and wound up pitching all seven innings.

July 31, 1985, Chicago White Sox 1, Boston 1, 7 innings, at Boston:

The game was played in unseasonably cool 66-degree temperatures and a steady rain, and the tying run was once again scored just before umpires halted play. Dave Sax, a catcher playing right field in place of Dwight Evans, who had left the game in the top of the seventh with a twisted knee, hit a sacrifice fly to

drive in Jackie Gutierrez. After a 78-minute rain delay the game was called at 11:34 PM.

September 8, 1985, Cincinnati 5, Chicago Cubs 5, 9 innings, at Chicago:

Pete Rose entered this game three hits short of Ty Cobb's hit record, and was originally not going to play. Lefthander Steve Trout was going to pitch for the Cubs, and Rose, now a player-manager, did not normally play against lefties. But Trout called in injured (he claimed he fell off his bicycle) and righty Reggie Patterson filled in. So Rose started, and singled in the first and fifth, tying Cobb. The day had started hot and muggy. In the eighth a tremendous wind- and rain-storm blew through, delaying the game two hours, and dropping the temperature from 88 to 58. It was as if Cobb himself, watching, was saying, you may break my record, but not today. The Cubs entered the ninth leading, 5-4, and brought in closer Lee Smith. Rose was the fourth scheduled hitter. Smith gave up three straight singles, tying the game. Rose came up with runners on first and second and struck out on a powerful Smith fastball. After the bottom of the ninth, at 6:09 PM, the game was suspended in still-lightless Wrigley Field. The league said that if the game was necessary to determine a division championship (the Reds were at the time still marginally in contention), it would be finished the day after the season ended. When this became unnecessary, the game was declared a tie. Interesting footnote: if you accept the new research showing Cobb's true hit total to be 4,190, then Rose really did break his record on this date, in the fifth inning, with a line single to right off Patterson. 28,269 *may* have witnessed this bit of revisionist history.

August 26, 1986, Toronto 6, Cleveland 6, 9 innings, at Cleveland:

The Blue Jays and Indians play to their second tie in a little more than two years. These are, through the end of 1995, the only ties in the history of the Toronto franchise. Again, the game was tied in the last inning, Cleveland blowing a three-run lead in the top of the ninth. Only nine players (Lloyd Moseby, George Bell, Cliff Johnson, Rick Leach, Willie Upshaw, Ernie Whitt, Julio Franco, Pat Tabler and Brook Jacoby) played in both games, even though they were just over two years apart.

April 23, 1988, Montreal 3, Philadelphia 3, 7 innings, at Philadelphia:

This otherwise nondescript game was the second of

a three-game series played in variable April weather in Philadelphia. Andres Galarraga, in what would become his first big year for the Expos (29 home runs), hit his fourth of the year and went three-for-three. With one out in the bottom of the seventh the rain came and the game could not be continued.

July 16, 1988, Los Angeles 2, Chicago Cubs 2, 8-1/2 innings, at Chicago:

The long history of lightless Wrigley Field and its quirks took a final bow only two weeks before the lights were turned on for the first time. The Cubs fashioned an early 2-0 lead, but the Dodgers tied it in the top of the sixth on a sacrifice fly by Tracy Woodson. Meanwhile, there was a rain delay of 28 minutes prior to the bottom of the eighth, and then, with skies darkening, Steve Sax grounded out for the first out of the ninth. It then started pouring. The lights had been completely installed, and in fact had been tested on non-game nights several times the previous week, and certified for game use. But after one hour and fifty-three minutes of rain, despite the fact that it was clearing (it was early evening by now), the game was called rather than take a chance on it going into long extra innings and having the umpires order the lights turned on.

May 28, 1989, Atlanta 3, St. Louis 3, 9-1/2 innings, at St. Louis:

The day started cloudy and cool and didn't get much better on this Sunday afternoon. 35,832 saw the Cards jump out to a quick 3-0 lead, with a run in the first and two in the third, all driven in by Pedro Guerrero, who was on his way to one of his best RBI years. But Geronimo Berroa's two-run double scored the tying runs in the top of the eighth. Vince Coleman doubled to lead off the bottom of the ninth, and was sacrificed to third, where he was stranded. At 4:12 PM, after nearly three hours of play, it began raining and at 6:06 PM, since it was getaway day for the Braves, the game was called .

June 5, 1989, Pittsburgh 3, Philadelphia 3, 7-1/2 innings, at Philadelphia:

A seesaw battle between the two Pennsylvania clubs. Pittsburgh jumped out to a 2-0 lead on a two-run single by John Cangelosi in the second. The Phils claimed the lead in the bottom of the sixth on a three-run homer by Dickie Thon, his third of the season. But the Bucs came right back to tie it in the seventh, Bobby Bonilla doubling in Jose Lind. After a leadoff walk in the bottom of the eighth, Jim

Leyland called in Randy Kramer from the bullpen. Rain, though, prevented Kramer from facing a batter, which resulted in his being credited with appearing in a game without throwing a pitch.

September 13, 1989, Pittsburgh 0, St. Louis 0, 5-1/2 innings, at St. Louis:

This is the only scoreless tie among the thirty-eight since 1969. Appropriately, there was really nothing at all of significance that happened here, in front of 28,561 soggy fans. Jose DeLeon gave up only one hit, a double to Buc pitcher Doug Drabek, and also walked Jay Bell and John Cangelosi. Drabek allowed four hits and a walk. Since this was the last scheduled game between the two clubs in St. Louis that year, and the Cardinals were still in a pennant race, 5-1/2 games out of first place at the time, and both teams had an open date the next day, it was made up then in front of only 1,519, with the Pirates winning 4-3.

May 28, 1993, Montreal 2, Chicago Cubs 2, 5 innings, at Chicago:

Remember, your raincheck is no good for another game if five innings are played (4-1/2 if the home team is ahead). And that seemed to be the main thing on Cub management's mind that day. With 28,523 tickets sold, and many future games sold out, the two teams were forced to slog through rain in the second, third and fifth innings, before the Cubs tied it on a sacé—fice fly by Dwight Smith in the bottom of the fifth. There had been three years and almost three months since the last tie game, the Pittsburgh-St. Louis game in September, 1989, the longest such stretch in baseball history.

April 6, 1994, St. Louis 8, Cincinnati 8, 5-1/2 innings, at Cincinnati:

This goofy, sloppy game was played in 38-degree temperatures and a steady rain, with an announced paid attendance of 20,179, though less than half that number actually showed up. They were "rewarded" by witnessing the highest scoring of the thirty-eight ties since divisional play began. Marge Schott, not wanting to issue refunds on this third day of the season, made the teams start, and umpires made the teams play through downpours that turned the mound into mud. The Reds piled up a 5-2 lead by the third, but St. Louis put up a five-spot in the fourth, with two-run singles by Erik Pappas and Ozzie Smith. In the bottom of that inning the Reds moved ahead, 8-7, but the Cards' Luis Alicea tied it with a sacrifice fly in the top of the fifth. Once again, sad to say, a players' strike enters into the story of this tie. It was to have been replayed as part of a doubleheader on August 19, but the date was cancelled by the strike.

July 17, 1995, Chi. White Sox 1, N.Y. Yankees 1, 6 + innings, at New York:

Nearly nine years had passed since the last American League tie, the longest such gap in league history. The game was sloppy in more ways than just the

weather. The White Sox managed thirteen baserunners (nine hits, four walks) off Andy Pettitte and the Yankees had seven (two hits, five walks). The only runs scored after a Ray Durham triple and an intentional walk to Frank Thomas; Durham was driven in on an infield out. For the Yankees Mike Stanley homered in the fourth. Don Mattingly had doubled for the other hit just prior to the rain.

No-Hitter Lollapaloosas Revisited

Another look at Ryan's no-hit likelihoods

Bob Brown

In a 1993 article entitled "No-Hitter Lollapaloosas," Neal Moran worked out, among other things, the chances that Nolan Ryan would pitch seven no-hitters in his career (BRJ, pp. 93-94). He estimated them to be around 48 percent ("Nearly an even-money bet," to use his exact words). Think about that for a moment. With the available supply of probability limited to 100 percent (a supply that must be sufficient to cover *all* the outcomes possible, 761 in Ryan's case), how could so much of it be concentrated at *one single point*, a point that one would not ordinarily associate with having much of a chance to happen. If there's one thing I've learned over the years in my work, it's this: The *farther* an outcome is from the mean, the *less* likely it is to happen (a sum of 12 on two throws of a single die, a verbal SAT score of 700, a GPA of 3.9, and nine heads in ten flips of a fair coin would all be good examples of this principle). What do you think now? Could Ryan have had a 48 percent chance of doing something this unusual? We'll look into that in a moment, but first let's review how Mr. Moran arrived at this figure.

Mr. Moran's approach—He begins by estimating Ryan's chances of *not* pitching a no-hitter in his career (10 percent), and thus concludes he has a 90 percent chance of pitching *at least one* before he retires. This is perfectly reasonable, but he then

proceeds to break up the 90 percent in a totally unreasonable way. To figure Ryan's chances of pitching seven no-hitters, he simply raises .90 to the seventh power (48 percent). How do you suppose he would have figured Ryan's chances of pitching, say, six no-hitters? My guess is he would have raised .90 to the sixth power (53 percent). Surely you see the flaw in this reasoning. *We've already accumulated more probability, 111 percent by my count, than the distribution can possibly hold* (and, keep in mind, there are still 758 probabilities we haven't calculated yet).

It appears that Mr. Moran is using the formula $P(k) = .9^k$, k=1, 2,… to estimate Ryan's chances of pitching k no-hitters in his career. But the probabilities .9, $.9^2$, $.9^3$, … will eventually *sum* to $.9/(1-.9) = 9$, which is absurd. In the next section, I'll show you how this difficulty can be overcome.

The correct binomial approach—In order to figure the chances that any pitcher will throw any number of no-hitters in his career, one merely needs to know two things: First, the number of hits he surrendered per nine innings (which can easily be converted to an opposition batting average, or OBA), and, second, the number of games he started in his career, n. Since the pitcher has, approximately, a 1-OBA chance of retiring any batter he faces, the probability he'll retire 27 batters without giving up so much as even one hit is $(1-OBA)^{27}$. Let this probability (of success) be symbolized by the letter p. That is:

Bob Brown is a statistics professor at Providence College.

$P(\text{no-hitter } \textit{in any start}) = (1\text{-OBA})^{27} = p.$

Now, assuming this p-value stays about the same over the pitcher's entire career, and that what happens in one game (success or failure) has no effect on what happens in any other, the probability that a pitcher will throw x no-hitters in n career starts, written P(x), is given by

$$P(x) = \frac{n!}{x!\,(n\text{-}x)!}\, p^x(1\text{-}p)^{n\text{-}x}, \quad x = 0, 1, 2, \ldots, n$$

Anyone who's ever taken a statistics course should be familiar with the formula above. It's the binomial probability distribution (the distribution commonly associated with repeated trials of an experiment).

For the garden-variety pitcher with OBAs in the range .250 to .260 and somewhere between 200 and 300 career starts, virtually all of the probability in the distribution is concentrated at just two points: about 90 percent at the point x=0; the remaining 10 percent or so at the point x=1.

Perennial all-stars, with OBAs in the range .230 to .250 and around 400 career starts, have an outside chance (2 percent) of pitching two no-hitters.

Hall of Famers, with OBAs under .230 and at least 250 starts, have a shot at three, perhaps even four, no-hitters before they're through (see Appendix II for a partial list). What do you think Nolan Ryan's distribution looks like? Let's find out.

An illustration: Nolan Ryan—Nolan Ryan may have been the most difficult pitcher to hit in baseball history. He gave up, on average, only 6.5 hits per 9 innings for an OBA of:

$$OBA = \frac{6.5}{27+6.5} = .194$$

meaning he had nearly an 81 percent chance of retiring any batter he faced. Hence, he had about three chances in 1000, $p = (.806)^{27} = .003$, of pitching a no-hitter in any one of his starts. Since Ryan started n=760 games, his chances of pitching x no-hitters can be found from the binomial formula:

$$P(x) = \frac{760!}{x!\,(760\text{-}x)!}\,(.003)^x(.997)^{760\text{-}x}, \quad x = 0, 1, 2, \ldots, 760$$

For x=0, we get:

$$P(x=0) = \frac{760!}{0!\;760!}\,(.003)^0(.997)^{760}$$
$$= (.997)^{760}$$
$$= .10$$

For x=1, we get:

$$P(x=1) = \frac{760!}{1!\;759!}\,(.003)^1(.997)^{759}$$
$$= .23$$

and so forth. Table 1 summarizes all the calculations for the possibilities x = 0, 1, 2, ... , 760 (all done on a hand-held calculator rounded to two places in, perhaps, five minutes).

Table 1.

Nolan Ryan's No-Hit Distribution

no-hitters, x	0	1	2	3	4	5	6	7	8 or more
Prob., P(x)	.10	.23	.27	.20	.12	.05	.02	.01	negligible

Hence, my suspicion was confirmed. Ryan had nowhere near a 48 percent chance of pitching seven no-hitters. It was closer to one percent.

One final example: Steve Carlton—To review just how easy it is to calculate these (binomial) probabilities, I've worked them out for HOFer Steve Carlton, who started n=709 games and gave up, on average, 8.06 hits per nine innings (OBA = .230). He had about one chance in a 1000, $p = (.77)^{27} = .0009$, of pitching a no-hitter in any one of them. Plugging into:

$$P(x) = \frac{709!}{x!\,(709\text{-}x)!}\,(.0009)^x(.9991)^{709\text{-}x}, \quad x = 0, 1, 2, \ldots, 709$$

yields the probabilities shown in Table 2.

Table 2

Steve Carlton's No-Hit Distribution

no-hitters, x	0	1	2	3	4 or more
Prob., P(x)	.53	.34	.11	.02	negligible

Mr. Moran's statement, "... it was about as likely for Ryan to have seven no-hitters as for Carlton to have only one!" (BRJ, 1993, p. 93) isn't supported by the math. Ryan's chances of pitching seven? About one percent. Carlton's chances of pitching one? Check the table above.

Appendix I: The Poisson Approximation to the Binomial

There is another way to figure the probabilities in Tables 1 and 2 above. A statistical distribution, the Poisson, closely approximates the binomial when p is small and n is large. The formula is:

$$P(x) = \frac{(np)^x}{(2.72)^{np}x!} , \quad x=0, 1, 2, \ldots$$

where, as before, n is the number of games started by the pitcher and p the small chance he has of throwing a no-hitter in any one of them.

Here's how the formula works. Let's use Carlton as an example. Substituting n=709 and p=.0009, we get:

$$P(x) = \frac{(.64)^x}{(2.72)^{.64}x!} = \frac{(.64)^x}{(1.90)x!}$$

Plugging in the x-values 0,1,2, and 3 yields, to two places, the exact same probabilities shown in Table 2! Want some practice? Use the formula:

$$P(x) = \frac{(2.29)^x}{(2.72)^{2.29}x!} = \frac{(2.29)^x}{(9.89)x!}$$

to approximate the probabilities shown in Table 1. You'll be pleasantly surprised.

Appendix II: No-Hit Distributions for Selected Pitchers

Pitcher	0	1	2	3	4	5 or more	n	p	np	$(2.72)^{np}$
Feller	.57	.32	.09	.02		n	484	.00115	.56	1.75
Ford	.64	.29	.06	.01		e	438	.001	.44	1.55
Gibson	.55	.33	.10	.02		g	482	.00122	.59	1.80
Johnson	.41	.37	.16	.05	.01	l	665	.00134	.89	2.44
Koufax	.48	.35	.13	.03	.01	i	314	.0023	.72	2.06
Maloney	.68	.26	.05	.01		g	262	.0015	.39	1.47
Palmer	.53	.34	.11	.02		i	521	.0012	.63	1.88
Seaver	.40	.37	.17	.05	.01	b	647	.0014	.91	2.49
Sutton	.51	.34	.12	.03		l e	756	.0009	.68	1.97

NO-HITTERS

Mr. Moran wrote that, "Ryan's seven no-hitters were 4.4 times as likely as the two by Maloney, ..." (BRJ, 1993, p. 94). *Actually, it was the other way around.* Maloney had a 5 percent chance of throwing two no-hitters; Ryan had only a 1 percent chance of throwing seven.

Ken Burns Commits an Error

Things weren't what they seemed

Leo Trachtenberg

To millions of baseball fans who saw Ken Burns' "Fourth Inning of Baseball: The American Epic," what appeared on our TV screens as the visual record of Babe Ruth's 1927 record-breaking sixtieth home run is accepted as truth. After all, we've been conditioned to believe that so-called documentary films give us the straight facts. And there it supposedly is, the shot of Babe slugging number sixty, palpable and vibrant, enlivening our screens, evocative of the great event. An event particularly captivating to those not yet born when Babe slammed his memorable homer, which means most viewers.

The trouble is that the movie film purportedly showing Babe socking number sixty is misleading. Indeed, what we've been given by Burns as the visual truth of Ruth's epic sixtieth is film that couldn't have been made on September 30, 1927, the day Ruth set his remarkable home run record.

To understand what the film makers have done with the supposed pictorial account of that famous 1927 homer—an event that climaxed the remarkable season of what has been called the greatest of ball clubs, the 1927 Yankees—let's examine both picture and track of the "Fourth Inning."

Here, shot by shot, is the sequence and narration in script form.

1: <u>TILT UP</u> ALONG THE EXTERIOR OF THE FACADE OF YANKEE STADIUM. IT IS FESTOONED WITH AMERICAN FLAG BANNERS.

<u>Narration</u>

"On September 30, the next to last day of the season, and needing just one more home run, he faced Tom Zachary of the Senators."

2: <u>LONG SHOT</u> FROM STANDS LOOKING TOWARDS HOME PLATE. THE STADIUM, FESTOONED WITH BANNERS, IS PACKED WITH FANS.

3: FULL LENGTH VIEW OF RUTH AT THE PLATE. THE STANDS IN THE BACKGROUND ARE FULL.

<u>Narration</u>

"The first Zachary offering was a fast one which sailed over for a called strike. The next one was high."

Leo Trachtenberg is the author of The Wonder Team, *a history of the 1927 Yankees.*

4: ANOTHER FULL LENGTH VIEW OF THE BABE AT THE PLATE: THE CAMERA IS SHIFTED SLIGHTLY TO THE LEFT. BABE SWINGS AND CONNECTS.

Narration

"The Babe took a vicious swing at the third pitched ball, and the bat connected with a crash that was audible in all parts of the stands."

5: LONG SHOT FROM STANDS. EXCITED CROWD IN FOREGROUND RISES.

6: CAMERA AT FIELD LEVEL ON LEFT FIELD SIDE OF DIAMOND. BABE CIRCLES BASES, TIPS HIS HAT, HEADS FOR THE DUGOUT.

Narration

"While the crowd cheered, and the Yankee players roared their greeting, the Babe made his triumphant, almost regal tour of the paths. And when he embedded his spikes in the rubber disc to officially complete homer sixty, hats were tossed in the air, papers were torn and tossed liberally, and a spirit of celebration permeated the place."

8: PAN SHOT OF PACKED STANDS.

9: CLOSE SHOT OF BABE SMILING.

Narration

"'Sixty, count em, sixty,' Babe shouted in the locker room. 'Let's see some other son of a bitch match that!'"

So what's wrong with the Burns film of Babe's sixtieth, a filmic image fostering the belief that what we're seeing is actual footage of the event?

For one thing, as far as we know, *no motion picture footage exists* of Ruth hitting his sixtieth homer. Authentic *still* photos of him walloping that round-tripper, and crossing the plate after he circled the bases, have been published many times. But to this day no film footage of the sixtieth home run has surfaced.

As for the shots of the packed stands, according to the New York *Times* story of October 1, 1927 (almost all the narration in the Burns film was taken from that story), only about 10,000 fans attended that game. Nor, as far as we know, wer the exterior and interior of Yankee Stadium decorated with banners that day.

The late Pete Sheehy, in 1927 a 16-year-old gofer, and later the Yankee clubhouse man, recalled in a 1984 interview, "We might have had about five or six thousand people. I was sitting there, and he hit his sixtieth home run. I was in the dugout. It was no big deal, next year he might hit sixty-two.... Of course there was a lot of hand-shaking. Today it would be a

madhouse."

Evidently the footage we see in the TV film was shot at some other, possibly later, date, perhaps at an Opening Day or a World Series. But the Burns film gives us the impression that we're watching film of the actual event, not footage passed off as the real thing.

It can be argued that Burns, by using footage taken of Ruth playing before a crowded and festive Yankee Stadium at some other time, is simply re-enacting that famous sixtieth shot. But if that was his intent he should have so informed the audience, not used substitute footage on trusting and unwitting viewers.

In a film that is touted as factual, that purports to give us a true history of a famous baseball happening, to visually misrepresent the facts is to mislead the public. Now millions of baseball fans unfamiliar with the reality, or the newspaper reporting of Babe's sixtieth—how Yankee Stadium looked on September 30, 1927, the size of the crowd, all the visual elements surrounding Ruth's record-breaking blast—will accept the Burns footage as an authentic record of the event.

We live in a TV-dominated age when much of what appears on the home screen is skewed, slanted, hoked up, often with deliberate intent to gull viewers. It's done during election campaigns by political spinmeisters; with so-called film biographies that falsify deeds and lives; with tendentious talk shows that influence or mislead, rather than inform. In too much of what's beamed to us on TV, it's the contrived image, not the unadorned truth. By giving us that misleading picture of a celebrated moment in baseball history Burns and his associates have slighted their obligation to historic authenticity.

"The historian judges the past and instructs the present for the benefit of the future," wrote the eminent German scholar Leopold von Ranke (1795-1886), generally recognized as the founder of the objective and scientific approach to the study and writing of history. Ranke cautioned us that the historian must give us the facts, the deeds, *"Wie es eigentlich gewesen."* The way it really was.

I don't know if Ken Burns and his coworkers came across von Ranke's dictum while making the "Fourth Inning of Baseball: The American Epic." But it might have curbed their impulse to diddle with the visual facts if someone had brought it to their attention when they were chronicling Babe Ruth's sixtieth. For what we've been given is not "The way it really was," but a pictorial invention.

Ken Burns' baseball series has many virtues: Why tarnish it with a major instance of false imagery?

Baseball's Most Complete Batters

Twenty-five since 1900

Mark VanOverloop

With more than five years of new research since I published my 1990 book *Baseball's Greatest Total Hitters*, I want to expand on my original top ten Power/Average hitters. This article ranks the players I think are the twenty-five most complete batters of all time. I determined the original top ten by using batting average plus home run percentage as the criteria. For this new list I include the two best traditional batting statistical measurements, Slugging Average (which encompasses Batting Average) and On-Base Percentage. The result is one easily computed, comprehensive measure of offense.

The starting point for the new rankings come from two formulas introduced in Leo Leahy's book *Lumber Men*:

Bases to Outs Ratio (BTOR)=(Total Bases+Bases on Balls)/Outs

Offensive Quotient (OQ)=Player's BTOR/League BTOR

OQ takes a player's BTOR and makes it relative to his era, to show how each player fared in comparison to the rest of the league during his career. The league average OQ is 100, so Babe Ruth's 218 OQ and Ted Williams' 210 (the only two players with an OQ of over 200) mean that Ruth's offensive productivity was 118 percent greater than that of his contemporaries, while Williams' was 110 percent above the norm.

Eight of my top ten Power/Average hitters (Ruth,

Williams, Lou Gehrig, Jimmie Foxx, Johnny Mize, Mel Ott, Hank Greenberg, and Willie Mays) rank among the twenty-five most complete batters, while the other two, Hank Aaron and Joe DiMaggio, rate the thirty-first and thirty-seventh spots, respectively. *Lumber Men* included players who played from 1876-1992, while my list includes only players from 1900-95. Barry Bonds' stats are updated and Frank Thomas is now included.

Just as in the vast majority of the charts, statistics, and offensive measures included in *Baseball's Greatest Total Hitters*, Ruth is for the most part ranked first. Williams is usually second behind Ruth (but in the few instances when the Babe slips to runner-up, Ted is in the top spot), with Gehrig very often third behind the Big Two.

In just his first five full seasons, Thomas has established himself as the most complete (Power+Average+Walks) batter since Ted Williams and, if he can maintain his current pace, one of the five or ten greatest hitters of all time. His .593 slugging average and .453 on base average are both the best since Williams retired thirty-five seasons ago.

Willie McCovey, Mike Schmidt, and Harmon Killebrew are ranked high despite their relatively low batting averages. (They all hit over 500 homers, resulting in lots of extra bases and total bases.) Out of respect for their awesome power they drew plenty of walks. McCovey and Killebrew played the bulk of their careers in the pitcher-dominated 1960's and early '70's when low batting averages were the league

Mark Van Overloop, the author of Baseball's Greatest Total Hitters, *is the founder/president of and an active player in of "A League of Our Own"—a 40+ men's baseball league in Park Ridge, New Jersey.*

norm, and their OQs reflect this.

Of the twenty-five most complete batters, twenty are enshrined in the Hall of Fame, and the two active players on the list (Thomas and Bonds) seem to be headed in that direction, barring disasters. Of the remaining three, one is Joe Jackson, who is barred. Dick Allen played his whole career during the pitcher-dominated 1960s through mid-1970s era, which held down all batting statistics. He also retired young, and he had a poor relationship with the press. Charlie Keller began his career with five very productive seasons by the age of 27, but missed most of the next two seasons serving in WWII, then came back to play his last full season in the year he turned 30. During his final six seasons, injuries limited him to an average of just 104 at bats. Over his six full seasons, Keller averaged 98 runs, 21 doubles, 10 triples, 25 homers, 98 RBI, 103 walks along with a .291 batting mark. If fate had let him continue that pace he would have been a legitimate Hall candidate.

To take the Offensive Quotient one step further, adjust each OQ by the player's home park factor. This results in Kiner and Wagner dropping out of the top twenty-five, being replaced by Willie Stargell, Jack Fournier, Hank Aaron, and Joe DiMaggio (a 3-way tie for 25th). With Aaron and DiMaggio included in this Park-Adjusted OQ, all ten of my original top ten Power Average hitters would be among the twenty-five most complete batters of all time, as Ruth and Williams would once again occupy their customary positions as leader and runner-up.

I was pleased to note the significant overlap between by lists, generated statistically, and the list Ted Williams put together for his Hitters' Hall of Fame. Williams included all of my top ten Power Average hitters (except for himself, out of modesty) among the top sixteen spots on his list. Thirteen of my top twenty-five are among his top twenty (again, not including himself). Five more players from Williams' list are on at least one of my top twenty-five OQ or Park-Adjusted OQ lists. This sort of consistency indicates that the approach I am using is a useful way to rank hitters over their careers.

25 Most Complete Batters Since 1900

	OQ	BTOR	SA	OBA	BA
Babe Ruth	218-#1	1.421-#1	.690-#1	.474-#2	.342-#6
Ted Williams	210-#2	1.366-#2	.634-#2	.483-#1	.344-#5
Lou Gehrig	177-#3	1.243-#3	.632-#3	.447-#3	.340-#11
Roger Hornsby	177-#3	1.096-#8	.577-#8	.434-#4	.358-#2
Frank Thomas	177-#3	1.242-#4	.593-#6	.453-#5	.323
Mickey Mantle	176-#6	1.097-#7	.557-#11	.423-#12	.298
Jimmie Foxx	173-#7	1.167-#5	.609-#4	.428-#6	.325-#25
Ty Cobb	170-#8	.980-#20	.512	.433-#5	.366-#1
Willie McCovey	169-#9	.929	.515	.377	.270
Johnny Mize	168-#10	1.010-#17	.562-#9	.397	.312
Stan Musial	166-#11	1.053-#10	.559-#10	.418-#15	.331-#20
Dick Allen	164-#12	.952	.534-#22	.381	.292
Joe Jackson	164-#12	.964-#24	.517	.423-#12	.356-#3
Mel Ott	162-#14	1.025-#13	.533-#24	.414-#17	.304
Tris Speaker	161-#15	.970-#22	.500	.428-#6	.345-#4
Mike Schmidt	160-#16	.966-#23	.527	.384	.267
Hank Greenberg	160-#16	1.120-#6	.605-#5	.412-#19	.313
H. Killebrew	159-#18	.940	.509	.379	.256
Hack Wilson	159-#18	.990-#19	.545-#15	.395	.307
Charlie Keller	159-#18	1.015-#16	.518	.410-#21	.286
Willie Mays	158-#21	.991-#18	.557-#11	.387	.302
Barry Bonds	157-#22	1.017-#14	.541-#17	.398	.286
Ralph Kiner	156-#23	1.029-#11	.548-#14	.398	.279
Frank Robinson	154-#24	.961-#25	.537-#19	.392	.294
Honus Wagner	154-#24	.830	.466	.390	.327-#23

Cleveland's Greatest Team

1995…so far

Vince Gennaro

The summer of '95 was a storybook summer in Northeast Ohio. The Cleveland Indians treated their long-suffering fans to a fairy tale season that included 100 wins (in a strike shortened 144-game season). Nearly thirty percent of those wins were earned in the Indians' last at bat, and a remarkable eight games ended with the thrill of a Tribe home run. The Indians displayed outstanding hitting and pitching, leading the American League in both batting average and earned run average. If the season had been of normal length, they would have challenged the '61 Yankees all-time team home run record. The Indians had their individual achievements too, as Albert Belle became the first player in baseball history to hit 50 home runs and 50 doubles in the same season.

This was a great Indian team, and it holds the promise of more success in the future. On the other hand, Cleveland baseball fans are already engaging in debate over how good the '95 club was in comparison to earlier great Indians squads. How does it compare to the astounding 1954 club that won a record 111 games, or the 1920 and 1948 world championship teams? Is the '95 team the greatest team in Cleveland history, or are we swayed to favor it because it's here and now after such a long dry spell?

We all know how difficult it is to compare great teams from different eras. It has always seemed to me that the fairest and most practical way to measure a team's greatness may be to compare it to the other teams it competed directly against.

I've attempted to do exactly that for the four top teams in Cleveland baseball history—the four pennant winners of 1920, 1948, 1954, and 1995. No other Indians teams were even close, statistically, to the accomplishments of these clubs. I created a formula that values both the end result—winning—*and* the means by which teams go about winning games—batting and pitching.[1] Instead of comparing the four teams' performances directly with each other, I looked at how each compared to the American League teams they played against.

To make my comparison, I weighted four categories: regular season winning performance (30 percent), batting (30 percent), pitching (30 percent), and postseason winning percentage (10 percent). Batting and pitching were further divided. Batting included runs per game, batting average, and slugging percentage, while pitching included hits per game, ERA, and strikeout-to-walk ratio. (For greater detail on the formula, see the notes at the end of this article.)

I've placed significant emphasis on the postseason because I believe that a team's claim to greatness is related to its success in its sport's premier event. I also believe, though, that this calculation should go beyond noting whether a team won or lost the Series,

I don't think that falling short of a world championship is a tragic flaw when measuring greatness. The four teams in our comparison did not compete for a world championship under similar circumstances.

Vince Gennaro, *a third baseman at heart, is a business executive in Cleveland.*

Baseball's postseason is divided into two eras—pre-1969 and 1969 to the present. Pre-1969 the *only* postseason was the World Series, and for much of that time (prior to 1960) only sixteen teams competed for the championship. For the 1920, 1948, and 1954 teams, a greater than .500 postseason winning percentage *literally* meant a world championship. Today nearly as many teams (fourteen) are competing for a league championship. In 1995, to win a World Series, a team had to win three short elimination series, instead of one. Simply put, while it might be a touch easier to win a division title in 1995 than a league championship in 1954, it's much tougher to win three postseason series than to win one. To me, postseason winning percentage seems the fairest way to compare the postseason adventures and accomplishments of teams in different eras.

The following (Table 1) are the key statistics used in evaluating each of the four Cleveland clubs:

Table 1.

	1920	1948	1954	1995
Regular Season Winning Pct.	.636	.626	.721	.694
Batting/Offense				
Runs/game	5.56	5.38	4.84	5.83
Batting Avg.	.303	.282	.262	.291
Slugging Pct.	.417	.431	.403	.479
Pitching/Defense				
Hits/game	9.5	8.0	7.7	8.8
ERA	3.41	3.22	2.78	3.83
SO/BB Ratio	1.16	0.95	1.40	2.08
Postseason Winning Pct.	.714	.667	.000	.600

The 1920 Cleveland club led all four Indians teams in batting average (.303) and postseason winning percentage, as it went 5-2 to win one of the last best-of-nine World Series. The stars of the club were Hall of Famer Tris Speaker, the player-manager who finished second in the league in batting at .388, and pitchers Jim Bagby (31-12) and Stan Coveleski (24-14). Bagby led the league in games, innings pitched, and wins. Several other players had solid years in a season marred by the death of infielder Ray Chapman. Third baseman Larry Gardner had one of his best seasons, hitting .310 and leading the Indians with 118 RBIs. Bill Wambsganss, of unassisted triple play fame, was the only regular to hit below .290. Pitcher Ray Caldwell, at the tail end of a twelve-year career, delivered his only 20-win season to help the cause.

The 1948 team was well balanced. Along with middle infielders Lou Boudreau and Joe Gordon, the team's stars included pitchers Bob Feller, Bob Lemon, and Gene Bearden, who won a combined 59 games. Lemon led the league in innings pitched, and Bearden in ERA. Cleveland finished the season in a dead heat with the Red Sox, and won the pennant in a one-game Fenway playoff. In the postseason, the '48 team bested the Boston Braves for Cleveland's second World Championship, behind the pitching of Lemon (2-0). (The only two times the Indians won the World Championship, they employed a player-manager—Speaker in '20 and Boudreau in '48.)

The 1954 club, with 111 wins and a .721 winning percentage, had the best record of any team since the 1909 Pirates. They also led our four Indians nominees in several pitching categories, but were winless in the World Series, as they were swept by the New York Giants. The batting stars included the league batting champ Bobby Avila, and home run and RBI leader Larry Doby. Pitchers Lemon, Early Wynn, and Mike Garcia, who combined for 65 wins, all had career years. Even the aging Bob Feller was 13-3 in the twilight of his glorious career.

The 1995 club led all four teams in runs per game and slugging percentage. In addition to Albert Belle, the Indians had five other starters who batted .300 or more, including second-year star Manny Ramirez, who batted .308 with 31 home runs and 107 RBIs. The '95 club also fashioned outstanding pitching, led by Orel Hershiser and Charles Nagy with matching 16-6 records. Jose Mesa headed baseball's best bullpen with 46 saves in 48 save opportunities and set the major league record for consecutive saves in one season. In the postseason they swept the Red Sox in the Division Series, beat Seattle 4-2 in the ALCS and lost to Atlanta 4-2 in the World Series.

Rather than compare these four teams directly to each other, let's look at how they compared to the teams *they* competed against. Instead of the *absolute* statistics, Table 2 shows the teams "index" of performance vs. the entire league (e.g., a 115 index indicates the Indians team outperformed the "average" AL team by 15 percent). The team with the highest Grand Total Index is judged to be the greatest team in Cleveland history.

Table 2.

	1920	1948	1954	1995
Regular Season Winning Pct.	127	125	144	139
Batting/Offense				
Runs/game	117	114	115	115
Batting Avg.	107	108	102	108
Slugging Pct.	108	113	108	112

Pitching/Defense

Hits/game	102	113	112	106
ERA	110	125	125	119
SO/BB Ratio	121	116	125	130
Postseason Winning Pct.	143	133	0	120
Grand Total Index	**118.9**	**119.7**	**111.9**	**122.7**

By this measure—a team's performance relative to its peers—the 1995 Indians are the greatest team in Indians history. Finishing second is the 1948 World Championship club, followed by the 1920 team and finally the 1954 team. The '95 team batted 11 percentage points higher than the next best-hitting team and 19 points higher than the American League average. Its .479 slugging percentage was 24 points higher than the next best Red Sox and 52 points higher than the AL average. Ironically, though, a team which earned most of its fame for its hitting and late-inning comebacks, actually dominated the AL in pitching. The staff yielded the fewest earned runs, and walks, and the lowest opposing batting average in the AL, while leading the league in saves and shut-outs. Its .694 regular season winning percentage, its respectable 9-6 postseason record, and its overall balance across all categories, clinch the distinction.

Others will have their own methods to rate Cleveland's teams, and will come to different conclusions. But I'm sure all long-suffering Indians fans hope the 1996 or 1997 Indians will end the debate, once and for all.

Notes:

Formula used to determine the Greatest Team in Cleveland Indians Baseball History:

30 percent: Index of regular season winning percentage to the AL average of .500

30 percent: Batting/Offense

   •Index of runs/game vs. the AL average (10%)

   •Index of batting average vs. the AL average (10%)

   •Index of slugging percentage vs. the AL average (10%)

30 percent: Pitching/Defense

   •Index of hits/game vs. the AL average (10%)

   •Index of ERA vs. the AL average (10%)

   •Index of strikeout-to-walk ratio vs. the AL average (10%)

10 percent: Index of post season winning percentage vs. average of .500

[1]In Harry Hollingsworth's book, *The Best and Worst Baseball Teams of All Time*, he cites analysis that, for the selected years analyzed, slugging percentage and ERA alone explain 84 percent of the variation in teams' winning percentage.

Rariden on Relief

Bill Rariden may be old enough to retire to his farm forever, as he threatens to do, but he knows a lot of wise things. He says:

"No matter how good a club's pitchers may be there are bound to be off days when they get knocked out or days when your team don't hit and it's the right move to send someone up to hit for the pitcher. If you have a good relief pitcher or two around you are fixed. A hurler who can go in there for a lead or stop the other fellows is worth more salary than any other pitcher. If you have not such an animal as a relief pitcher around you must send in one of the regulars and thus break up the regular order in which they are being worked, or worse yet, send in some pitcher who doesn't fill the bill. There's nothing more effective in a pitching way than to have four men who can be worked in regular order. A good relief pitcher enables a manager to keep his men going that way. Relief pitching is a trade all by itself. If more pitchers specialized in it or were trained in it we would have tighter baseball." (The Sheffield, Alabama Standard, May 6, 1921.)

—Jimmie Purvis

Tomorrow the World

Welcome to the Fairbanks Airtank

Don Nelson

Sometime in the future there may be major league baseball teams in Tokyo, Mexico City and Rome (I could imagine that). And maybe in Havana, Fairbanks and Shanghai (harder to imagine). But stranger things have happened. The technology is already available: fast, convenient travel for the teams (New York to Rome in five hours by supersonic jet); instant communications by satellite and the internet; climate-controlled stadia for the spectators. (I have a suggestion for the name of the farthest-north arena: The Fairbanks Airtank.)

The politics aren't quite right for all of these cities right now. There was a day not long ago when it was easy to go to Havana and impossible to enter Shanghai. That situation is reversed today, even though Cuba is only ninety miles from our shores and China is a whopping 6,000 miles distant.

The major league map today is already quite extensive, stretching from Seattle to Montreal and from San Diego to Miami. The baseball map through 1952 defined a much smaller world (see Map 1). The longest trip then was the 1,000 miles between St. Louis and Boston. Today, when the Giants play the Expos, they must traverse 2,500 miles to get there. The pre-1953 major league baseball map on the one hand was a strange concept of the National Pastime and on the other made great sense for that era.

The majors' map remained unchanged for fifty

years, between the time the Baltimore American League club moved to New York in 1903 and the Boston National League club vacated that city for Milwaukee in 1953. In succeeding years, the map was redrawn again by the move of St. Louis (AL) to Baltimore in 1954 and Philadelphia (AL) to Kansas City in 1955. But these dislocations stretched the boundaries very little—a bit to the north of Chicago and a little west of St. Louis. The Browns–Orioles migration was an internal switch. Every city that had a team or teams before the migrations still had one.

The real revolution began in 1958 when the Brooklyn Dodgers and the New York Giants fled clean across the country to Los Angeles and San Francisco.

Let's deal with the strangeness of that 1903-53 map. It consisted of ten cities in seven states and the District of Columbia, bounded roughly by the Mississippi River on the West, the Ohio and Potomac Rivers on the South, the Great Lakes and Canada on the North and the Atlantic Ocean on the East. Everything west and south of those boundaries (about 88 percent of the area of the forty-eight states) was excluded from major league competition.

Considering the transportation and communication of the time, it might be fair to say that each major league city had a "coverage" area of about 100 miles in all directions. That being the case, the coverage area extended into parts of thirteen additional states in the Northeast and Midwest, still a small chunk of the geography of the forty-eight United States.

Don Nelson, who has had several articles in SABR publications over the years, is still retired, still living in Fairfax, Virginia, and still (rats!) a Cub fan.

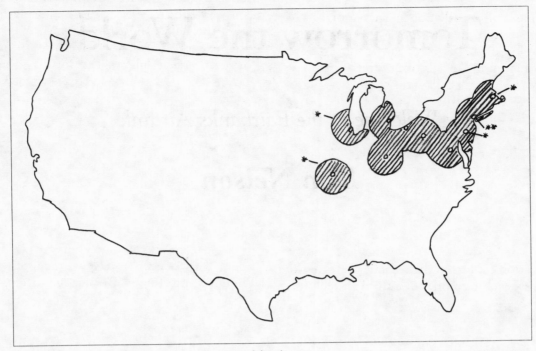

Map 1

Nonetheless, this distribution of teams made some sense. All of the largest cities of the '30s and '40s except Los Angeles and San Francisco were represented. All of the largest population states except California and Texas were at least partly covered. Figuring a population area a little bigger than that covered by the circles on the map (all of the seven major league states plus part of the people living in the other thir-

teen), about half the population had reasonable access to major league ball.

The trouble with California and Texas was that they were too far away to be reached conveniently by rail. Another consideration was that day games played in the hot South and Southwest summers could be brutal for ballplayers and fans alike.

Of course, it wasn't as if 90 percent of the country

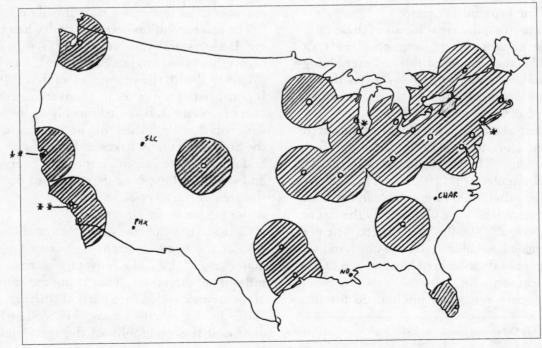

Map 2

didn't have baseball at all. Southerners got to see major league ball in preseason spring training games and some of the other parts of the country were treated to barnstorming exhibitions after the end of the regular season in the fall. And there were some forty minor leagues operating out of about 300 cities from coast to coast and border to border.

Technological advances—I would say that two air technologies—air travel and air conditioning—had more to do with expanding the major league map than anything else. Air travel cut the travel time to the West Coast and Texas to hours instead of days. Air conditioning was an indirect stimulus, making the Sunbelt more livable and contributing to growth of large population centers in the steamier parts of the country. This is reaching a bit, but a third air technology—air waves—also contributed. Radio and television made fans all over the country wonder: Why can't we have a major league team, too?

Map 2 shows the approximate major league "coverage" of the mid-'90s. It assumes that the coverage radius for each city, considering modern transportation and communication, is at least half again as large as it was prior to 1953. Most major metropolitan areas of the nation now have teams. All the pre-1953 cities except Washington still have at least one team. Most of the people in the forty-eight contiguous states have reasonable access to live major league action and virtually everybody can see it live on TV. Approximately 40 states now are within reach of the 150-mile rings, double the number before 1953. But there are still plenty of gaps in the coverage in the Southeast, Great Plains, Rocky Mountains, and mid-north Pacific coast.

A look at Map 2 shows why Denver and Miami were good choices in the last expansion. Denver, especially, may have a huge drawing circle around it, judging from attendance there. And since a large population center and "coverage" are important, Phoenix and Tampa Bay are good choices for the 1998 expansion. So for the next expansion? If population is the overriding factor, then why not Washington? If "coverage" area is most important, then perhaps Charlotte or Salt Lake City are potential attendance winners.

By the Numbers

Baseball is looking at different numbers than the other two top professional sports.

For baseball, you need the potential for 50,000 seats over eighty open dates a season, for a total potential attendance of 4,000,000. (Toronto has done that.)

For basketball, you're looking at the potential for 20,000 seats over forty open dates, for a total attendance of 800,000.

For football, it's 75,000 seats over eight open dates, for a total attendance of 600,000.

So, a major league baseball team today has to have the potential to draw five to six times more fans than its basketball or football competition.

Baseball could consider the experience of other professional sports cities when it comes to expansion:

"Open" cities with football teams only: Buffalo, Jacksonville, New Orleans.

"Open" cities with basketball teams: Orlando (a leader for the year 2000 expansion), Portland, Sacramento, San Antonio, Salt Lake City, Vancouver.

"Open" cities with both basketball and football teams: Charlotte, Indianapolis, Washington.

Whether Fairbanks or Honolulu ever has a major league baseball team is a pretty far-out question, but it's an American question. Whether Tokyo and London do, that's an international question.

—D.N.

Normalized Winning Percentage

A *significant improvement upon an old idea*

Bill Deane

Although most baseball observers realize winning percentage is a less than reliable tool for rating pitchers—due chiefly to its team-dependency—they continue to use it nonetheless. And, if we are going to use a flawed tool, we might as well try to improve upon it, which I think I've done with a statistic I call "normalized winning percentage." NWP projects how a pitcher might perform on a .500-team, thus putting all hurlers, past and present, on an even plane of comparison. I offer it as the ultimate tool for evaluating a pitcher's ability to win.

The concept for NWP starts out by comparing a pitcher's won-lost record to that of his team, neutralizing the impacts of a team's offense and defense on its pitchers' records. This idea is hardly new: Ted Oliver used it in his *Kings of the Mound* in 1944; David Neft and Richard Cohen used it in *The Sports Encyclopedia Baseball* in 1973; Merritt Clifton used it in *Relative Baseball* in 1979; Pete Palmer used it in *The Hidden Game of Baseball* in 1984. Each of these men analyzed the data differently, but each overlooked one basic problem: a pitcher on a poor team has more room for improvement than one on a good team.

Consider the performances of Steve Carlton in 1972, and Greg Maddux in 1995. Carlton had a 27-10 (.730) record for the last-place Phillies, who were a woeful 32-87 (.269) in games in which Lefty did not get a decision. Carlton's percentage, therefore, ex-

ceeded his team's by a whopping 461 points out of a possible 731. On the other hand, it is hard to imagine anyone having a better pitching season than Maddux had, when he went 19-2 with an ERA (1.63) more than 2.5 runs better than the league's. Yet, Maddux's winning percentage was "only" 328 points above that of his Braves (71-52, .577, without Greg's decisions). Moreover, even if Maddux had been a perfect 21-0, he would have fallen short of Carlton's 461-point cushion. The point here is not to diminish Carlton's achievement, but to illustrate the potential inequity in this type of comparison.

NWP attempts to correct this inequity by measuring by how much a pitcher has exceeded his team's performance, dividing the result by how much he *could* have done so, and scaling the result as if he had pitched for an average (.500) team. Thus, a hurler who posts a .520 percentage for a .400-team gets credit for the same NWP score (.600) as a .600-pitcher on a .500-team, or a .680-pitcher on a .600-team—because each has exceeded his team's percentage by 20 percent of the potential room for improvement.

For a pitcher whose win percentage exceeds his team's, the formula for NWP is as follows:

$$\text{Average Pct.} + \frac{[(\text{Pitcher Pct.} - \text{Team Pct.}) \times (\text{Perfect Pct.} - \text{Average Pct.})]}{(\text{Perfect Pct.} - \text{Team Pct.})]}$$

Rather cumbersome but, since "Average Pct." is al-

Bill Deane is a freelance baseball writer, researcher, and consultant based near Cooperstown, New York. He spent eight years as Senior Research Associate for the National Baseball Library and Archive.

ways equal to .500 and "Perfect Pct." is always equal to 1.000, we can simplify the formula as follows:

$$NWP = .500 + \frac{\text{Pitcher Pct.} - \text{Team Pct.}}{2 \times (1.000 - \text{Team Pct.})}$$

For a pitcher whose percentage is lower than his team's, the converse-NWP formula is applicable:

$$NWP = .500 - \frac{\text{Team Pct.} - \text{Pitcher Pct.}}{2 \times \text{Team Pct.}}$$

To put the NWP formula into practice, let's take a look at Mike Mussina's 1995 performance for the Orioles. Mussina compiled a 19-9 (.679) log, while his team was 71-73 overall. Subtracting his decisions, the Orioles had a 52-64 record for a .448 percentage. Mussina's NWP is calculated as follows:

$$NWP = .500 + \frac{.679 - .448}{2 \times (1.000 - .448)}$$

$$\text{or } .500 + .231/1.104$$

Mussina's resultant NWP (.709) was one of the top six in the majors last year; a list of the 1995 leaders accompanies this article.

I developed the concept for NWP over a decade ago. The formula has undergone several minor refinements over the years, and undoubtedly has room for more. NWP's biggest weakness is that it assumes all pitching staffs to be created equal, so that an average pitcher on a poor staff (e.g., Toronto's Pat Hentgen) can appear better than an excellent pitcher on a great staff (Atlanta's John Smoltz). While this creates some aberrant single-season results, things tend to even out over a pitcher's career.

Adaptations—To figure how a pitcher might have fared on something other than a .500 team—for example, Carlton on the '72 NL champion Reds—simply substitute the desired percentage (.617, in this case) for "Average Pct." (.500) in the NWP formula. Carlton's projected percentage here is .858, or about a 32-5 record.

To adapt the NWP formula to a "replacement-level," choose a value for that level—say, .350 (meaning that we might expect a replacement-level pitcher on a .500 team to win 35 percent of his decisions). Divide that value by .500 (leaving .7 in this example), and multiply the result times "Team Pct." in both the numerator and denominator of the NWP formula.

NWP can be, and has been, incorporated into what analyst Pete Palmer calls "wins above team" (WAT), the number of victories a pitcher contributes over what an "average" pitcher might. Palmer revised his formula to include mine in *Total Baseball*. The formula for WAT (for pitchers with higher percentages than their teams) is as follows:

$$WAT = \text{Pitcher decisions} \times \frac{\text{Pitcher Pct.} - \text{Team Pct.}}{2 \times (1.000 - \text{Team Pct.})}$$

NWP gives Carlton's 1972 season a score of .815, while Maddux's 1995 campaign checks in at .887. But, because Carlton maintained his excellence over a greater number of decisions, he beats out Maddux in WAT, 11.7 to 8.1.

A list of the all-time leaders in NWP, including WAT, accompanies this article. Lefty Grove posted the best career normalized winning percentage (.643), while Cy Young accumulated the most wins above team (99.7). Each of the fifteen leaders is in the Hall of Fame and, as a group, their careers are evenly distributed between each decade from the 1900s to the 1970s (as opposed to conventional measures of pitching, which suggest that all of the best hurlers toed the rubber before 1920).

Current pitchers with strong chances of making the list are Boston's Roger Clemens (182 wins, a .654 NWP, and 43.1 WAT through 1995) and the Braves' Maddux (150, .606, 25.7). Other actives who have consistently recorded high NWPs include the Mariners' Randy Johnson (.644), the Yankees' David Cone (.616) and Jack McDowell (.579), the Rockies' Bret Saberhagen (.592), the Braves' Tom Glavine (.589), the Indians' Orel Hershiser (.583), and the Angels' Mark Langston (.581). Younger hurlers who have shown promise include Baltimore's Mike Mussina (.716), Kansas City's Kevin Appier (.620), and Florida's John Burkett (.602).

Leaders In Normalized Winning Percentage, With Wins Above Team

Bill Deane, with assistance from Pete Palmer

1995 Leaders (Minimum 13 Wins or 18 Decisions)

Pitcher	Club	W- L	TEAM	NWP	WAT
Randy Johnson	SEA (A)	18- 2	79-66	.902	8.05
Greg Maddux	ATL (N)	19- 2	90-54	.887	8.13
David Cone	TOR-NY (A)	18- 8	(a)	.729	6.17
Kenny Rogers	TEX (A)	17- 7	74-70	.722	5.33
Jaime Navarro	CHI (N)	14- 6	73-71	.714	4.28
Mike Mussina	BAL (A)	19- 9	71-73	.709	5.84
Erik Hanson	BOS (A)	15- 5	86-58	.708	4.15
Todd Stottlemyre	TOR (A)	14- 7	67-77	.707	4.35
Pat Rapp	FLA (N)	14- 7	67-76	.705	4.31
Ramon Martinez	LA (N)	17- 7	78-66	.703	4.88
Denny Neagle	PIT (N)	13- 8	58-86	.700	4.19
Pete Schourek	CIN (N)	18- 7	85-59	.680	4.49
Mark Langston	CAL (A)	15- 7	78-67	.674	3.83
Hideo Nomo	LA (N)	13- 6	78-66	.671	3.25
Alex Fernandez	CHI (A)	12- 8	68-76	.635	2.71
Pedro Martinez	MON (N)	14-10	66-78	.632	3.18
Kevin Appier	KC (A)	15-10	70-74	.628	3.20
Tom Glavine	ATL (N)	16- 7	90-54	.608	2.49
Jim Bullinger	CHI (N)	12- 8	73-71	.606	2.13
Al Leiter	TOR (A)	11-11	56-88	.604	2.29
Tim Wakefield	BOS (A)	16- 8	86-58	.600	2.40
Carlos Perez	MON(N)	10- 8	66-78	.600	1.80

(a) Cone's overall team percentage, weighted for his number of decisions with each club, was .433.

All-Time Leaders (Minimum 200 Wins Since 1900)

Pitcher	W	L	WAT	NWP
Lefty Grove	300	141	62.9	.643
Grover Alexander	373	208	81.6	.640
Whitey Ford	236	106	44.4	.630
Walter Johnson	417	279	90.0	.629
Cy Young	511	316	99.7	.621
Christy Mathewson	373	188	64.9	.616
Tom Seaver	311	205	58.9	.614
Juan Marichal	243	142	38.7	.601
Bob Feller	266	162	36.8	.586
Carl Hubbell	253	154	34.6	.585
Joe McGinnity	246	142	32.4	.584
Warren Spahn	363	245	45.8	.575
Ted Lyons	260	230	36.2	.574
Bob Gibson	251	174	31.0	.573
Jim Palmer	268	152	30.2	.572

Note: although Young and McGinnity started their careers before 1900, they are included because each won at least 200 games after that year. Their statistics include pre-1900 records.

All Star Games at Home

How hometown heroes fare

Ron Kaplan

Major leaguers are supposed to have an edge when playing in front of the home crowd, especially pressure-packed situations such as the World Series or All Star Games. In the Series, the star player is surrounded by a familiar supporting cast, as well as the season-long direction of his manager. But what happens when the midsummer classic takes place in his familiar environs?

Ever since White Sox third sacker Jimmy Dykes stroked two hits and scored one of the American League's four runs in the inaugural All Star Game at Comiskey Park in 1933, several players have come to the fore to uphold the glory of their league before their hometown faithful. More than a few have also failed to live up to their status in the eyes of the rest of the country. Few, however, have been out-and-out goats.

Batters in these circumstances have hit an un-All Star-like .238 in the 65 games. They scored 98 runs, rapped out 89 hits and batted in a paltry 38 runs. Of the hits seven were doubles and one was a three-bagger. Those who were lucky enough to blast homers before their home town crowds include Joe DiMaggio, Mickey Owen, Ted Williams (twice), Stan Musial, George Kell and Vic Wertz, Larry Doby and Al Rosen (also twice), Harmon Killebrew, Frank Howard, and Hank Aaron.

All Star pitchers have fared little better. In all, they accounted for five wins and five losses on the strength of 101.1 innings, yielding 43 earned runs and 85 safeties. The strikeout-to-walk ratio was pretty good: 80 K's to 32 free passes.

Carl Hubbell performed the All Star Game's most famous feat in 1934 at his New York Giants Polo Grounds, when he struck out Ruth, Gehrig, Foxx, Simmons, and Cronin in order. Unfortunately, Hub's temporary teammates could not hold on to a 4-0 lead, and the American League won their second straight game.

Johnny Vander Meer was the starting and winning pitcher for the National League in Cincinnati in 1938. The author of back-to-back no-hitters that season shut down the AL on one hit and no walks in his three innings.

In Yankee Stadium the following year, Joe DiMaggio and George Selkirk drove in two of the AL's runs on the way to a 3-1 victory. DiMaggio's contribution was a solo home run in the fifth. Red Ruffing, the starting pitcher for the AL, struck out four in his three innings of work.

The All Star Game returned to the Polo Grounds in 1942. While first baseman Johnny Mize and rightfielder Mel Ott started for the NL, it was Mickey Owen, their Brooklyn Dodger rival, who provided the only spark for the squad with a pinch hit homer. The Dodgers supplied five additional players to the roster, including starters Arky Vaughan at third, center fielder Pete Reiser and left fielder Ducky Medwick.

Ron Kaplan lives in Upper Montclair, New Jersey.

Billy Herman and Pee Wee Reese also appeared in the game. The cross-river Yankees chipped in four starters: Tommy Henrich, DiMaggio, Joe Gordon, and Spud Chandler, the winning pitcher.

Perhaps the most impressive individual achievement by an All Star at home was registered by Ted Williams, who returned from World War II in spectacular style in 1946. The Splendid Splinter accounted for four hits, including two home runs, scored four runs and drove in five before the frantic Fenway fans, leading his squad to a 12-0 shellacking of the beleaguered NL hurlers. Dom DiMaggio (CF), Johnny Pesky (SS), and Bobby Doerr (2B) also were among the starters for the AL.

In 1948, Stan Musial homered and drove in the only runs for the NL in its 5-2 loss in St. Louis. The fans must have been pleased, even if he did play for the Cardinals rather than the Browns, who hosted the game.

It was only fitting that Jackie Robinson should become the first black player to appear in All Star competition. Despite his double and three runs scored as a starter in the 1949 game, the AL won, 11-7, at Ebbets Field. Don Newcombe took the loss, giving up three hits, one walk, and two runs in less than three innings.

Tiger fans roared when third baseman George Kell and rightfielder Vic Wertz socked homers in the 1951 game at Briggs Stadium. That was about all they had to be happy about, as the NL turned the tables, 8-3. Fred Hutchinson, who would manage the 1962 NL All Star team, was one of the victimized moundsmen, yielding three runs on three hits and two walks in three innings.

Three years later Cleveland's Al Rosen and Larry Doby combined for three homers and six RBI to lead the AL squad to an 11-9 victory in Municipal Stadium. Rosen, who played both first and third, socked a pair of round trippers and knocked in five runs. Doby's was a pinch-hit blast. Starting second sacker Bobby Avila added a pair of RBIs on the strength of three hits. All told, the Indian's batters accounted for seven of the team's seventeen hits, four of the eleven runs, and eight RBIs.

In 1955, Milwaukee's Gene Conley earned the victory for the NL, 6-5, by striking out the side in the 12th inning at Milwaukee's County Stadium. Hank Aaron entered the game as a pinch runner and went on to collect two hits, score one run and drive in another.

Don Drysdale got the starting nod in the second game of the 1959 All Star competition (the contest expanded to two games from 1959-1962). He struck out five in three innings, but he also gave up three runs on four hits and three walks, and was charged with the loss.

In the first game of the 1960 series, played in Kansas City, Bud Daley, the lone K.C. Athletics representative, walked one and fanned two in closing the contest, won by the NL, 5-3. In the second game at Yankee Stadium, five Yankee starters (Roger Maris, Mickey Mantle, Moose Skowron, Yogi Berra, and Whitey Ford) could muster just two hits. Ford, the losing pitcher, yielded five hits and three runs in three innings.

On the other side of the continent the next year, Stu Miller, the Giant's diminutive reliever, became something of a dubious legend when he was blown off the mound by the strong Candlestick Park winds. Though charged with a balk, he was still the winning pitcher in the 5-4 game.

Johnny Callison deserves honorary mention, even if he wasn't a member of the host Mets in 1964: he blasted a three-run homer in the ninth inning to cement the NL's 7-4 win while wearing a New York batting helmet. Ron Hunt became the first Met to start in an All Star Game, getting one hit in three at-bats.

Harmon Killebrew belted a homer for his Twins fans in 1965, but it wasn't enough, as the NL beat the AL, 6-5, in Minnesota's Metropolitan Stadium.

Following a delay of several days because of rain in 1969, Frank Howard rewarded the patient Washington fans, smashing a long home run in his only at bat of the contest, won by the NL, 9-3.

Native Cincinnatian Pete Rose played both left and right fields in the 1970 All Star Game, held in the brand-new Riverfront Stadium. His bruising, run-scoring, game-winning collision at the plate with Cleveland's Ray Fosse is still seen in videos of baseball's most famous plays.

In 1972, as he was closing in on the all-time homer record, Hank Aaron added one more four-bagger, helping the NL win, 4-3, at Atlanta's Fulton County Stadium.

Philadelphia was the logical choice to host the All Star Game in the country's bicentennial year. Greg Luzinski was the only starter among the five Phillies who played, but Dave Cash was the only home team player to scratch out a hit in the 7-1 victory over the AL.

Five Yankees appeared before the New York crowd in 1977, as their league lost once again, 7-5. Willie Randolph started at second and got one hit in five trips to the plate. Reliever Sparky Lyle was touched for three hits and two runs in two innings.

None of the Dodgers' All Star representatives managed a hit in the 1980 contest held in the Chavez Ravine ballpark. Members of the ignominious group included starters Davey Lopes, Reggie Smith, and Steve Garvey. On a happier note, Jerry Reuss picked up the 4-2 victory, striking out the side in his one inning of work.

Two years later, Montreal's Steve Rogers was the starting and winning pitcher at Stade Olympique. Starters Andre Dawson and Gary Carter and substitutes Tim Raines and Al Oliver combined for three hits in ten at bats.

Baltimore fans roundly booed Cito Gaston, the manager of the 1993 AL squad, when he declined to bring pitcher Mike Mussina, the team's sole representative, into the game held in brand new Camden Yards. That several of Gaston's own Blue Jays were included on the squad added to the crowd's ire.

The complete listing of how home-town players fared in All Star competition through 1995 follows:

		AB	R	H	RBI	Comments:

1933, Comiskey Park, Chicago (AL) AL 4, NL 2

		AB	R	H	RBI	Comments:
White Sox:	Al Simmons, OF	4	0	1	0	
	Jimmy Dykes, 3B	3	1	2	0	
Cubs:	Gabby Hartnett, C	1	0	0	0	
	Woody English, PH	1	0	0	0	
	Lon Warneke, P	4 IP, 6H, 1R, 2K				

1934, Polo Ground, New York (NL) AL 9, NL 2

		AB	R	H	RBI	
Giants:	Mel Ott, OF	2	0	0	0	
	Bill Terry, 1B	3	0	1	0	
	Carl Hubbell, P	3 IP, 2H, 2BB, 6K				Starting pitcher; es-

tablished the record for consecutive strikeouts. After the first two batters reached base, Hubbell struck out Ruth, Gehrig, and Foxx. To start the 2nd inning, he fanned Simmons and Cronin.

Dodgers:	Van Lingle Mungo, P	1 IP, 4H, 4R, 2BB, 1K				Losing pitcher.
	AL Lopez, C	Did not play				
Yankees:	Lefty Gomez, P	3 IP, 3H, 4R, 1BB, 1K				Starting pitcher.
	Red Ruffing, P	1 IP, 4H, 3R, 1BB				Singled and drove in

a run in only AB.

	Babe Ruth, OF	2	1	0	0	
	Lou Gehrig, 1B	4	1	0	0	
	Bill Dickey, C	2	1	1	0	
	Ben Chapman, OF	Did not play				

1935, Municipal Stadium, Cleveland AL 4, NL 1

	Joe Vosmik, RF	4	1	1	0	
	Mel Harder, P	3 IP, 1H, 1K				Pitched final three

innings after Gomez' 6.

Earl Averill, OF

1936, Braves Field, Boston (NL) NL 4, AL 3

Braves:	Wally Berger	Did not play				
Red Sox:	Rick Ferrell, C	2	0	0	0	
	Jimmie Foxx, 1B	2	1	1	0	Singled as PH in 7th.
	Lefty Grove, P	3 IP, 3H, 2R, 2BB, 2K				Starting and losing

pitcher for AL.

1937, Griffith Stadium, Washington, DC AL 8, NL 3

	Rick Ferrell	Did not play				
	Wes Ferrell	Did not play				
	Buddy Myer	Did not play				

1938, Crosley Field, Cincinnati NL 4, AL 1

	Ival Goodman, RF	3	0	0	0	
	Ernie Lombardi, C	4	0	2	1	
	F. McCormick, 1B	4	1	1	0	
	J. Vander Meer, P	3 IP, 1H, 1K				Starting and winning

pitcher.

	Paul Derringer, P	Did not play				

1939, Yankee Stadium, New York (AL) AL 3, NL 1

Yankees:	Red Rolfe, 3B	4	0	1	0	
	Joe DiMaggio, CF	4	1	1	1	Homered in 5th
	Bill Dickey, C	3	1	0	0	
	George Selkirk, LF	2	0	1	1	
	Joe Gordon, 2B	4	0	0	0	
	Red Ruffing, P	3 IP, 4H, 1R, 1BB, 4K				Starting pitcher
	Frank Crosetti, SS	Did not play				
	Lefty Gomez, P	Did not play				
	Johnny Murphy, P	Did not play				
Giants:	Mel Ott, CF-RF	4	0	2	0	
	Harry Danning, C	Did not play				
	Bill Jurges, SS	Did not play				
Dodgers:	Dolph Camilli, PH	1	0	0	0	
	Babe Phelps, PH	1	0	0	0	
	C. Lavagetto, 3B	Did not play				
	Whitlow Wyatt, P	Did not play				

1940, Sportsmans Park, St. Louis (NL) NL 4, AL 3

Cardinals:	Johnny Mize, 1B	2	0	0	0	Starter
	Terry Moore, CF	3	0	0	0	Starter
Browns:	G. McQuinn, 1B	Did not play				

1941, Briggs Stadium, Detroit AL 7, NL 5

	Rudy York, 1B	3	0	1	0	Starter
	Al Benton, P	Did not play				
	Birdie Tebbetts, C	Did not play				

1942, Polo Grounds, New York (NL) AL 3, NL 1

Giants:	Johnny Mize, 1B*	2	0	0	0	Starter
	Mel Ott, RF	4	0	0	0	Starter
	Willard Marshall, PH	1	0	0	0	

Dodgers:	Billy Herman, 2B	1	0	0	0	
	Arky Vaughan, 3B	2	0	0	0	Starter
	Pete Reiser, CF	3	0	1	0	Starter
	Ducky Medwick, LF	2	0	0	0	Starter
	Pee Wee Reese, SS	1	0	0	0	
	Mickey Owen, PH	1	1	1	1	Homered as a PH.
Yankees:	Tommy Henrich, RF	4	1	1	0	Starter; doubled
	Joe DiMaggio, CF	4	0	2	0	Starter
	Joe Gordon, 2B	4	0	0	0	Starter
	Spud Chandler, P	4 IP, 2H, 2K				Starting and winning

pitcher.

1943, Shibe Park, Philadelphia, (AL) AL 5, NL 3

Athletics:	Dick Siebert, 1B	1	0	0	0	Starter
Phillies:	Babe Dahlghren, 1B	2	0	0	0	Hit into DP.

1944, Forbes Field, Pittsburgh NL 7, AL 1

	Vince DiMaggio, CF	0	0	0	0	
	Bob Elliott, 3B	3	0	0	0	Starter
	Rip Sewell, P	3 IP, 1BB, 2K				

1945, No Game

1946, Fenway Park, Boston (AL) AL 12, NL 0

Red Sox:	Dom DiMaggio, CF	2	0	1	0	Starter
	Johnny Pesky, SS	2	0	0	0	Starter
	Ted Williams, LF	4	4	4	5	Starter; enjoys trium-

phant return from military service. His two homers before the home crowd make for the most dramatic individual All Star performance.

	Bobby Doerr, 2B	2	0	0	0	Starter
	Rudy York, 1B	2	0	1	0	
	Hal Wagner, C	1	0	0	0	
Braves:	Johnny Hopp, CF	2	0	1	0	Starter
	Phil Masi, C	2	0	0	0	

1947, Wrigley Field, Chicago (NL) AL 2, NL 1

Cubs:	Andy Pafko, CF	2	0	1	0	
	Phil Cavarretta, 1B	1	0	0	0	K'd as PH
White Sox:	Luke Appling, PH	1	1	1	0	Singled as PH.

1948, Sportsmans Park, St. Louis (AL) AL 5, NL 2

Browns:	Al Zarilla, RF	2	0	0	0	
Cardinals:	R. Schoendienst, 2B	4	0	0	0	Starter
	Stan Musial, LF-CF	4	1	2	2	Starter, HR.
	Enos Slaughter, RF	2	0	1	0	Starter

1949, Ebbets Field, Brooklyn AL 11, NL 7

Dodgers:	Pee Wee Reese, SS	5	0	0	0	Starter
	Jackie Robinson, 2B	4	3	1	0	Starter (1st black

man to appear in AS Game); double.

	Gil Hodges, 1B	3	1	1	0	

	Roy Campanella, C	2	0	0	0	
	Preacher Roe, P	1 IP				
	Don Newcombe, P	2.2 IP, 3H, 2R, 1BB, 3K				Losing pitcher.
Giants:	Johnny Mize, 1B	2	0	1	0	Starter
	Willard Marshall, RF	1	1	0	0	Starter
	B. Thomson, PH	1	0	0	0	
	Sid Gordon, 3B	2	0	1	0	
Yankees:	Joe DiMaggio, RF	4	1	2	3	
	Yogi Berra, C	3	0	0	0	
	T. Henrich, OF	Selected as starter; did not play.				
	Vic Raschi, P	3 IP, 1H 3BB, 1K				Finished game.
	Allie Reynolds, P	Did not play				

1950, Comiskey Park, Chicago (AL) NL 4, AL 3

White Sox:	Ray Scarborough, P	Did not play				
Cubs:	Hank Sauer, RF	2	0	0	0	
	Andy Pafko, CF	4	0	2	0	Starter

1951, Briggs Stadium, Detroit NL 8, AL 3

	George Kell, 3B	3	1	1	1	Starter; homer.
	Vic Wertz, RF	3	1	1	1	Starter; homer.
	Fred Hutchinson, P	3 IP, 3H, 3R, 2BB				

1952, Shibe Park, Philadelphia (NL) NL 3, AL 2

Phillies:	Granny Hamner, SS	1	0	0	0	
	Curt Simmons, P	3 IP, 1H, 1BB, 3K				Starter
	Robin Roberts	Did not play				
Athletics:	Bobby Shantz, P	1 IP, 3K				Game called after 5 inn.

1953, Crosley Field, Cincinnati, NL 5, AL 1

	Ted Kluszewski, 1B	3	0	1	0	Starter
	Gus Bell, CF	3	0	0	0	Starter

1954, Municipal Stadium, Cleveland AL 11, NL 9

	Bobby Avila, 2B	3	1	3	2	Starter
	Larry Doby, CF	1	1	1	1	Homered as PH.
	Al Rosen, 1B-3B	4	2	3	5	Starter; 2 HR.
	Bob Lemon, P	.2 IP, 1H				
	Mike Garcia	Replaced on squad by Sandy Consuegra				

(White Sox)

NOTE: Best performance by home teammates.)

1955, County Stadium, Milwaukee NL 6, AL 5 (12 inn.)

	Eddie Mathews, 3B	2	0	0	0	Starter
	Hank Aaron, RF	2	1	2	1	Entered game as PR.
	Johnny Logan, SS	3	0	1	1	
	Del Crandall, C	1	0	0	0	Started in place of

Roy Campanella.

	Gene Conley, P	1 IP, 3K				Winning pitcher;

fanned side in 12th.

1956, Griffith Stadium, Washington NL 7, AL 3

Roy Sievers, PH   1   0   0   0

1957, Busch Stadium, St. Louis AL 6, NL 5

Stan Musial, 1B   3   1   1   0   Double

Wally Moon, PH   1   0   0   0

Larry Jackson, P   2 IP, 1H, 1BB

Hal Smith, C   Did not play

NOTE: 7 of 8 starting position players elected by fans were members of the Cincinnati Reds.

1958, Memorial Stadium, Baltimore AL 4, NL 3

Gus Triandos, C   2   0   1   0   Starter

Billy O'Dell, P   3 IP, 2K   Finished game; sac bunt.

1959, Forbes Field, Pittsburgh Game 1: NL 5, AL 4

Dick Groat, PH   0   0   0   0   Sac. as PH.

Bill Mazeroski, 2B   1   0   1   1

Elroy Face, P   1.2 IP, 3H, 3R, 2BB, 2K

Smoky Burgess, C   Did not play

1959, Memorial Coliseum, Los Angeles Game 2: AL 5, NL, 3

Junior Gilliam, 3B   2   1   1   1   Entered the game with walk as PH.

Wally Moon, LF   2   0   0   0   Starter

Charlie Neal, 2B   1   0   0   0

Don Drysdale, P   3 IP, 4H, 3R, 3BB, 5K Starting and losing pitcher.

1960, Municipal Stadium, Kansas City Game 1: NL 5, AL 3

Bud Daley, P   1 IP 1 BB, 2K   Finished game.

1960, Yankee Stadium, New York Game 2: NL 6, AL 0

Roger Maris, RF   4   0   0   0   Starter

Mickey Mantle, CF   4   0   1   0   Starter

Moose Skowron, 1B   1   0   1   0   Starter

Yogi Berra, C   2   0   0   0   Starter

Whitey Ford, P   3 IP, 5H, 3R, 1K   Starting and losing pitcher.

Elston Howard, C   Did not play

Jim Coates, P   Did not play

1961, Candlestick Park, San Francisco Game 1: NL 5, AL 4

Willie Mays, CF   5   2   2   1   Starter, double.

Orlando Cepeda, LF   3   0   0   0   Starter

Mike McCormick, P   3 IP, 1 H, 1R, 1BB, 3K

Stu Miller, P   1.2IP, 1R (0 ER), 1BB, 4K   Winning pitcher; blown off mound by Candlestick winds.

1961, Fenway Park, Boston Game 2: AL 1, NL 1

Don Schwall, P   1   0   0   0

3 IP, 5H, 1R, 1BB, 2K, 1HB

NOTE: Game called (rain) after 9 inn.

1962, D.C. Stadium, Washington Game 1: NL 3, AL 1

Dave Stenhouse, P   Did not play

1962, Wrigley Field, Chicago Game 2: AL 9, NL 4

Cubs: Ernie Banks, 1B   2   1   1   0   Triple

Billy Williams, LF   1   0   0   1

George Altman, PH   1   0   0   0

White Sox: Luis Aparicio, SS   2   0   0   0   Starter

Ray Herbert, P   1   0   0   0

3 IP, 3H   Winning pitcher

1963, Municipal Stadium, Cleveland NL 5, AL 3

Mudcat Grant*, P   Did not play

1964, Shea Stadium, New York (NL) NL 7, AL 4

Ron Hunt, 2B   3   0   1   0   First Met to start an AS game; John Callison swatted the game-winning home run while wearing a Mets batting helmet.

1965, Metropolitan Stadium, Minneapolis NL 6, AL 5

Tony Oliva, RF   2   0   1   0   Double

H. Killebrew, 1B   3   1   1   2   Homer

Zoilo Versalles, SS 1   0   0   0

Earl Battey, C   2   0   0   0   Starter

Jim Hall, CF   2   1   0   0

Mudcat Grant   2 IP, 2H, 1BB, 3K

1966, Busch Stadium, St. Louis NL 2, AL 1

Tim McCarver, C   1   1   1   0

Curt Flood, PH   1   0   0   0

Bob Gibson, P   Replaced on squad by Phil Regan

1967, Anaheim Stadium NL 2, AL 1 (15 inn.)

Don Mincher, PH   1   0   1   0

Jim Fregosi, SS   4   0   1   0

Jim McGlothlin, P   2 IP, 1H, 2K

1968, Astrodome, Houston NL 1, AL 0

Rusty Staub, PH   1   0   0   0

1969, Robert F. Kennedy Stadium, Washington NL 9, AL 3

Frank Howard, LF   1   1   1   1   Starter; homer.

Darold Knowles, P   .2 IP

1970, Riverfront Stadium, Cincinnati NL 5, AL 4 (10 inn.)

Pete Rose, RF-LF,   3   1   1   0   Collided with Ray Fosse to score winning run.

Tony Perez, 3B	3	0	0	0		Starter
Johnny Bench, C	3	0	0	0		Starter
Jim Merritt, P	2 IP, 1H, 0R, 1K					
Wayne Simpson, P	Did not play					

1971, Tiger Stadium, Detroit AL 6, NL 4

Al Kaline, RF	2	1	1	0	
Bill Freehan, C	3	0	0	0	Starter
Mickey Lolich, P	2 IP, 1H, 1R, 1K				Finished game.

1972, Atlanta Fulton County Stadium NL 4, AL 3

Hank Aaron, RF	3	1	1	2	Starter; homer.

1973, Royals Stadium, Kansas City NL 7, AL 1

Cookie Rojas, 2B	0	0	0	0	
John Mayberry, 1B	3	0	1	0	Double
Amos Otis, CF	2	0	2	1	Starter; drove in lone AL run.

1974, Three Rivers Stadium, Pittsburgh NL 7, AL 3

Ken Brett, P	2 IP, 1H, 1BB			Winning pitcher

1975, Milwaukee County Stadium NL 6, AL 3

George Scott, 1B	2	0	0	0	
Hank Aaron, PH	1	0	0	0	Lined out in final AS appearance.

1976, Veterans Stadium, Philadelphia NL 7, AL 1

Dave Cash, 2B	1	1	1	0	
Greg Luzinski, LF	3	0	0	0	Starter
Bob Boone, C	2	0	0	0	
Larry Bowa, SS	1	0	0	0	
Mike Schmidt, 3B	1	0	0	0	

1977, Yankee Stadium, New York NL 7, AL 5

Willie Randolph, 2B	5	0	1	0	Starter
T. Munson, PH	1	0	0	0	K'd as PH in 9th.
Reggie Jackson, RF	2	0	1	0	Starter
Graig Nettles, 3B	2	0	0	0	
Sparky Lyle, P	2 IP, 3H, 2R, 1K				

1978, San Diego Stadium NL 7, AL 3

Dave Winfield, LF	2	1	1	0	
Rollie Fingers, P	2 IP, 1H, 1K				

1979, Seattle Kingdome NL 7, AL 6

B. Bochte, PH-1B	1	0	1	1	Also had Sac hit.

1980, Dodger Stadium, Los Angeles NL 4, AL 2

Davey Lopes, 2B	1	0	0	0	Starter
Reggie Smith, CF	2	0	0	0	Starter

Steve Garvey, 1B	2	0	0	0	Starter
Bill Russell, SS	2	0	0	0	Starter
Bob Welch, P	1	0	0	0	
	3 IP, 5 H, 2 R, 1 BB, 4 K				
Jerry Reuss, P	1 IP, 3K				Winning pitcher.

1981, Municipal Stadium, Cleveland NL 5, AL 4

Bo Diaz, C	1	0	0	0	
Len Barker, P	2 IP, 1K				

1982, Olympic Stadium, Montreal NL 4, AL 1

Tim Raines, LF	1	0	0	0	Starter
Al Oliver, 1B	2	1	2	0	Double
Andre Dawson,* CF	4	0	1	0	Starter
Gary Carter, C	3	0	1	0	Starter
Steve Rogers, P	3 IP, 4H, 1R, 2K				Starting and winning pitcher.

1983, Comiskey Park, Chicago (AL) AL 13, NL 3

White Sox:	Ron Kittle, LF-RF	2	1	1	0	
Cubs:	Leon Durham, RF	2	0	0	0	
	Lee Smith, P	1 IP, 2H, 2R, 1K				

NOTE: 50th Anniversary Game

1984, Candlestick Park, San Francisco NL 3, AL 1

Chili Davis, PH	1	0	0	0	
Bob Brenly, PH	1	0	0	0	

1985, Hubert H. Humphrey Metrodome, Minneapolis NL 6, AL 1

Tom Brunansky, RF	1	0	0	0	

1986, Houston Astrodome AL 8, NL 2

Glenn Davis, PH	1	0	0	0	
Kevin Bass, PH	1	0	0	0	
Mike Scott, P	1 IP, 1H, 1R, 2K				

1987, Oakland Coliseum

Mark McGwire, 1B	3	0	0	0	
Jay Howell, P	2IP, 3 H, 2 R, 2 ER, 0 K, 3 BB				Losing pitcher by virtue of truly dreadful inning, allowing N.L. to score twice with two outs in the top of 13th.

1988, Riverfront Stadium, Cincinnati AL 2, NL 1

Barry Larkin, SS	2	0	0	0	
Chris Sabo, PR	0	0	0	0	
D. Jackson, P	Did not play				

1989, Anaheim Stadium, AL 5, NL 3

Devon White, CF	1	0	0	0	

1990, Wrigley Field, Chicago (NL) AL 2, NL 0

Cubs:	Ryne Sandberg, 2B	3	0	0	0	Starter

Andre Dawson, RF	2	0	0	0	Starter
Shawon Dunston, SS	2	0	0	0	
White Sox: Ozzie Guillen, SS	2	0	0	0	Starter
Bobby Thigpen, P	1 IP, 1K				

1991, Toronto Skydome AL 4, NL 2

Joe Carter, LF	1	1	1	0	
Roberto Alomar, 2B	4	0	0	0	Starter
Jimmy Key, P	1 IP, 1H, 1K				

1992, Jack Murphy Stadium, San Diego AL 13, NL 6

Tony Fernandez, SS	2	1	1	0	
Tony Gwynn, RF	2	0	0	0	Starter
Fred McGriff, 1B	3	0	2	1	Starter
Benito Santiago, C	1	0	0	0	Starter
Gary Sheffield, 3B	2	0	0	0	

1993, Camden Yards, Baltimore AL 9, NL 3

Cal Ripken, Jr., SS	3	0	0	0	Starter
Mike Mussina, P	Did not play. Baltimore fans boo A.L. manager Gaston for not using Mussina.				

1994, Three Rivers Stadium, Pittsburgh

Carlos Garcia, 2B	2	0	1	0	Picked off first by Randy Johnson.

1995, The Ballpark at Arlington

Ivan Rodriguez, C	3	0	0	0	Starter
Kenny Rogers, P	1 IP, 1H, 1R, 1ER, 1K				Gave up solo homer to Piazza in 7th.

* Johnny Mize (Cards and Giants), Jim Grant (Indians and Twins) and Andre Dawson (Expos and Cubs) are the only players to appear before two different home crowds.

Inter-city rivalries include Yankees-Dodgers-Giants in New York; Yankees and Mets in New York; White Sox and Cubs in Chicago; Braves and Red Sox in Boston; Cardinals and Browns in St. Louis. They do not include such match-ups as Indians-Reds or Pirates-Phillies.

Base Ball in Ancient Rome
by W.F. Kirk

When Julius Caesar was a kid, and Brutus was another,
And each imagined he possessed a spear that knew no brother,
These noble Romans chose up sides, all on a summer day,
And hurried in a corner lot hard by the Appian Way.

Tiberious Dooley played first base on Captain Caesar's team.
Herminius Clancy covered short and did it like a dream.
Horatius Flanigan played left—that garden was his home.
And Marcus Shay in center field tore up the Latin loam.

Vicinius Cogan, tall and broad, was Caesar's pitching kid,
And with his Roman spitball most astounding things he did,
While Claudius McGinnity, a twirler tried and true,
Struck out the might Julius and a number of his crew.

The game was nearly over and the score was three to three,
When Caesar, sliding into third, spiked Brutus on the knee.
The game broke up and Brutus snarled,
"Some day I'll get you, Kid,"
Which history informs us that in later years he did.

—Jack Carlson, *from the Dayton Herald, May 2, 1902*

Patching Up the Playoffs

Getting the best teams into post-season play

Bob Boynton

Major league baseball's new postseason—with its three divisions, a wild card, and an extra round of playoffs—suffers from some serious logical and structural deficiencies. Because the divisions are based on a nearly balanced, round-robin schedule, their geographical labels are meaningless. Even worse, their constitution is unfair. The divisions are meaningless because, just as if geography were ignored and the teams were randomly reassigned to new divisions, there are no advantages related to constrained geography (e.g., reduced travel expenses and minimal disruption of circadian rhythms). The system is unfair because, by allowing a first-place team in a weak division to enter the playoffs at the expense of a better team in a stronger one, it perpetuates a defect that has plagued the two-divisional setup for a quarter century.

The fair way—League moguls have decided that, in order to maintain competitive interest in a fourteen-team league, four of these teams should participate in postseason play. This seems to be a reasonable number, so let's work with it. The truly equitable procedure for selecting these four teams would dispense entirely with preset divisions. Standings of all fourteen teams would be published as a single list throughout the season, with the top four teams at the finish moving into postseason competition. A preliminary round of playoffs would follow between

Bob Boynton is an emeritus professor at UC San Diego who has been an active member of the Ballparks and Bibliography Commitees since joining SABR in 1990.

teams One and Four, and another between teams Two and Three, with the winners competing in the League Championship Series to determine who moves on to the World Series. This straightforward scheme guarantees that the four best teams in the league, truly defined by winning percentage over the long regular season, are certain to be the ones admitted to postseason play. There is potential inequity in any system that can produce a different outcome.

Looking back—The future, of course, is unpredictable, but lessons can be learned by examining the past. I have done this by retroactively analyzing the final standings of the American League over the nineteen seasons, starting in 1977, that it has been playing a roughly balanced schedule.

Let's take a look at the AL's 1984 season to see how inequities of postseason selection can occur for each assumed divisional structure. The final standings for the two divisions that were actually used that year are shown in Table 1. The problem is obvious. The imbalance between divisions in 1984 was so great that the five best teams in the league were all in the East. Kansas City in the West—despite finishing with only the sixth-best record in the league at .519—was admitted to postseason play ahead of Toronto, which finished second with .549.

Consider what the outcome would have been had the current three-divisional scheme been employed in 1984, as shown in Table 2. The three divisions yield an even worse outcome by causing a *double* inequity.

Table 1.

Actual 1984 American League standings.

	G	W	L	Pc	GB
East					
Det	162	104	58	.642	-
Tor	163	89	73	.549	15
NY	162	87	75	.537	17
Bos	162	86	76	.531	18
Bal	162	85	77	.525	19
Cle	163	75	87	.463	29
Mil	161	67	94	.416	36.5
West					
KC	162	84	78	.519	6
Cal	162	81	81	.500	3
Min	162	81	81	.500	3
Oak	162	77	85	.475	7
Sea	162	74	88	.457	10
Chi	162	74	88	.457	10
Tex	161	69	92	.429	14.5

Table 2.

1984 American League standings, retroactively based on three divisions.

	G	W	L	Pct	GB
East					
Det	162	104	58	.642	-
Tor	163	89	73	.549	15
NY	162	87	75	.537	17
Bos	162	86	76	.531	18
Bal	162	85	77	.525	19
Central					
KC	162	84	78	.519	-
Min	162	81	81	.500	3
Cle	163	75	87	.463	9
Chi	162	74	88	.457	10
Mil	161	67	94	.416	16.5
West					
Cal	162	81	81	.500	-
Oak	162	77	85	.475	4
Sea	162	74	88	.457	7
Tex	161	69	92	.429	11.5

With Toronto as the wild card, division winners California and Kansas City both enter the playoffs ahead of New York and Boston—teams with better records that finished third and fourth respectively in the overall standings.

Table 3 summarizes the two- and three-division outcomes for all nineteen seasons. Wherever a pair of teams is listed, an inequity has occurred: the the team at the top would (or did) qualify for postseason play at the expense of the superior team below.

This data can be summarized as follows. Of the nineteen seasons listed, the old system, with one winner in each of two divisions, yields iniquitous results eleven times. The current system of three fixed divisions does so only nine times, but with much more striking inequities on four occasions. The double-displacement already discussed for 1984 includes California, a .500 team, as a qualifier. In addition, there are three other seasons (1983, 1987, and 1994) in which teams that did not win more than half of their regular season games would have participated in the postseason. By contrast, the worst case for two divisions is Kansas City in 1984 at .519. This is not surprising, because the greater the number of teams in a division, the less likely it becomes that all of them will have losing seasons.

Averting disaster—If there was any saving grace to the strike that ended the ugly 1994 season prematurely, it was that Texas did not enter the postseason, as it otherwise would have, with a record well below

.500. The owners lucked out in 1995, when the new system was belatedly implemented for the first time, because there was no inequity in either league, whereas there would have been in both leagues under the old two-divisional system. But luck is not perpetual, and if the current playoff system is witlessly continued, disasters similar to those cited will inevitably occur.

Why not have the top four teams meet? With fourteen teams ordered in a single list throughout the season, the pennant race might *seem* less exciting than when standings are artificially split into three divisions. Actually, the season-ending scramble for fourth place, in what might become known as "the prestigious first division," probably would be very similar to the wild card frenzy provided by the current system. In keeping the standings, as suggested in Table 4, the first division teams could be separated from the others by a dividing line, and GBFD would mean "Games Behind [entry into] the First Division."

Even if the Lords of Baseball don't want to take this route, they could significantly improve the three-divisional scheme merely by insisting that a legitimate divisional "winner" must win more often than it loses. (Could anyone in his right mind actually quarrel with this?) By this rule, for example, Texas, otherwise a divisional "winner" in 1983 with a horrible .475 record, would be disqualified and replaced by the next best team that was a *real* winner that year (New York, at a respectable .562).

Table 3.

Inequities of postseason assignments resulting from use of two systems for creating divisions among fourteen teams. In each column, for each year, the first team or teams listed qualify for postseason play at the expense of the other team or teams listed. "No inequity" means that the four teams in the league with the highest winning percentages qualify for postseason play. The two-divisional system existed from 1977 through 1993; the three-division system was inaugurated in 1994.

Year	A 2 Divisions	B 3 Divisions
1977	no inequity	Tex .580
		Bal or Bos .602
1978	Mil .574	Tex or Cal .537
	Bos .607	Mil .574
1979	Cal .543	Cal .543
	Mil .590	NY .556
1980	KC .599	Oak .512
	Bal .617	Mil .531
1981	no inequity	no inequity
1982	Cal .574	no inequity
	Bal .580	
1983	no inequity	Tex .475
		NY .562
1984	KC .519	Cal .500 & KC .519
	Tor .549	Bos .531 & NY .537
1985	KC .562	no inequity
	NY .602	
1986	no inequity	Cle .519
		Tex .537
1987	Min .525	Oak .500
	Tor .593	NY .549
1988	Bos .549	no inequity
	Min .562	
1989	Tor .549	no inequity
	KC .568	
1990	Bos .543	no inequity
	Chi .580	
1991	no inequity	no inequity
1992	no inequity	no inequity
1993	no inequity	no inequity
1994	no inequity	Tex .456
		KC .557
1995	Sea .545	no inequity
	Bos .597	

Return to an unbalanced schedule?—For several years after both major leagues expanded to six teams in each of two divisions, the schedules called for more games to be played within than between divisions. A return to an unbalanced schedule would make the

Table 4.

American League standings for the 1984 season, without preset divisions.

	G	W	L	Pct	GBFD*
Det	162	104	58	.642	-
Tor	163	89	73	.549	-
NY	162	87	75	.537	-
Bos	162	86	76	.531	-
Bal	162	85	77	.525	1
KC	162	84	78	.519	2
Cal	162	81	81	.500	4
Min	162	81	81	.500	4
Oak	162	77	85	.475	9
Cle	163	75	87	.463	11
Sea	162	74	88	.457	12
Chi	162	74	88	.457	12
Tex	161	69	92	.429	16.5
Mil	161	67	94	.416	18.5

*Games Behind First Division

geographical divisions more meaningful. For example, consider the following scheme for a fifteen-team league (likely by 1998) with three divisions:

Within Divisions:
18 games (9 home, 9 away) against each of 4 teams = 72 games (36 home, 36 away)

Between Divisions:
8 games (4 home, 4 away) against each of 10 teams = 80 games (40 home, 40 away)

Total:
152 games (76 home, 76 away)

This 152-game schedule would be similar in length to the classic 154-game slate that lasted fifty years, and a return to a shorter regular season would of course improve the odds of finishing the World Series before snow flies. Teams would be on the road in distant places for only 26 percent of their games. On the other hand, it might seem undesirable to play only four home games against ten of the fourteen other teams, and the owners probably would be reluctant to accept the revenue loss resulting from ten fewer regular season contests.

Four leagues?—Looking ahead to the possibility of thirty-two major league teams by the end of the century, these could be divided into four separate, geographically concentrated, eight-team leagues, each of which would adopt the classic 154-game balanced schedule that calls for twenty-two games with each opponent. Playoffs would be scheduled between A and B, and also C and D, with the winners meeting to determine who goes to the World Series. Admittedly, there are disadvantages associated with this scheme. The idea runs directly counter to the owners' current obsession with interleague play. Because there is no way to judge relative performance between teams in completely separate circuits, equity would not be tested during the regular season. (This of course is hardly new, having been true throughout the century for the two major leagues.) Another objection might be that, with four leagues, hometown fans would dislike being able to watch only a quarter of the major league teams.

But there is a positive side. Interleague competition throughout a long post-season probably would enhance interest in these special contests, and there could also be expanded All-Star play. During "All-Star Week," teams selected from Leagues A and B could meet on Tuesday, those from C and D, on Wednesday, and the winners could play on Thursday to determine the All-Star Championship Team. (And there would be enough extra money to compensate the winning players.)

Options—The major league playoff scheme belatedly implemented in 1985 is ill-considered and inequitable. Better alternatives are possible. The simplest and best of these would schedule playoffs among the top four teams as defined by winning percentage during a season of balanced, round-robin play. If use of the current fixed three-divisional scheme continues, as it probably will, retroactive analysis indicates that equity of outcome would be considerably improved, and justice better served, simply by disqualifying phony division "winners" who actually fail to win more than half of their games, but profit from fortuitous assignment to small, weak divisions. A return to an unbalanced schedule, and the partitioning of teams into four separate leagues are additional possibilities.

Lady Base Ballists in Quad

DANVILLE, IL, June 9—The "Ladies" Base Ball Club, composed of women from Chicago and Cincinnati, defeated the Danville Browns by a score of 23 to 12 to an attendance of 2,000.

Last evening state's attorney Blackburn swore out a warrant for their arrest for unlawfully disturbing the peace and good order or society. Officer Patterson arrested them as they were leaving town in carriages for Covington, Indiana.

—Ray Schmidt, from the Ottumwa (Iowa) Daily Democrat, June 11, 1890

The Iron Men of Pitching

Not who you might think

Guy Waterman

Who is the Cal Ripken of pitchers? That is, which pitcher never missed a start for the longest consecutive streak?

It's a tough question to answer with certainty without an exhaustive and tedious search of day-to-day box scores for years on end. Someday some tireless SABR researcher will do that work. In the meantime, for those of us who are lazier but still curious: Is there a shortcut to answering this question?

One obvious route is to look at annual starts and see how long each pitcher started a sufficient number of games each year so that we may assume he never missed his turn. That sounds simple—until we come to grips with the next question: How many starts per year constitute a full season? A season in which we may feel safe in saying that pitcher never ducked a starting assignment?

When I began to ponder this question, I made an assumption that I'll bet many SABR researchers would share: That today's standard five-day rotation has replaced a standard of every four days which prevailed earlier in this century. As I delved into the GS (Games Started) records, however, I was surprised to find that there is very little evidence to support this Theory of the Iron Age. The hardest-working starting pitchers of the 1920s and 1930s consistently recorded fewer annual starts than those of the 1960s and 1970s.

The difference seems to be far greater than the difference between the 154-game schedule and 162 games.

On my first pass through the numbers, I began by assuming a four-day rotation for the 154-game schedule, or (allowing for some slippage) 35 starts per season; and, somewhere after the Year of the Pitcher (1968) and the changes in its wake, a gradual scaling back to five-day rotations for 162 games, or (again granting some leeway) 30 starts per season. The results catapulted a flock of 1970s stars (Carlton, Seaver, Sutton, the Perry brothers, the Niekros) into the top spots, with a seasoning of nineteenth century veterans thrown in at odd intervals (Young, Keefe, Nichols, Galvin). The highest ranks for anyone in the entire half-century between 1910 and 1960 were Walter Johnson, who came in a distant 22nd, and Wilbur Cooper, barely in sight at 35th.

Whenever results like that pop off the page, one should start asking questions. Did my statistical method load the dice against the stars of what many consider baseball's golden age? (Not iron, apparently, but still golden.)

The answer is yes. One complication, of course, is that many starters of the pre-1950 years also put in several relief appearances. Grove, Hubbell, and others often started, say, 30-32 games in a season, but relieved in another 5-15 games. Before he missed time in 1934, Grove averaged 31 starts per years—plus an average of 13-14 relief appearances. Detroit's wartime pennant-winning tandem of Hal Newhouser and Dizzy Trout displayed awesome workhorse propensi-

Guy Waterman is a backwoods Vermont homesteader whose previous published writings have been about ragtime, politics, mountain climbing, and baseball.

ties not confined to starts. In 1944 Newhouser started 34 games, Trout 40—impressive enough. But Prince Hal also relieved in thirteen games, Trout in nine.

In contrast, the leading post-1950 starters seldom relieved, with a few exceptions like Bob Lemon, Early Wynn, and Phil Niekro. (Niekro missed being the only man in the twentieth century to go ten straight years with at least 36 starts per year, only because he made just 30 starts in 1973—but appeared in 12 games in relief!) Once established as starters, Carlton, Seaver, and Sutton virtually never relieved—Carlton not once between 1972 and 1986, a period of fifteen years and 515 starting assignments.

Facts like these, and the obvious inaccuracy of my original Iron Age assumptions, suggested the need for a fresh start, this time holding the starting requirements constant. But at what level? Not an easy choice. To require 35 starts per year will surely penalize the 1920s-1930s stars who relieved between starts. To ease off to 30 seems excessively permissive, especially for 162-game schedules, not something Ripken or Gehrig would approve. No simple answer suggests itself, and I am inclined to be suspicious of complex assumptions. They feed the delusion that we have taken into account all the complex variables in this endlessly complex game of the real world, when it is unlikely we are that wise.

So...presented on the next page are two tables, one based on fairly stringent requirements, the other more lax. Table 1 requires 35 starts for 162-game schedules, 33 for 154 games (and proportional adjustments for the short seasons of 1901-03, 1918-1919, 1981, and 1994-1995). Table 2 requires only 31 starts for 162 games, 30 for 154. Two other things to mention:

First, all nineteenth century records are withheld and treated separately in Table 3 later. A glance at the number of annual starts before 1900 versus after makes it very clear that entirely different credentials are needed. This is not intended to dismiss the great nineteenth century pitchers, but only to present their records separately. Any reader may compare the top nineteenth century streak (Cy Young's 590-639) with the twentieth century leaders: Young easily beats all comers in Table 1, but ranks fourth in Table 2. Seven other nineteenth centurions crash Table 1, while Tim Keefe and Kid Nichols continue to place high when stacked against Table 2.

Second, in all these tables, two numbers are shown, labelled "Min" (minimum) and "Max" (maximum). The minimum represents the total number of starts in all (consecutive) years where that pitcher met the minimum requirements each year. The maximum is

that figure plus the starts in years just before and after. This is because we do not know (without checking daily records) when, during those years, the streak began and ended. It could have been anywhere from none at all to all of those starts. In all cases, pitchers are ranked (arbitrarily) by their maximum figures.

Tables 1 and 2, the Cal Ripkens and Lou Gehrigs and Deacon Scotts and Steve Garveys and Billy Williamses of pitching, are on the next page.

Readers may draw their own conclusions from these tables. Here are some that struck me:

1. A bad conscience compels me to confess to two negative points, the most important being that no one listed here did what Gehrig and Ripken did. Pitchers starting regularly still do get days off to rest. What Ripken accomplished stands by itself in baseball lore, and no comparison of apples with oranges should detract from his great achievement.

Commenting on a draft of this article, SABR's founder, L. Robert Davids, reminded me that when professional major league baseball started—under significantly different conditions—most teams had only one regular pitcher, and George Bradley did in fact do what Ripken did for 88 games (all 64 in 1876 and all until July 13, 1877).

2. A further negative aside: These tables are a crude, and really only a preliminary, way of getting at the iron men of starting pitchers. For example, Pete Palmer has generously provided data to show that Johnson was out for three weeks in 1909 and missed two starts in 1911—interruptions that should throw him off the list, but that aren't sufficiently reflected in the numbers. Palmer also identified missed starts by Young in 1895 and 1900 (see Table 3 below). So it is clear that the technique I use here gives an approximation at best, subject to significant error.

Having loudly acknowledged these limitations, however, I am irresistibly tempted to go on to some more positive comments, to wit:

3. Isn't it nice to have an all-time list that doesn't begin with Mathewson and Johnson and then proceed through the same old litany of Hall of Famers? Isn't it grand to see Bob Friend and Claude Osteen in an all-time top ten? And Mel Stottlemyre and Rick Reuschel ranked ahead of Bob Feller? Even ol' Bobo up there in nineteenth place?

Table 1.

Twentieth century pitchers with longest streaks of continuous starts

Criteria: 35 starts per year for 162-game seasons; 33 starts per year for 154-game seasons; proportionally lower numbers for shortened seasons

Min=total starts for years of continuous streak

Max=that plus starts for years before and after

Rank	Pitcher	Period	Years	Min	Max
1.	Christy Mathewson	1903-1914	12	449	505
2.	Walter Johnson	1909-1919	11	397	441
3.	Gaylord Perry	1966-1975	10	382	440
4.	Jim Bunning	1958-1967	10	369	425
5.	Don Drysdale	1959-1967	9	352	412
6.	Ferguson Jenkins	1967-1975	9	350	391
7.	Bob Friend	1956-1964	9	344	388
8.	Joe McGinnity	1899-1907	9	361	381
9.	Frank Viola	1984-1992	9	320	383
10.	Claude Osteen	1964-1971	8	305	367
11.	Catfish Hunter	1969-1976	8	301	357
12.	Mel Stottlemyre	1965-1973	9	329	354
13.	Rick Reuschel	1973-1981	9	318	336
14.	Phil Niekro	1974-1980	7	280	332
15.	Robin Roberts	1950-1956	7	269	332
16.	Steve Carlton	1971-1977	7	264	331
17.	Jack Powell	1897-1904	7	276	328
18.	Bob Feller	1938-1948*	7	274	321
19.	Bobo Newsom	1936-1942	7	256	312
20.	Mickey Lolich	1969-1974	6	244	310

*Feller's wartime interruption not deducted from his streak.

Table 2.

Twentieth century pitchers with longest streaks of continuous starts

Criteria: 31 starts per year for 162-game seasons; 30 starts per year for 154-game seasons; proportionally lower numbers for shortened seasons

Min=total starts for years of continuous streak

Max=that plus starts for years before and after

Rank	Pitcher	Period	Years	Min	Max
1.	Don Sutton	1969-1987	19	644	687
2.	Gaylord Perry	1966-1983	18	634	660
3.	Steve Carlton	1968-1984	17	600	644
4.	Warren Spahn	1947-1963	17	592	633
5.	Christy Mathewson	1901-1914	14	523	548
6.	Phil Niekro	1974-1986	13	466	522
7.	Vic Willis	1898-1909	12	453	476
8.	Tom Seaver	1967-1979	13	449	475
9.	Robin Roberts	1949-1960	12	434	472
10.	Walter Johnson	1909-1919	11	397	441
11.	Jim Bunning	1957-1967	11	399	428
12.	Don Drysdale	1959-1968	10	383	424
13.	Claude Osteen	1964-1973	10	371	423
14.	Catfish Hunter	1967-1976	10	370	417
15.	Mike Moore	1984-1994	11	367	413
16.	Bob Friend	1956-1965	10	368	408
17.	Frank Viola	1983-1992	10	354	405
18.	Dave Stieb	1982-1990	9	364	391
19.	Ferguson Jenkins	1967-1975	9	350	391
20.	Early Wynn	1951-1960	10	346	390

4. Mike Moore in Table 2?!? There's a surprise: a man widely criticized for inflated ERAs in recent years. Maybe his managers know something that is eluding SABRmetricians.

5. How about the continued poor showing of pitchers from the 1920s and 1930s? The highest ranks of anyone with streaks in those two decades are Feller and Newsom, in Table 1. No one from the 1920s-1930s makes Table 2. Coming closest are Stan Coveleski (#22), Bucky Walters (#27), and Carl Hubbell (who straggles in at #30).

What about other stars of the 1920s-1930s? For example, those who regularly were among the leaders in Complete Games, like Burleigh Grimes, Dazzy Vance, Paul Derringer in the NL, or Lefty Grove, Ted Lyons, Wes Ferrell in the AL? Or all those great Yankee mound stars of that era?

On examination, none of these great stars put together a consistent streak of starts for more than four or five years. Grimes led in complete games four years, but tailed off to 29 starts in 1926. Derringer was inde-

fatigable in 1936, 1938, 1939, and 1940, leading the league in starts three of those years, but he only started 26 games in 1937. Ferrell led in complete games three years in a row, but on either side of that streak made only 23 and 26 starts. The others had off-years too: Vance in 1926, Lyons in 1931, Grove in 1934. Grove, of course, was also handicapped by being held in the minors about five years after he was ready to win big in the majors.

Feller's inclusion in Table 1 incidentally may be questioned. SABR's Vermont historian Dominick Denaro has challenged my assumption that Feller should not be penalized for the wartime rest. Denaro has compiled an interesting list of pitchers with most innings pitched as a teenager (since 1920). Feller tops the list—and is the only one of the seven with more than 200 teenage IP who did not develop serious arm trouble by age 25. Denaro suggests that Feller's time off due to wartime service may well have saved him from a similar fate.

Those Yankee stars? Though four made it to the Hall of Fame (Lefty Gomez, Waite Hoyt, Herb

Pennock, Red Ruffing), they typically started 30-31 games, Hoyt 32 three times, none ever more than 34. Maybe the Yanks had such depths of starting pitching that they could afford to give them all plenty of rest. A nice luxury, but not something that occurred to their teammate on first base.

6. Speaking of whom, compare the number of years involved for pitchers versus position players. Gehrig's streak lasted thirteen, almost fourteen, seasons. Ripken had fourteen full seasons going into 1996. The pitchers? For the twentieth century results vary widely with the assumed minimum number of starts, from Mathewson's twelve years in Table 1 to Sutton's almost unbelievable nineteen years in Table 2.

Think what that last number means. If a 31-game standard is reasonable—an arguable point—Sutton went out there time after time for nineteen long years without once begging off. *Nineteen years!* That is a very long time in any profession, any form of human endeavor, to go out every single time it's your turn and do something as demanding, indeed punishing, as starting a game against major league batters.

In my opinion, the leaders in these lists deserve immense respect for such a lifetime achievement.

Now back to the nineteenth century. Before 1900 many pitchers started more than once every four days—a whole lot more. So, where a nineteenth century pitcher's starts dropped more than 20 percent

below his average 'til then, let's assume he missed some turns. (First check whether his team played a lot fewer games that year, in which case cancel this proviso.) Thus for example: Mickey Welch was cruising along at more than 50 starts per year during the mid-1880s, then suddenly tailed off to 40 in 1887. Forty starts would represent a busy year in 1987 (indeed!), but in 1887, for a man who had been starting more than 50? Not something Gehrig or Ripken would have done. So for Table 3 let's say that a 20 percent drop below average suggests the likelihood that starts were missed. The resulting nineteenth century leaders are shown in Table 3.

What about today's ongoing streaks? Due to publishing deadlines, this article can only report through the 1995 season. The longest streaks still alive at that point are presented in Table 4. The name at the top of the list will surprise no one. Nor will the fact that three of the top six are from the Braves' fabulous rotation. Odd that Glavine and Smoltz carry identical numbers into 1996. More interesting, perhaps, is the presence of the old Latin pro, Dennis Martinez. At age 41 in 1996, his chances of moving up into the all-time leaders may be lower than some of the others. But being over 40 didn't stop Phil Niekro for many years.

The performance of Niekro, Sutton, and other later twentieth century heroes surely invites us to question our frequent assumption that modern players are wimps, fleeing to the Disabled List at the first sight of

Table 3.

Nineteenth Century Pitchers with longest streak of continuous starts

Criteria: minimum of 35 starts per year
No decline of more than 20 percent from previous average
Min=total starts for years of continuous streak
Max=that plus starts for years before and after

Rank	Pitcher	Period	Years	Min	Max
1.	Cy Young	1891-1904	14	590	639
2.	Tim Keefe	1881-1889	9	475	517
3.	Kid Nichols	1890-1899	10	440	467
4.	Pud Galvin	1879-1884	6	371	414
5.	Old Hoss Radbourn	1882-1887	6	350	410
6.	Amos Rusie	1890-1895	6	330	389
7.	Gus Weyhing	1887-1893	7	341	375
8.	John Clarkson	1885-1889	5	310	367
9.	Silver King	1887-1892	6	309	336
10.	Ted Breitenstein	1893-1898	6	262	318

Table 4.

Ongoing Streaks: Longest streak of continuous starts going into 1995

Criteria: 30 starts per year through 1993
21 starts in 1994, 27 starts in 1995
Min=total starts for years of continuous streak
Max=that plus starts for years before and after

Rank	Pitcher	Period	Years	Min	Max
1.	Greg Maddux	1988-	8	265	292
2.	Doug Drabek	1988-	8	256	284
3.	Dennis Martinez	1988-	8	248	270
4.	David Cone	1989-	7	218	246
5.	Tom Glavine	1990-	6	190	219
	John Smoltz	1990-	6	190	219
7.	Jack McDowell	1990-	6	191	215
8.	Greg Swindell	1990-	6	178	206
9.	John Burkett	1990-	6	187	187
10.	Tom Candiotti	1991-	5	152	181

blood, while yesterday's Men of Steel played hurt, never whimpered, and went out there, day after day for entire careers. Not so. The DADFEC Award (that's for "Day After Day For Entire Careers") goes not to Ed Walsh, Burleigh Grimes, Carl Hubbell, and Iron Man McGinnity, but rather to Don Sutton, Phil Niekro, Gaylord Perry, and Steve Carlton.

I should like to emphasize that, in most respects I do not share the common view that all moderns are "better" than all ancients. I have always been of the "Good Old Days" school. But I have to admit that these numbers give me a new respect for many pitchers of the recent past—men who deserve to stand with the GODS (stands for "Good Old Days") of the more hallowed yesteryears.

Note:

The author is indebted to several knowledgeable SABR members who critiqued a draft of this article and suggested changes which are incorporated, several of which are explicitly identified in the text. Critics included SABR founder L. Robert Davids, *Total Baseball*'s Pete Palmer, Publications Director Mark Alvarez, and Larry Gardner (Vermont) Chapter experts Nathan Brubaker, Dominick Denaro, and Tom Simon. Their help in no way implies endorsement. Responsibility for remaining errors and weaknesses in analysis is exclusively the author's.

Tim Keefe

Transcendental Graphics

Great Managers

What makes skippers Hall of Fame caliber?

Steve Charak

Earl Weaver's selection to the Hall of Fame raises an interesting question. People generally agree that 3,000 hits, 500 home runs, or 300 wins by a pitcher virtually guarantee a player's entrance. The Hall also requires, with the special exception of Addie Joss, ten full years in the major leagues.

What criteria put a manager at that level? And who are those of Hall of Fame caliber?

I suggest that two simple but rare criteria put a manager in the Hall of Fame class: First, two World Series titles, and second, ten years as a manager

Among managers active in 1995 only four have led teams to two or more championships. Sparky Anderson, Tom Lasorda, Tom Kelly, and Cito Gaston.

Write Sparky's ticket now. He's in. Lasorda is a lock, too. Some people think he isn't a smart manager, but anyone who can win a World Series with Mickey Hatcher hitting third has something figured out.

Kelly will have ten years' service by the end of 1996. His opposing manager in the 1987 Series, Whitey Herzog, taught the world about building your team around your home park. Kelly took it all the way. In 1987 and 1991, Kelly won championships without winning a road game.

Gaston isn't considered by many to be a great one. Some people wonder if he makes any managerial decisions at all. But he has won two World Series titles.

He's had gifted players, and he avoided getting in the way of his talent. Gaston has not yet managed for ten years, and it's too soon to know if he'll make it.

Among those who've managed in the past thirty years, Dick Williams, Walt Alston, Danny Murtaugh, and Ralph Houk achieved the two championship milestone. Alston is in the Hall. The other three qualify.

Williams took a talented though somewhat disorganized A's team and led it to consecutive championships. And he might have won a few more had he been willing to stick around. Despite a slight character flaw—an inability to get along with just about anyone—Williams managed to win two other pennants.

When your team is outscored 55-27 over seven games, you can't expect to win. But Murtaugh's 1960 Pirates won their first championship in thirty-five years against a high-powered Yankee team. Eleven years later, the Murtaugh-led Pirates came from behind to beat the Orioles.

Houk is an unique case. He won World Series titles in his first two years as a manager, and a third pennant in his third year. He never won another one. Many believe he inherited a great Yankee team and that anyone could have managed it successfully.

It wasn't that simple. Houk made some improvements on Casey Stengel's managing (which got pretty ragged during his last couple of years with the Yankees and really ragged with the Mets). Chief among his changes was making Whitey Ford a regular starter.

Steve Charak is author of Story Problems of the Outrageous Kind. *He is the founder and publisher of* Young Voices *Magazine.*

Ford never won twenty games playing for Stengel. He never started that often. In 1962, Houk had to find a replacement for his shortstop, and he did.

Among those no longer managing, my choices of Hall of Fame caliber managers are Anderson, Houk, Herzog, Murtaugh, Williams, and Billy Southworth

Among those still managing, I think Lasorda, Kelly, and LaRussa qualify.

Herzog won only one Series, but he was an innovator. He took advantage of his home field. He brought in players who would excel on Astro-Turf (Ozzie) while unloading malcontents (Templeton) and over-the-hill players (Simmons). He also used his players wisely, such as starting Andujar on three days' rest and Bob Forsch on four days rest in 1982.

LaRussa has won a single World Series so far, but he is still active. He is the right manager for our time. He seems to get along well with players who make a gazillion times more than he does. He got the most out of Dave Stewart, and he managed to get the most out of players like Rickey Henderson and Jose Canseco while (usually) ignoring their attitudes.

Now that Atlanta has won a World Series, Bobby Cox may have achieved this level. Cox has some negatives. He probably should have won in 1991. He didn't win a pennant when he managed in Toronto. But he turned Toronto around before taking over a last-place Braves club and turning it into the team of the '90s.

Seventeen managers have won two or more World Series. Of those who are no longer managing only Billy Southworth, Bill Carrigan (who didn't manage for ten years), Murtaugh, Williams, and Houk are not in the Hall of Fame.

Southworth was the managerial equivalent of Hal Newhouser. Southworth won three successive pennants with the Cardinals, from 1942-44. These pennants came during the war years, which for many people diminished their credibility. Also, it was thought that Branch Rickey's farm system, with its steady supply of talent, kept the team stocked with quality players when other teams were depleted. But as Newhouser went on to win twenty games after the War, Southworth did win one more pennant, with the Braves in 1948. He is Hall of Fame caliber.

Two Managers who didn't win two World Series are in the Hall of Fame, and I consider them both questionable. Leo Durocher was flamboyant, managed mainly in New York, with all that means, was involved in some of the game's great moments, and he did win three pennants and one World Series. But there are better managers on the outside looking in.

Al Lopez is the managerial equivalent of Fred Lindstrom, someone who had some good statistics (in his case, as a manager), but who doesn't belong among the true greats. Yes, Lopez did win two American League pennants, the only two that Stengel didn't win from 1949-1960. But he never won a Series. A perennial also-ran.

Gene Mauch is often touted as a managing great. He has been described as the "best manager never to have won a pennant," and the guy who "knew the rule book inside and out."

Mauch may have been the best manager never to have won a pennant, but he still never won a pennant. He may have known the rule book inside and out, but in 1964 he didn't know well enough to give his two best pitchers—Jim Bunning and Chris Short—adequate rest.

A manager's job is to win, and Mauch didn't.

Managers who have won at least two World Series titles

Manager	Series Wins	Pennants	Hall of Fame?
Walter Alston	4	7	Yes
Sparky Anderson	3	5	No
Bill Carrigan	2	2	No
Frank Chance	2	4	B
Cito Gaston	2	2	A
Bucky Harris	2	3	Yes
Ralph Houk	2	3	No
Miller Huggins	3	6	Yes
Tom Kelly	2	2	A
Tom Lasorda	2	4	A
Connie Mack	5	8	Yes
John McGraw	3	9	Yes
Joe McCarthy	7	9	Yes
Bill McKechnie	2	4	Yes
Danny Murtaugh	2	2	No
Billy Southworth	2	4	No
Casey Stengel	7	10	Yes
Dick Williams	2	4	No
Leo Durocher	1	3	Yes
Al Lopez	0	2	Yes
Earl Weaver	1	4	Yes

A=Still active as manager

B=In Hall of Fame as a player

From Their Lips to Your Ears

Voices of the game and how they do it

Mark Simon

With the growth of television and everything that comes with it (cable, satellite dishes, etc.), there seems to be less appreciation for baseball on the radio than there used to be, especially from younger fans. Most of my college friends have no desire to listen to an Ernie Harwell, a Ken Coleman, or a Gary Cohen. Yet, radio baseball play-by-play remains an art, and many people are enamored of the voices that have filled the airwaves. With this in mind, I thought I would talk to some of the many artists who paint or have painted the daily picture on the radio, and find out how they do their daily work.

Preparation—The motto of the big league broadcaster could be borrowed from the Boy Scouts—"Be Prepared." There is nothing more important to a broadcaster than the preparation that he has brought to the booth.

"You don't prepare for a baseball broadcast on the day of a game," says New York Mets voice Gary Cohen. "You prepare by studying the game from the time you were a little kid. You can't learn baseball as an adult. You can't develop the love necessary for being a broadcaster as an adult."

"When you're doing baseball, you're immersed in the game," says former Red Sox broadcaster Ken Coleman. "You're in it twenty-four hours a day seven days a week. You're always preparing material you might use on a broadcast."

One thing broadcasters consider an absolute necessity is a love for the game. "You have to have a love for the game," Cohen says. "You have to have an understanding of the game. If you don't, you'll be exposed very quickly."

To enrich their understanding, many broadcasters read and keep files. Cohen reads six or seven newspapers a day, making notes as he goes along. Most broadcasters also keep index cards. "I've always had an index card on every player, with basic stats, an anecdote or two, and some cards with stories I may want to recall," says former Detroit Tigers broadcaster Ernie Harwell.

Kansas City Royals broadcaster and former college baseball player Denny Matthews keeps scouting reports on each player. "They come from the club," he says. "I get them from the advance scouts. I evaluate players, too. Once you've seen them for a while, you know what they can or cannot do. Once you see them fifty to sixty games, you can evaluate them."

With times changing, some broadcasters have gone to the electronic age. Red Sox broadcaster Joe Castiglione carries an electronic version of *The Baseball Encyclopedia* to every game.

Broadcasters also make sure they have all the books they'll need with them. The standard library includes the requisite scorebook (many of which are custom designed), a rule book, a record book, and the NL Green Book and/or the AL Red Book. The broadcast-

Mark Simon, a college senior and sports director of WTSR Radio (91.3 FM). He hopes someday to be the radio voice for the New York Mets and the New York Knicks.

ers are also supplied with lots of statistical notes and background by the ballclubs. Some broadcasters keep extra material available. "I have a looseleaf notebook with all the Mets game-by-game results since 1962 just in case you need to jog your memory," says Cohen. "I also have a pitchers line by line going back in some cases through their entire career."

"I keep a home run book," says Castiglione. "Where they went, who they were hit off. I also keep [track of] wall balls at Fenway."

The part of preparation that most of the broadcasters enjoy most is what Cohen refers to as "kibitzing and talking." Most broadcasters arrive at the stadium at least three hours before a game, and they sit and chat with whatever baseball people they can find. "The most fun time is hanging around the batting cage and the dugout," says Castiglione. "That's where you get a lot of information you can't read in periodicals and journals."

Some take advantage of every second they have to make sure they are adequately prepared. On the drive to and from the ballpark, Coleman listened to the innings he had broadcast. "I try to avoid using the same phrases too often. I try to check on my energy level, comfort level, pausing, and phrasing."

Much of this preparation is never used directly. But the voices don't think that their background work is a waste of time. "I may carry an item with me that I think is of interest for two to three weeks, but I have to wait for a situation to come up in a game that I can relate it to," says San Francisco Giants broadcaster Hank Greenwald. "It may not happen for a while. You let the game dictate what you do."

Calling the game —The voices and styles of different broadcasters give the games they handle distinct flavors. Most don't aim for a specific audience, because they feel this can be a distraction. Harwell is one who forms a composite picture. "There are all kinds of people you talk to. You have to please a college professor with your grammar and a veteran baseball player with your baseball knowledge. You have to introduce baseball to kids who have never been subjected to baseball before. You have to have material to appeal to the casual listener as well as to a real fan."

Castiglione recognizes the older fans who are listening. "One of our great callings is to provide a service to the elderly, the blind, the shut-ins. We always try to keep those people in mind." But he also realizes they need to pay attention to the young fans. "Every day someone is listening to a baseball game for the first time in their life, and you're going to have a large influence on them if they enjoy baseball and learn from it."

Baseball is a slow-moving sport and the good announcers have styles that allow the listener to take in all aspects of the game, while maintaining a solid rhythm.

"My philosophy is that the game is paramount and that the announcer is secondary," says Harwell. "Most people tune in not to hear Ernie Harwell, they tune in to know who is playing and what the score is."

"My idea is to make the game as vivid as I can, with the description of each play," says Castiglione. "You have to be ready to capitalize when there is action because most of the game is not action.

"You try to make it as descriptive as possible," he says, "No two ground balls to shortstop are exactly the same. If it's an exciting play, you go back and recapitulate the play so people listening with half an ear can pick up what they may have missed."

"[The person listening] has got to be able to see in his mind more clearly than if he's watching on television because the imagination is more vivid," says Greenwald. "I will try to start the description with the pitcher himself because it's important for the listener to get a sense of timing. In his mind, nothing happens until the pitcher throws the ball. If you haven't described the release of the ball, 'The 1-2 pitch is fouled back' is a bit abrupt.

"Baseball is a game of peaks and valleys. It sort of runs along like life itself. There are big moments and there are very dull moments," says Harwell. "I try to keep it as simple as I possibly can. The simpler the better. When you get too fancy, you find yourself in trouble. The play-by-play has to be laid out in brief, concise, simple terms.

"When you do radio you have a canvas that is completely empty. You have to make use of the imagination of the listener," he says.

Since a baseball game unfolds gradually, a broadcaster needs an intense focus to stay with the game. "It is so easy to let your mind wander," says Cohen. "People ask me what qualities you need to do this—concentration is at the top of the list."

"When you are doing a game, your concentration level is such that you are completely involved in describing what you see," says Coleman. "Thoughts flash in and out of your mind and you use them."

Most broadcasters agree that being yourself is the most important quality that they can bring to the table. "I'm not one of those guys who goes completely bananas when a home run is hit or a double play is made," says Harwell. "My voice will rise with the crowd and the excitement of the game. It has to be natural. It can't be forced.

"You don't try to be funny, be an expert, be a manager, or be anything you aren't. The best compliment anyone can pay you is that you sound like yourself—that you sound no different on the air than off the air. If you try to copy somebody, you'll only be second best."

"You have to be comfortable on the air and be true to yourself," says Cohen. "The people most successful in this business are those who let their own personality shine through."

While these announcers feel that what they say is important, they also feel that what they don't say is very important. "Silence is one of the most effective tools an announcer can use," says Harwell. "The fan needs a little rest for the ears, and I think a pause or silence can set up a play more dramatically than anything else."

Sometimes there is also a need for the announcer to "lay out" and let the crowd roar.

Ernie Harwell

"Once you establish what happened, let the crowd do its thing because the people listening are probably doing the same thing," says Matthews. "I'm not paid to yell and scream. I'm paid to tell you what happens so you can yell and scream."

Every announcer has to deal with statistics. Some use them more than others. Some like different ways of using them. "The best way to deal with them is to relate them to something else, to humanize them," says Greenwald. "Rather than saying Hank Aaron hit 755 home runs, I'd rather be able to say 'If you mea-sure the distance he covered circling the bases, it would be like a guy running from San Francisco to San Jose.'

"I try to use as few statistics as I can. I don't like to use too many statistics because when people listen they can't absorb them. You can't take all that stuff in at once," says Harwell.

Statistics are just one of many ingredients that enhance a broadcast. "The easiest part of the business is to describe what happens on the field," says Greenwald. "The toughest part is filling time between pitches, making that interesting to people. A sport like basketball carries the announcer, but an announcer has to carry baseball because nothing happens. The amount of time the ball is in play is less than five minutes. The rest is what you make it."

Another way broadcasters fill time is through storytelling. Many broadcasters such as Waite Hoyt and Harry Heilmann, were well known for their tales and every broadcaster considers the story to be a valuable tool.

"I'm pretty well known as a storyteller and believe in setting the game in a historical perspective," says Harwell. "I might discuss the origin of the Texas Leaguer or why we have foul-pole screens. I don't let it interfere with the play by play. I use that material early in the game, then later when the game begins to develop it becomes a story in itself."

Most fans lose interest when a team is struggling. The announcer can't. "There's nothing like the excitement of a pennant race," says Castiglione. "The excitement speaks for itself. But if you're thirty games out in September, you still might see something today that you've never seen before. There's always a reason to be interested."

"Anybody can sound good if the team wins 100 games a year," says Greenwald. "The real opportunity for you is when you have a bad team. If you get people saying the team isn't really good, but these guys are fun to listen to, you've earned your stripes. [When the team is bad] you look at the season not in terms of the standings. Every day you may go out and see a terrific game. Even in the course of a 100-loss season most games are decided by one or two runs. Forget the standings. They're not relevant anymore."

Like anybody else, broadcasters have good days and bad days. "Some nights you're not as sharp as others," says Matthews. "Some days you're really sharp, some you're really dull. Most of the time you're somewhere in between. The average listener probably doesn't know, but I know."

One thing that can make for a bad night is a string of broadcaster mistakes. But most have found that a mistake isn't necessarily a bad thing.

"The public forgives errors if they are human errors," says Harwell. "[They] don't forgive a lack of knowledge of the game, or someone who acts like he knows more than he does."

"If it's something silly, you try to make light of it," says Castiglione. "It's a good way to laugh at yourself and to establish yourself as a real person. People don't like robots."

Even hard-core fans will tune in and out of games. This makes providing the score all the more important. "I try to pride myself on giving the score a lot more than anyone else," says Harwell. "Because I feel, one, people don't listen very carefully and when you give the score they don't hear it, and two, a lot of people are in and out of the room."

When the score is close, many fans like to second guess the decisions of the men on the field. But all of the broadcasters agreed that that was not part of their job. "The job is to report what you see. You're not hired to coach or manage. You can suggest options or alternatives, but you're not hired to second-guess," says Coleman.

Wrap-Up—These men realize that they are providing an important service to many people and they get great enjoyment from carrying baseball through good times and bad.

"Part of the attraction of baseball is the quality of soap opera," says Cohen. "Each day relates to the one before it and the one after it. It becomes an interwoven fabric relating to what happened the day before, the week before, the month before. It all takes shape in an interesting fashion. It's not just the broadcast of the game. It's the broadcast of the season that's the attraction to the listener."

"You have to remember to have fun," says Castiglione. "We're not talking about disarmament or world events. The thing to remember is to have fun with it. It's baseball. It's a fun game."

Timeless Quotes

"Salaries must come down or the interest of the public must be increased in some way. If one or the other does not happen, bankruptcy stares every team in the face."

—*Albert Spalding, 1881*

"These kids today; they won't learn. You can't tell them. You can't teach them. It's not the same as it used to be. Those were the good days. Now they don't care."

—*Stuffy McInnis, Harvard coach, 1950*
—Norman Macht

Quad and Quint Crown Winners

A short list of greats

Sheldon Miller

A lot is made of the Triple Crown winners—those who lead the league in home runs, RBIs, and batting average in the same season.

I thought it would be interesting to investigate other versatile players. I decided on a Quadruple Crown and a Quintuple Crown consisting of doubles, triples, stolen bases, batting average, and on-base percentage. I wanted to put a premium on a player's ability to get on base and move along even if he is not a power hitter or playing in an age of long hits.

I began with the beginning of the National League back in 1876 and included all years up to the present. I also included all the other leagues usually considered major leagues (UA: 1884, AA: 1882-1891, PL: 1890, AL: 1901-Present, and FL: 1914-1915).

The results were very interesting. The number of qualifying candidates closely matched the number of Triple Crown winners. Eleven players qualified for the Quadruple Crown and two of those players also qualified for the Quintuple Crown.

Honus Wagner in 1908 and Ty Cobb in 1917 led their league in all five categories: doubles, triples, batting average, on-base percentage, and stolen bases. Ty Cobb was the only player in American League history to qualify for both the Quadruple Crown (in 1911 and 1917) and the Quintuple Crown (in 1917).

Benny Kauff proved what a dominant player he was in the Federal League in 1914 by winning the Quadruple Crown. Honus Wagner was the only player to win three times (the Quadruple Crown in 1904, 1907, and 1908 and the Quintuple Crown in 1908). Stan Musial was the only other player to win the Quadruple Crown more than once (1943 and 1948).

Five players (Barnes, O'Neill, Hornsby, and Musial twice) fell short of the Quintuple Crown by not leading in stolen bases. Three (Wagner twice, and Kauff) missed out because they didn't lead in triples. One (Cobb) failed to lead the league in on-base percentage. The list of winners follows, and on the next page is a complete chart with runners up in each category.

Quadruple and/or Quintuple Crown Winners

Leading or tied for league lead in doubles (2B), triples (3B), batting average (BA), on-base percentage (OBP), and stolen bases (SB)

Player	Yr.	Lg.	Categories	Crown
Ross Barnes	1876	NL	2B, 3B, BA, OBP	Quadruple
Tip O'Neill	1887	AA	2B, 3B, BA, OBP	Quadruple
Honus Wagner	1904	NL	2B, BA, OBP, SB	Quadruple
Honus Wagner	1907	NL	2B, BA, OBP, SB	Quadruple
Honus Wagner	1908	NL	2B, 3B, BA, OBP, SB	Quad./Quint.
Ty Cobb	1911	AL	2B, 3B, BA, SB	Quadruple
Benny Kauff	1914	FL	2B, BA, OBP, SB	Quadruple
Ty Cobb	1917	AL	2B, 3B, BA, OBP, SB	Quad./Quint.
Rogers Hornsby	1921	NL	2B, 3B, BA, OBP	Quadruple
Stan Musial	1943	NL	2B, 3B, BA, OBP	Quadruple
Stan Musial	1948	NL	2B, 3B, BA, OBP	Quadruple

Sheldon Miller is a computer programmer/analyst and has been a member of SABR since 1984.

Winners and runners up in each Quadruple Crown category

Player	Yr./Team/Lg.	2B	3B	BA	OBP	SB
Ross Barnes	1876 Chi. (NL)	Barnes, Chi. 21 Hines, Chi. 21 Higham, Har. 21	Barnes, Chi. 14 Hall, Phi. 13	Barnes, Chi. .429 Hall, Phi. .366	Barnes, Chi. .462 Hall, Phi. .384	
Tip O'Neill	1887 StL. (AA)	O'Neill, Stl, 52 Lyons, Phi. 43	O'Neill, StL. 19 Poorman, Phi. 19 McPhee, Cin. 19 Kerins, Lou. 19 Davis, Bal. 19 Burns, Bal. 19	O'Neill, StL. .435 Browning, Lou. .402	O'Neill, StL. .490 Browning, Lou. .464	Nichol, Cin. 138 Latham, StL. 129 Many players O'Neill, Lou. 30
Honus Wagner	1904 Pit. (NL)	Wagner, Pit. 44 Mertes, NY 28	Lumley, Brk. 18 Wagner, Pit. 14	Wagner, Pit. .349 Donlin, Cin., NY. .329 Beckley, StL. .325	Wagner, Pit. .423 Thomas, Phi. .416	Wagner, Pit. 53 Dahlen, NY 47 Mertes, NY 47
Honus Wagner	1907 Pit. (NL)	Wagner, Pit. 38 Magee, Phi. 28	Ganzel, Cin. 16 Alperman, Brk. 16 Wagner, Pit. 14 Beaumont, Bos. 14	Wagner, Pit. .350 Magee, Phi. .328	Wagner, Pit. .408 Magee, Phi. .396	Wagner, Pit. 61 Magee, Phi. 46 Evers, Chi. 46
Honus Wagner	1908 Pit. (NL)	Wagner, Pit. 39 Magee, Phi. 30	Wagner, Pit. 19 Lobert, Cin. 18	Wagner, Pit. .354 Donlin, NY .334	Wagner, Pit. .415 Evers, Chi. .402	Wagner, Pit. 53 Murray, StL. 48
Ty Cobb	1911 Det. (AL)	Cobb, Det. 47 Jackson, Cle. 45	Cobb, Det. 24 Cree, NY 22	Cobb, Det. .420 Jackson, Cle. .408	Jackson, Cle. .468 Cobb, Det. .467	Cobb, Det. 83 Milan, Was. 58
Benny Kauff	1914 Ind. (FL)	Kauff, Ind. 44 Evans, Brk. 41	Evans, Brk. 15 Esmond, Ind. 15 Kenworthy, KC 14 Kauff, Ind. 13	Kauff, Ind. .370 Evans, Brk. .348	Kauff, Ind. .447 Evans, Brk. .416	Kauff, Ind. 75 McKechnie, Ind. 47
Ty Cobb	1917 Det. (AL)	Cobb, Det. 44 Speaker, Cle. 42	Cobb, Det. 24 Jackson, Chi. 17	Cobb, Det. .383 Sisler, StL. .353	Cobb, Det. .444 Speaker, Cle. .432	Cobb, Det. 55 E. Collins, Chi. 53
Rogers Hornsby	1921 StL. (NL)	Hornsby, StL. 44 Kelly, NY 42	Hornsby, StL. 18 Powell, Bos. 18 Grimm, Pit. 17 Frisch, NY 17 Bigbee, Pit. 17	Hornsby StL. .397 Roush, Cin. .352 McHenry StL. .350	Hornsby StL. .458 Youngs, NY .411	Frisch, NY 49 Carey, Pit. 37 Many players Hornsby, StL. 13
Stan Musial	1943 StL. (NL)	Musial, StL. 48 Herman, Brk. 41 V.DiMaggio, Pit. 41	Musial, StL. 20 Klein, StL. 14	Musial, StL. .357 Herman, Brk. .330	Musial, StL. .425 Galan, Brk. .412	Vaughan, Brk. 20 Lowrey, Chi. 13 Many players Musial, StL. 9
Stan Musial	1948 StL. (NL)	Musial, StL. 46 Ennis, Phi. 40	Musial, StL. 18 Hopp, Pit. 12	Musial, StL. .376 Ashburn, Phi. .333	Musial, StL. .450 R. Elliott, Bos. .423	Ashburn, Phi. 32 Reese, Brk. 25 Many players Musial, StL. 7

The Other Veeck

Reviving the Cubs

Eddie Gold

It's a shame that William Louis Veeck is known primarily as Bill Veeck's father. The "other" Veeck took a floundering Cubs organization and built it into the flagship of the National League for two decades.

Veeck, who served as president of the club from 1917 to 1933, never went tieless, coatless or was open-shirted. He wore a starched collar, but was no stuffed shirt. The senior Veeck did not pull any promotional stunts like exploding scoreboards, dancing clowns, or prancing midgets. But he was the first to have his team broadcast games (1922) in the face of furious protests from every owner. And Veeck brought a regular Ladies Day to Chicago as femme fans flocked to the friendly confines every Friday.

Mr. Veeck, who wrote a sports column under the name "Bill Bailey" for the Chicago *American*, criticized the Cubs in a series of columns that caught the eye of owner William Wrigley.

"All right, if you're so smart why don't you come and do it," said Wrigley. Veeck did, and Wrigley, an avid fan, left the running of the Cubs to his new president.

Success didn't come quickly or easily. In 1925 the Cubs hit rock bottom, finishing in the cellar for the first time in their history.

Veeck's biggest mistake was naming veteran shortstop Rabbit Maranville playing-manager, replacing Bill Killefer on July 6. The Maranville reign started off with a bang as the Cubs slugged the Dodgers, 10-5 at Ebbets Field. Naturally, the Rabbit went out to celebrate. He and a few teammates hopped into a taxi with Times Square as their destination. When they didn't leave a tip, the cab driver became miffed and a fight ensued with everyone winding up in the hoosegow.

The final straw came when Maranville raced through a Pullman train, anointing the passengers with "holy water" from a spittoon.

After the Cubs slipped into the cellar, Veeck hastily replaced the Rabbit at the helm with former Pirates catcher George Gibson. Then followed Veeck's master stroke. It was reported the Yankees were eyeing Louisville manager Joe McCarthy to replace the ailing Miller Huggins. Veeck had a secret meeting with McCarthy at French Lick, Indiana, in September, 1925. They kept the signing secret until the season ended.

The Cubs had a good nucleus with catcher Gabby Hartnett, first baseman Charlie Grimm plus pitchers Charlie Root and Guy Bush. But they lacked the leadership and it was McCarthy's job to provide it.

Veeck and McCarthy's first move was to draft stump-like slugger Hack Wilson from Toledo for $7,500. Wilson went on to clout 56 homers and drive in a major league record 190 runs in 1930.

The pair continued to put the pieces together, grabbing Indy outfielder Riggs Stephenson for $20,000 and plucking shortstop Woody English from Toledo and pitcher Pat Malone from Minneapolis.

Eddie Gold is a sportswriter for the Chicago Sun-Times.

Then they engineered the deal with the Pirates for Kiki Cuyler, who rounded out an all-star outfield with Stephenson and Wilson.

But the Cubs were a player away from the pennant. Wrigley insisted on the acquisition of second baseman Rogers Hornsby from the Braves for five players and $200,000.

In 1929, the Cubs roared to their first pennant in eleven seasons. Hornsby, Wilson, Cuyler, Stephenson and Grimm formed the Cubs' own version of "Murderer's Row," while the pitching of Root, Bush and Malone led them to a 98-54 record. In four years Veeck and McCarthy had lifted the club from the bottom to the top.

After the Cubs dropped the World Series to the Athletics in five games and finished a disappointing second in 1930, Wrigley, over Veeck's objections, re-placed McCarthy as manager with Hornsby. McCarthy went on to win eight pennants and seven World Series with the Yankees.

Wrigley died prior to the 1932 season, at age 70, leaving Veeck to carry on. Veeck dismissed Hornsby on August 2 and turned over the management to Grimm. The Cubs pulled themselves together under Jolly Cholly and won the pennant with an influx of new players that included the double play duo of Billy Jurges and Billy Herman, plus third baseman Stan Hack and pitcher Lon Warneke.

Veeck died of leukemia at age 56 on October 4, 1933, in Chicago. But he left a baseball legacy— Barnum Bill Veeck, who installed the famed Wrigley Field scoreboard and planted the ivy vines before moving on to greener pastures.

A Lynching on Sunday

Three weeks after arresting NY State League president Haas for allowing an illegal Sunday ball game to be played in Albany in 1894, Police Chief Lynch vowed he would arrest eight players on Sunday, June 3. Albany manager Billy Arnold got wind of this, so he had eight "dummies" take the field. Lynch had them arrested and taken to court, where he learned they weren't the real players. Lynch returned to Riverside Park, grabbed the first three players he could catch, and hauled them away. This action did not have the desired effect. Chief Lynch returned to find that the game was in the fourth inning and the gates were locked. Learning of his presence, the players hid behind the right field fence. The chief scaled the fence, arrested Jack Messitt of Albany, and made yet another trip to court. When the angry Lynch returned again with reinforcements, the game was in the seventh inning. This time, both clubs decided to call the game rather than risk spending the night in jail.

—Tony Kissel

Wyoming Major Leaguers

Cowboy ballplayers

Mike Patchen

Wyoming is the least populated state in the union. Yet in 1995 there were three native-born Wyomingites who played in the major leagues, two others who went to the University of Wyoming and still another who lived in Wyoming for part of his life. Mike Devereaux, now with the Orioles, and pitcher Tom Browning were both born in Casper. Expo Mike Lansing was born in Rawlins. Art Howe, Oakland manager and former hitting coach for the Colorado Rockies, and Jeff Huson of the Orioles both attended the University of Wyoming. Mark Lee, a former relief pitcher for Baltimore, lived in Casper for a part of his life.

Wyoming does not have spring weather conducive to high school baseball. The only competitive baseball is T-Ball through American Legion and Senior Babe Ruth in the summer. Wyoming only has collegiate baseball at UW and has had only one professional team in state history—the 1941 Cheyenne Indians of the Western League. (The minor league Cheyenne Indians are not to be confused with the Cheyenne Indians semipro team that operated in Wyoming's capital for over four decades. For an article on the 1941 Indians by Joe Naiman see the *SABR Minor League History Journal*, Vol 2, Number

Mike Patchen *is an attorney in Gillette, Wyoming. This is his first article for any publication. His fondest baseball memory is listening to Vin Scully and Jerry Doggett call Los Angeles Dodgers games on KFI Radio. He would like to acknowledge the help of other SABR members: Pat Doyle, Paul Jacques, Jerry Jackson, Richard Obrand, Bill Felber, Charlie Garahan, Tom Bourke, John Dowling, Blake Spurney, David Ball, Ray Nemec, and C. Stanley Gilliam.*

1). It appears that only three of the Indians made the major leagues after they played in Cheyenne. Bill L. Evans played briefly for the White Sox in 1949 and for Boston in 1951. He pitched in only thirteen games, with a record of 0-1. George Milstead pitched for the Cubs from 1924 through 1926. From Texas, he was known as "Cowboy." He pitched in thirty-six games, with a 3-7 record. John Kerr was the player-manager of the 1941 Indians. He played for Detroit, the White Sox, and Washington from 1923 through 1934. He was on the 1933 Senators World Series team, and got into one game of the fall classic, running for Fred Schulte in the tenth inning of Game Five. Kerr married Walter Johnson's niece, Olive.

There was a Cheyenne team in the 1912 Rocky Mountain League, replacing Pueblo, Colorado on June 27. Cheyenne went 3-0 before the league folded on July 4. Manager Ira Bidwell kept his team in town as the semipro Cheyenne Indians.

Native-born Wyomingites with major league experience are rare. The first was Robert Harris, who pitched in the 1930s and 40s for the Tigers, Browns, and A's. The Gillette native soon moved to Nebraska where, as an adult, he spent winters trapping animals. After the 1942 season, he went into the military for three years. When he came back Connie Mack cut him, claiming he had hurt his arm in the Navy. Harris sued under the GI Bill of Rights and won a settlement of $5,000.

Dick Ellsworth came from the small ranching town of Lusk. Ellsworth pitched for five different teams

Transcendental Graphics

Dick Ellsworth

over his major league career. He won 22 games for the 1963 Cubs and then lost 22 in 1966. He also went 15-0 pitching his Fresno, CA high school team to the San Joaquin Valley title. One poll listed Ellsworth as the greatest player from Wyoming.

The next native to make the major leagues was Jan Dukes from Cheyenne. Jan pitched for the Senators in 1969 and '70 and the Rangers in 1972. He says that his biggest thrill in baseball was striking out Carl Yastrzemski with the bases loaded in a game in late 1969. The '70s saw three native-born Wyomingites make the big leagues. Dan Spillner of Casper made his debut in 1974 with the Padres. He went on to pitch for San Diego, Cleveland, and the White Sox over his eleven-year career. In his debut, he allowed four runs in less than an inning against Houston. Two players born in Cheyenne, Dennis DeBarr and Rick Sofield, reached the majors two years apart. DeBarr was 0-1 in fourteen relief appearances for Toronto in 1977. He was 11-2, with a 2.36 ERA and 10 saves

with Montgomery of the Southern League in 1976. Sofield played for the Twins 1979-81. He hit .247, with 9 homers and 49 RBIs in 131 games in 1980, his only full year in the big leagues. He had eight years in the minors with seven clubs.

Browning, Devereaux, Lee, and Bill Wilkinson of Greybull started their big league careers in the '80s. Bill, the grandson of former major leaguer Jim Bluejacket, pitched for Seattle in 1985, '87, and '88. His best year was 1987, when he had 10 saves and a 3.66 ERA. Bill's brother Brian pitched in the Mariner system but never made it to the Big Show. Devereaux started his career in the Dodger organization and played for Los Angeles before being traded to Baltimore, where he sparkled in 1992 with 24 homers, 107 RBIs, 180 hits, and a .276 average. He became the first Orioles center fielder to have 100 RBIs in a season. He signed with the White Sox as a free agent in 1995 and was traded to Atlanta in August of that year.

Lee started in the Tiger organization, but debuted with the Royals in 1988. He also pitched for the Brewers in 1990 and 1991. He was with the Orioles in 1995. He was considered Wyoming's best amateur pitcher in 1980.

Browning pitched for the Reds and was a 20-game winner his rookie year. Browning also threw a perfect game and won a World Series game. The Royals signed him as a free agent after the 1994 season. He retired at the end of 1995.

Lansing made his major league debut in 1993 and had the honor of being the very first batter for the very first Colorado Rockies home game. He attended Wichita State when the Shockers won the College World Series, but was injured and didn't play.

Non-native connections—Although only ten players who made the major leagues were born in Wyoming, a number of others have called Wyoming home at some time in their life. The University of Wyoming produced several big leaguers. Art Howe is probably the best known, having played for eleven years, managed for four years and coached for three more besides being a scout for the Dodgers. The UW grad with the most promise was Greg Brock, who came up through the Dodgers organization and was touted as the replacement for Steve Garvey. Greg hit 20 homers his rookie season and 21 in 1985, but he eventually was traded to Milwaukee and closed out his career in the White Sox minor league system.

Three other players from UW also made the major leagues. Jeff Huson came up through the Montreal system before being traded to Texas. He played for the Rangers in 1990-93. He was then traded to Baltimore where he played in 1995. Pat House, who lives in Idaho, pitched for Houston in 1967-68. House was called up part way through the 1967 season and faced the Giants in his first big league appearance. In the seventh inning, with runners on first and second, Pat was called in. He promptly got Willie McCovey to hit back to the box, Jim Ray Hart to pop to third, and Tom Haller to ground to first. He also pitched a no-hitter in the Pioneer League. Paul Fitzke, who had an outstanding football career for UW, pitched one game for the Indians in 1924. He lasted four innings, allowed five hits with a strikeout and three walks.

Retirees—Several ex-major leaguers live in the Cowboy State today. Woodie Held lives on a ranch near Dubois. Held played from 1954 through 1969. He had several good years for the seven different teams he called home. Bud Daley, who won the fifth game of the 1961 World Series, resides in Lander. He once said his greatest thrill in baseball was driving in the winning run (after fouling off seven pitches) at his state high school championship game. Daley pitched for Wilson High School in Long Beach, California and was the Southern California Player of the Year in 1950.

Mike Blyzka lives in Cheyenne. He played for the 1953 Browns and the 1954 Orioles. He was part of the largest major league trade—eighteen players in 1954. Mike was sent to Denver, the Yankees Triple A club. He loved the Rocky Mountains and stayed. Gerald Nyman, who lives in Jackson Hole, played two years for White Sox in 1968 and '69 and for the Padres in 1970. He has coached in the minor leagues with his most recent stint as a pitching coach for the Eugene Emeralds in 1995.

There have been other players who called Wyoming home. Mike Epstein, lived in Lusk. Mike played from 1966-74 for five different teams. Bob Cerv lived in Cheyenne in the early 50s. Cerv played from 1951 through 1962. Ben Hunt, who died in Greybull, played two seasons—1910 for the Red Sox and 1913 for the Cardinals. (For a great article on Hunt by Dick Thompson, see *The Baseball Research Journal* No. 22.).

Postretirees—Besides Hunt, three other major leaguers died in Wyoming. Ed Murray played one game for the Browns on June 24, 1917. He struck out in his only time at bat and then in the ninth inning of the game with Detroit, Grover Hartley pinch-hit for him. Ed, at shortstop, did have one assist in the game. He later lived in Cheyenne and the insurance agency he founded still conducts business. Bill Meehan died in Douglas. He pitched one game for the 1915 A's. He started, lasted four innings, gave up seven hits and three walks, struck out four, and was charged with the loss. His son still lives in Douglas. The most tragic death was that of Ed Kennedy, who played thirteen games (short, third and the outfield) for the 1884 Cincinnati Unions. Kennedy was a newspaper owner in northern Kansas. He was offered a job at the Cheyenne newspaper as a pressman. When he arrived in Cheyenne he stepped off the train onto the platform and dropped dead of apoplexy. Kennedy had played for the Cincinnati Unions in 1884.

High schoolers—Besides Lansing, Devereaux, Browning and others, two former big leaguers went to high school in Wyoming. The most successful was Jim "Death Valley" Scott who pitched nine seasons for the White Sox from 1909-1917. He had two 20-win seasons (1913 and 1915) and was among league leaders in several categories in those years. Scott attended high school in Lander. He pitched a nine inning no-hitter on May 14, 1914, but then gave up two hits in the tenth. He went on to umpire in the minors before making the major leagues in 1930-31. His nickname came from similarity to the name of Walter Scott, the original Death Valley Scotty.

Mark Knudson went to high school in Casper. Knudson pitched for Houston and Milwaukee from 1985-91. He started in just over half of his 117 pitching appearances and is now a broadcaster in Denver.

Semipro connections—Despite the lack of a long playing season, the Cowboy State has seen some great semipro action. The most notable team was the Cheyenne Indians. The Indians produced several regional tournament champions and several of their players went on to professional careers. Casper and Greybull also produced championship teams who took the Denver *Post* tournament in the late '30s. The Midwest Refinery league, made up of teams sponsored by the Midwest Oil Company, was the most notable of the semipro leagues in Wyoming. Its players worked in the oil fields of Wyoming and played baseball when they weren't working.

Several players from the Midwest League and the Indians saw action in the major leagues. The most notable was Claude Hendrix, who pitched for Cheyenne in 1910. He went on to pitch for the Pirates and Cubs, as well as being one of the best pitchers in the Federal League, starring for the Chifeds. Others who played semipro ball in Wyoming were Ben Hunt, Jim Bluejacket, and Claud "Bob" Linton who had at least seventeen years in professional baseball but only one year—1929—in the major leagues. He played seventeen games for the Pirates, hitting just .111. He was also a minor league manager for three years.

Bluejacket's real name was James Smith. However when he played ball in Bartlesville, Oklahoma, in 1908, the only clothing he had was a Navy uniform. He was called Bluejacket and he adopted that name as his own. Despite twelve years in organized ball, he only appeared one year in the National League (Cincinnati in 1916 for three games) and two years for Brooklyn in the Federal League. In his Brooklyn debut he won 2-0 on a six-hitter in which he picked off two baserunners.

George "Zip" Zabel pitched for Cheyenne in 1912 and holds a major league record for pitching 18.1 innings in relief in one game for the Cubs in 1915. Rolla "Lefty" Mapel pitched for the Browns in 1919. He too played semipro ball in Wyoming. In the Denver *Post* tournament of 1915, Mapel struck out 27 batters in twelve innings. Ray "Lefty" Boggs played in the Midwest League for a month before being called up to play for the Boston Braves. He appeared in just four games and walked seven batters in his five innings of work.

Lynn was known as Jim "Lefty" Scoggins. He pitched one game for the White Sox. On August 26, 1913, he started a game against Washington. According to the Washington *Evening Star*, Scoggins (the article lists him as Linn Scroggins) walked Danny Moeller, the first batter he faced. Eddie Foster then reached base on a throwing error by Buck Weaver. When Scoggins went 3-0 on Clyde Milan, he was relieved by Ed Cicotte, who finished the walk to Milan. Washington scored five runs in the top of the first including scores by Moeller, Foster, and Milan. Thus Scoggins lost his only major league appearance. *Total Baseball* only gives Scoggins one walk but it seems he should have two in his brief appearance.

Other Cheyenne Indians who played major league baseball are Ralph Glaze (Red Sox, 1906–1908), Art "Six O'clock" Weaver (four teams, 1902–1908), and Jimmy Whelan (Cardinals, 1912). Glaze later coached at Baylor, Drake, and USC, where he was also the Athletic Director. Whelan had only one at bat in the majors.

Devereaux, Hendrix, Kerr, Cerv, Daley, Epstein, and Browning all played in the World Series (Hendrix got a hit off Babe Ruth in the fourth game of the 1918 Series).

A number of Wyoming men played minor league ball and there have been a number of semipro teams in the state. Additional information is always welcome. Despite the lack of professional ball in Wyoming, and the state's sparse population, Wyoming has contributed to baseball in the United States, and its people love the game. Paul Jacques, a Laramie photographer is putting together a pictorial history of baseball in Wyoming in an effort to preserve the history of the game in the Cowboy State.

The All Stars of the Past 65 Years

A method to cacluate the best players since 1930

Alan S. Kaufman
and James C. Kaufman

Selecting all-time all-stars creates debates about the relative merits of this home run hitter from the 1930s and that batting champion from the 1980s. How do you choose an All Star outfielder when you compare a slugger like Reggie Jackson, a speedster like Rickey Henderson, and a batting champ like Tony Gwynn? Or when you compare a great offensive shortstop from the past generation (Ernie Banks) to a defensive whiz from the current generation (Ozzie Smith)? The answer should reside in finding common units of comparison, units that can effectively cut across eras and give weight to all aspects of baseball ability. Such a metric should emphasize recognition of a player's ability relative to other players from his era. We suggest three:

• Finishing among the top 10 in Most Valuable Player (MVP) elections;

• Being selected for the NL or AL All Star team at midseason; and

• Being selected to *The Sporting News* (*TSN*) All Star team at the end of the season.

We contend that players who are frequently considered the top men at their positions can stake a claim

Alan S. Kaufman *and* ***James C. Kaufman*** *are the authors of* The Worst Baseball Pitchers of All Time *(McFarland, 1993), an updated version of which was published in 1995 by Citadel Press. They have written for* Playboy, Baseball Digest, NINE, Baseball Quarterly Reviews, *and many other publications. They are frequent contributors to Baseball Research Journal. Alan is the author of psychological tests and books that are used throughout the world and is a Senior Research Scientist for PAR, Inc., in Odessa, Florida. James, an aspiring playwright, is a Teaching Fellow at Yale University in the Department of Cognitive Psychology.*

to an all-time All Star team regardless of when they played. The same rationale applies to those who regularly rank among the top finishers in MVP elections. Therefore, we selected All Star teams based on a consensus of these aspects of recognition. The MVP has been awarded in each league under its present voting procedures since 1931, and the All Star Game has been played since 1933. *The Sporting News* has selected an All Star team since 1925, although only a single ML team was chosen until 1960.

The All Star teams that we chose based on these criteria had to exclude players who excelled before 1930, such as Babe Ruth, Ty Cobb, and Christy Mathewson. We limited the candidates to those players who began their careers about 1930 or later. We included Mel Ott, Jimmie Foxx, and Carl Hubbell, who became regulars in 1928, along with Bill Dickey (1929), Joe Cronin (1929), Earl Averill (1929), Lefty Gomez (1931), Dizzy Dean (1932), Luke Appling (1932), Arky Vaughan (1932), Hank Greenberg (1933), and Ducky Medwick (1933). We excluded Charlie Gehringer (1926), Paul Waner (1926), Lou Gehrig (1925), Mickey Cochrane (1925), Lefty Grove (1925), and Al Simmons (1924).

For MVP rankings we developed a point system patterned after the one actually used to select MVPs. We allotted players 14 points for each MVP award they won, 9 points for each second-place finish, 8 points for third place, 7 points for fourth place, 6 points for fifth place, 5 points for sixth place, 4 points for seventh place, 3 points for eighth place, 2 points for ninth place, and 1 point for tenth place.

MVP rankings favor pitchers whose careers were mostly prior to 1956, because there was no separate award for hurlers. However, since 1956, when the Cy Young award was instituted, many MVP voters have de-emphasized pitchers, believing that pitchers have their own award. Consequently, we added a fourth criterion for selecting the best righthanded and left-handed pitchers of the past 65 years: performance in actual and hypothetical Cy Young elections. We used the point system we developed previously (*BRJ*, 1995), which allotted 5 points for each actual or hypothetical Cy Young award that a pitcher won, 4 points for tying for an award, 3 points for each second-place finish, 2 points for tying for second place, and 1 point for each third-place finish.

For the All Star team criterion, we gave players 1 point for each All Star team for which they were selected, regardless of whether they were replaced due to injury or otherwise did not get into the game (including the 1945 teams, even though no game was played). Players earned a maximum of 1 point per season between 1959 and 1962, when two All Star Games were played, if they were selected for either or both games. We used the lists of players included in *Total Baseball* (4th ed.), along with the 1995 All Star rosters, as the data source. Players who had a few excellent seasons prior to the first All Star Game in 1933 (notably Dickey, Cronin, Foxx, Hubbell, and Ott) were given special consideration when this criterion was used to select our All Star teams.

For the *TSN* teams, we again gave 1 point for each selection, and gave special consideration to players whose selections were primarily or exclusively before 1961, when a single ML team was chosen.

We gave credit to a player for making the All Star team or the *TSN* team regardless of the position he played that season. Thus, Dave Parker earned 6 points based on 5 selections as an outfielder and 1 as a DH; Stan Musial earned 12 points, 9 as an outfielder and 3 as a first baseman. Both Parker and Musial were classified as outfielders. However, some players starred at two or more positions in several different seasons or made the All Star or *TSN* teams as DH. To accommodate these players, we selected DHs for our All Star teams. Notable players included in this category were Pete Rose, Harmon Killebrew, Robin Yount, Elston Howard, Harvey Kuenn, Paul Molitor, and Joe Torre. Rod Carew was considered only as a second baseman because 7 of his 9 *TSN* selections came at that position, with only 2 coming at first base. Similarly, Ernie Banks was categorized as a shortstop because he

earned all 48 of his MVP points while at that position, not at first base.

As shown in Table 1, we selected first, second, and third All Star teams based on each of the three criteria; the criterion of Cy Young points was also used for pitchers. Foxx, Musial, Mays, and Rose made the first team for each separate criterion. Berra, Carew, Schmidt, Ripken, and Williams were first-team selections for two out of three criteria, and Feller made the first team based on three of the four criteria for pitchers. Although Foxx was named to nine All Star teams, he was given the nod over Garvey and Mize (each named to ten teams) because his slugging feats between 1929 and 1932 (when he averaged 39.5 home runs, 141 RBI, and a .337 batting average) would have made him an easy choice for four more teams had the All Star game been played prior to 1933. Similarly, Dickey and Ott had four All Star caliber years between 1929 and 1932 (Dickey batted .310 to .339 and Ott drove in 115 to 151 runs), facts that were taken into consideration in Table 1. Hubbell also had some good years between 1929 and '32, but the first of his five 20-win seasons did not occur until 1933, so little correction was necessary in the rankings.

We used the All Star teams selected by the various criteria in Table 1 as raw materials for choosing consensus teams. That is to say, we allotted 5 points for each first-team selection, 3 points for each second-team selection, and 1 point for each third-team selection. Table 2 synthesizes data from the several criteria and presents our consensus first and second All Star teams for players whose careers began about 1930. Most consensus first-team All-Stars easily outdistanced the player or players who made the second team. Closest races were for catcher, with Yogi Berra edging Dickey and Johnny Bench; third base, with Mike Schmidt besting Brooks Robinson; and the third outfield spot, with Ted Williams surpassing Hank Aaron.

All consensus first-team selections are in the Hall of Fame except for the gambling Rose and the still-active (and automatic selection) Cal Ripken. Among second-team choices, only Nellie Fox and Steve Garvey are not in Cooperstown. Fox, with 74.7 percent of the vote in his last year of eligibility, came as close as one can without enshrinement, and Garvey is still on the Hall of Fame ballot. Another second baseman, Joe Gordon, merits Hall of Fame consideration based on the data in Table 1. Gordon made the *TSN* team an impressive six times when only one team was chosen, and also ranks among the second-base leaders on our other two criteria. Overall with our system, Gordon outranks Hall of Fame second basemen Bobby Doerr, Billy Herman, and Red Schoendienst.

Players on the two consensus All Star teams span the 65 years rather evenly. The teams include a total of twenty-seven players—nine whose careers began in the late 1920s to the early 1940s (Foxx, Musial, Williams, Feller, Dickey, Mize, Cronin, DiMaggio, Hubbell); nine who had their best years in the 1950s and 1960s (Berra, Mays, Spahn, Fox, B. Robinson, Banks, Aaron, Mantle, Killebrew), and nine whose careers were mainly between 1970 and 1995 (Carew, Schmidt, Ripken, Rose, Bench, Garvey, Morgan, Seaver, Carlton). Ripken's selection over Hall of Fame shortstops Banks, Cronin, Boudreau, Aparicio, Reese, Vaughan, and Rizzuto attests that his greatness is not defined only by his iron-man streak. Although Cronin was penalized to some extent because the inaugural All Star Game did not occur until 1933, his seven selections to the AL squad is probably equivalent to the ten and eleven selections for Banks, Aparicio and Reese (see Table 1); he would not have matched the thirteen selections for Ripken and Ozzie Smith. Based on the criteria used in our analysis, Cronin would not likely have overtaken Ripken as the top shortstop of the past 65 years even if the All Star Game and MVP elections had occurred in the late 1920s, and if two *TSN* teams, not one, had been chosen during Cronin's career.

Among players on the two consensus All Star teams, only Ripken, still active in 1996, played in the decade of the 1990s. Consequently, we developed Table 3, which presents a consensus All Star team for players from the 1980s and 1990s based on the same criteria used previously. To be eligible for this team, players had to begin their careers in the 1980s or '90s, or they had to play in at least twelve of the sixteen seasons from 1980 to 1995. Gary Carter beat out Carlton Fisk for this team and George Brett edged Wade Boggs. Murray, Ripken, Sandberg, and Yount had little competition. Kirby Puckett and Parker were easy choices for the outfield, with Barry Bonds besting Tony Gwynn and Dave Winfield for the third slot. On the pitching staff, Greg Maddux, by virtue of four *TSN* selections and four straight Cy Young awards, easily beat out Roger Clemens for the righthanded pitcher on the team. No recent lefthanded pitcher ranked very high among southpaws over the past 65 years, but Fernando Valenzuela gets the nod for the modern team based on his fourteen Cy Young points and six All Star selections. Jimmy Key made three

TSN teams to Fernando's two, but Key (and two-time *TSN* nominees Tommy Glavine, Danny Jackson, Frank Viola, and Chuck Finley) fell short on the other criteria.

Will any currently active players challenge any members of the two consensus All Star teams shown in Table 2? Maddux certainly has a shot. Bonds' 58 MVP points and five *TSN* selections during his first ten years are extremely impressive, although he will have to maintain nearly that pace for another decade to displace any of the six superstar outfielders from their perches. Other bona fide contenders are Frank Thomas at first base and Barry Larkin at shortstop. Two-time MVP Thomas has accumulated 42 MVP points in only six seasons and could certainly wind up in Table 2 ahead of Garvey, Mize, Murray, and even Foxx before he retires. And 1995 NL MVP Larkin's six *TSN* selections in ten seasons make him a contender for the future.

Obviously, there are many ways to choose All Star teams and to compare players from one generation to another. We have offered one such approach, and believe that our consensus teams are solid and well-rounded and could compete with any team, anytime, anywhere.

Table 1

All Star Teams Based on Points Earned in MVP (and Cy Young) Elections, Number of Years on All Star Teams and Number of Years on The Sporting News (TSN) Teams.

*Denotes playing career began prior to 1st All Star Game (1933)

**Denotes that all, or virtually all, *TSN* selections occurred before 1961 (when only one ML team was chosen)

Catcher	MVP Points		All Star Years		TSN Teams	
1st Team	Berra	75	Berra	15	Bench	7
			Dickey*	11	Dickey**	6
2nd Team	Bench	43	Bench	14	Carter	6
	Campanella	43			Berra**	5
3rd Team	Dickey	29	Freehan	11	Fisk	5
	Carter	27	Fisk	11	Campanella**	4
			Carter	11	Freehan	4
					Munson	4

First Base	MVP Points		All Star Years		TSN Teams	
1st Team	Foxx	57	Foxx*	9	Foxx**	5
2nd Team	Greenberg	52	Garvey	10	Hernandez	5
	Murray	51	Mize	10		
3rd Team	Thomas	42	Murray	8	Cepeda	4
	Garvey	38	Hodges	8	McCovey	4
	Mize	35	Vernon	7	Powell	4
			York	7	Garvey	4

Cepeda	7	Cooper	4
		Mattingly	4
		Kluszewski**	3
		Mize**	3

Second Base

	MVP Points		All Star Years		TSN Teams	
1st Team	Morgan	45	Carew	18	Carew	9
2nd Team	Fox	34	Fox	12	Gordon**	6
	Carew	33				
3rd Team	Gordon	29	Sandberg	10	Richardson	6
	Sandberg	28	Morgan	10	Sandberg	6
			Herman	10	Morgan	5
			Schoendienst	10	Fox**	4
			Gordon	9	J. Robinson**	4
			Doerr	9		

Third Base

	MVP Points		All Star Years		TSN Teams	
1st Team	Schmidt	73	B. Robinson	15	Schmidt	10
2nd Team	B. Robinson	52	Schmidt	12	B. Robinson	9
			Brett	12		
3rd Team	Brett	44	Boggs	11	Boggs	7
			Kell	10	Kell**	6
			Santo	9		
			Mathews	9		

Shortstop

	MVP Points		All Star Years		TSN Teams	
1st Team	Banks	48	Ripken	13	Ripken	8
			Smith	13	Cronin**	7
2nd Team	Boudreau	39	Banks	11	Larkin	6
	Ripken	36	Aparicio	10		
			Reese	10		
			Cronin*	7		
3rd Team	Stephens	33	Vaughan	9	Aparicio	5
	Reese	29	Concepcion	9	Smith	5
	Cronin	26	Marion	8	Rizzuto**	4
			Stephens	8	Banks	4
			Boudreau	8		

Outfield

	MVP Points		All Star Years		TSN Teams	
1st Team	Musial	105	Aaron	21	T. Williams**	12
	T. Williams	99	Mays	20	Musial**	12
	Mays	97	Musial	20	Mays	11
2nd Team	Mantle	89	Yaz	18	Aaron	9
	Aaron	85	T. Williams	17	J. DiMaggio **	8
	J. DiMaggio	82	Mantle	16	Rice	6
			Ott	12*	Puckett	6
					Parker	6
					Medwick**	5
3rd Team	F. Robinson	67	R. Jackson	14	Mantle	5
	Ba. Bonds	58	J. DiMaggio	13	R. Jackson	5
	R. Jackson	50	Kaline	13	Kaline	5
	Rice	50	Winfield	12	Clemente	5
	Kaline	49	Clemente	12	Oliva	5
	Stargell	47	F. Robinson	12	Gwynn	5
	Clemente	46	Gwynn	11	Ba. Bonds	5
	Parker	46			Kiner**	4
	Puckett	42			Averill**	4

Designated Hitter

	MVP Points		All Star Years		TSN Teams	
1st Team	Rose	55	Rose	17	Rose	6
	Killebrew	54				
2nd Team	Yount	28	Killebrew	11	Yount	4
					Killebrew	4
					J. Torre	4
3rd Team	E. Howard	23	J. Torre	9	H. McRae	3
	J. Torre	20	E. Howard	9	Baylor	3
			Kuenn	8	Molitor	3
			T. Perez	7	Baines	3
					T. Davis	3
					Luzinski	3

Righthand Pitcher

	MVP Pts.		All Star Years		TSN Teams		C. Y. Pts.	
1st Team	Feller	39	Seaver	12	Feller**	5	Feller	24
2nd Team	D. Dean	36	Marichal	9	Palmer	5	Seaver	22
					Roberts**	4	Palmer	22
							G. Maddux	21
3rd Team	Eckersley	31	Drysdale	8	Seaver	4	Clemens	19
	Walters	28	Feller	8	Marichal	4	Roberts	17
	Roberts	28	Gibson	8	G. Maddux	4	D. Dean	16
			Hunter	8	D. Dean**	3	Walters	15
			Ryan	8	Lemon**	3		
					M. Cooper**	3		

Lefthand Pitcher

	MVP Pts.		All Star Years		TSN Teams		C. Y. Pts.	
1st Team	Hubbell	43	Spahn	14	Carlton	7	Spahn	33
2nd Team	Newhouser	39	Carlton	10	Spahn**	5	Carlton	21
			Hubbell*	9			Koufax	19
3rd Team	Koufax	32	W. Ford	8	Hubbell**	4	Newhouser	16
	Spahn	30	L. Gomez	7	R. Guidry	4	Hubbell	15
			Newhouser	7	W. Ford	4		
			Pierce	7	Koufax	4		
					Newhouser**	3		

Note: MVP points allot 14 points for each MVP award, 9 points for each 2nd place finish, 8 points for each 3rd place finish, etc. Number of years on All Star teams equals the number of years selected for the All Star game (whether or not they played). Number of *TSN* teams equals the number of times they were selected for the *TSN* All Star Team. Cy Young points allot 5 points for each actual or hypothetical award, 4 points for tying for an award, 3 points for a second-place finish, etc.

Table 2

All Star teams for the past 65 years, based on MVP (and Cy Young) elections, number of years on All Star teams and number of years on TSN teams (total points in parentheses).

Position	First Team	Second Team
Catcher	Yogi Berra (13)	Johnny Bench (11)
		Bill Dickey (11)
First Base	Jimmie Foxx (15)	Steve Garvey (5)
		Johnny Mize (5)
Second Base	Rod Carew (13)	Joe Morgan (7)
		Nellie Fox (7)
Third Base	Mike Schmidt (13)	Brooks Robinson (11)
Shortstop	Cal Ripken (13)	Ernie Banks (9)
		Joe Cronin (9)
Outfield	Stan Musial (15)	Hank Aaron (11)
Outfield	Willie Mays (15)	Mickey Mantle (7)
Outfield	Ted Williams (13)	Joe DiMaggio (7)
Designated Hitter	Pete Rose (15)	Harmon Killebrew (11)
RH Pitcher	Bob Feller (16)	Tom Seaver (9)
LH Pitcher	Warren Spahn (14)	Steve Carlton (11)
		Carl Hubbell (10)

Note: Points are assigned as follows: 5 points for each first-team selection, based on: (a) MVP points, (b) number of All Star teams, and (c) number of TSN teams; 3 points for each second-team selection; and 1 point for each third-team selection. For pitchers, additional points (5, 3, or 1) are earned for All Star teams based on Cy Young points. Maximum score is 15 points for a non-pitcher and 20 points for a pitcher.

Table 3

All Star team for the 1980s and 1990s, based on MVP (and Cy Young) elections, number of years on All Star teams and number of years on TSN teams.

Position	Player
Catcher	Gary Carter
First Base	Eddie Murray
Second Base	Ryne Sandberg
Third Base	George Brett
Shortstop	Cal Ripken
Outfield	Kirby Puckett
Outfield	Dave Parker
Outfield	Barry Bonds
Designated Hitter	Robin Yount
RH Pitcher	Greg Maddux
LH Pitcher	Fernando Valenzuela

Note: To be eligible for this modern team, players either had to begin their careers in the 1980s or 1990s, or they had to play at least 12 seasons between 1980 and 1995.

Major Personnel Changes and Team Performance

Do big changes make a big difference?

Daniel Boyle

From the cry of "Break up the Yankees" to the sentiment, "We finished last with you, we can finish last without you," change has been a constant throughout baseball history. From Connie Mack selling off his star Athletics not once but twice, through numerous mediocre or worse teams making wholesale personnel moves in hopes of a real championship chance, to Charlie Finley allowing his A's to disperse in free agency, baseball lore is full of examples of dramatic team changes. Any winning team has to balance the fear of growing old together against the possibility of breaking up a solid nucleus prematurely in making decisions about the year ahead. Any losing team has to evaluate whether a nucleus is really present, or whether it might be better to start all over again.

Which course is best? What happens to a team that decides, or is forced, to make changes in personnel? This paper proposes a definition of a "major personnel change" and then examines what happened to the teams meeting this definition.

What is change?—The first step in this analysis is to settle on a definition of a major change. Since the idea for this project came in the early 1980s, when the Giants changed their entire starting rotation and the Reds their starting outfield over the same winter, I adopted a definition based on position. A team "changed" if any one of the following was completely different:

1. its starting infield;
2. its starting outfield;
3. its top four pitchers;
4. its top three pitchers and its catcher.

Starting infield, outfield, and catcher were determined by the annual team lineups listed in *The Baseball Encyclopedia*. In cases where the choice of a starter at a given position based on at bats differed from the choice based on games played, continuity was assumed. In other words, all players had to be clearly supplanted at their respective positions for a team to meet one of the criteria. Pitchers' rankings were based on innings pitched.

Obviously, this is not the only, or even necessarily the best, definition of change. The Athletics teams cited in the opening paragraph from the World War I, Depression, and free-agent eras all fail to meet any of the criteria, since these teams were generally disassembled over a period of years. In measuring year-to-year changes in teams and their performance, this definition does allow us to isolate clear instances of teams in flux and to analyze the outcomes. By looking at extreme examples, we may gain some insight into how wholesale changes affect performance in the following season.

Before and after records were compared as a measure of the results of team changes. For example, the 1912 New York Yankees finished at .329. In 1913, the Yankees' starting infield was completely different, and

Daniel Boyle lives in San Diego.

they compiled a .377 winning percentage, an improvement of .048. Teams' winning percentages are used throughout the analysis, to normalize for number of games played. However, results are presented in terms of both winning percentage and number of wins in a typical 162-game season, a more readily understandable measure. In the above example, the Yankees' improvement was equivalent to eight more wins in a 162-game season.

What happened, and does it matter?—I examined all teams in the American, National, and Federal Leagues and the American and Union Associations for continuity from year to year from 1876 through 1993. A total of 289 teams met at least one of the criteria for change. The average result of these 289 teams was an improvement of .008 (+1 win), which certainly seems to fall within normal season-to-season fluctuations.

The picture is different if we consider the kinds of teams making major changes. Presumably, a poor team would not be affected in the same way as a good team by, for example, changing its entire infield. If the 289 teams are stratified into winning and losing teams, the effects of major changes are clarified.

Not surprisingly, most of the 289 teams had losing records. It is much more common to make changes when things are not going well on the field. As Table 1 shows, the 217 losing teams produced an average improvement in the following year of .032, or +5 wins. A more dramatic effect is seen in the sixty-six teams with winning records which met at least one criterion. These teams saw their records plummet by an average of -.074 (-12 wins). The remaining six teams with a .500 mark saw an improvement of .028 or +4 wins. Since the .500 teams more closely resemble the losing teams, they are grouped with these teams in subsequent breakdowns by league, by year and by type of change.

Table 1.

Change in Performance Based on Team Record

Category	Number of Teams	Average Change in Percentage	Average Change in # of Wins
All Teams	289	+.008	+1
Winning Teams	66	-.074	-12
Losing/.500 Teams	223	+.032	+5
Losing Teams	217	+.032	+5
.500 Teams	6	+.028	+4

Note that while the difference in performance for winning and losing teams is remarkable, this alone is

not sufficient proof that the performance changes were different from what might have happened if the teams had not made major personnel changes. One could argue for a tendency toward the mean, a likelihood that poor teams will improve and good teams get worse. Bill James hazarded a guess in an early *Statistical Abstract* that in any given year, a team will end up five games closer to .500 than in the preceding year. Tendency toward the mean is a recognized mathematical concept, and must be addressed in an analysis of this type.

What is missing from the simple analysis of winning and losing teams cited above is a control group. In order to gauge the statistical significance of these performance differences, team making personnel changes must be considered an experimental group and compared to a control group of teams not making such changes.

I drew up the control group by going through each of the 289 teams in the experimental group and selecting the team in its league with the most similar record. For various reasons, a match could not be made for all 289 teams; for example, if an eighth place and a seventh place team both made major personnel changes, the sixth place team was selected for the control group as a match for the seventh place team, and no match was made for the last place team. The result was a control group consisting of 237 teams. Of the fifty-seven teams in the winning team control group, the average change in team record for the next season was +.003, or +1 win, while the average change for the 180 teams in the losing control group was +.005 or +1 win.

I then compared the year-to-year changes in record for the experimental or changed teams to the changes for the control or unchanged teams, using a statistical method known as the two-tailed test of means. The results of this test are shown in Table 2. The misfortunes of winning teams making major changes were confirmed by the statistical test. The decline in winning team's performance is significant at the p=.01 level (t statistic > 2.58), meaning that the probability that this decline is due to chance alone is less than one percent. On the other hand, the good fortune of losing teams making major changes is not statistically significant even at the p=.1 level, meaning that there is a greater than ten percent probability that the improvement is due to chance. In fact, the probability is approximately 26 percent. Thus, the five-game improvement in a changed nonwinning team's record is not statistically different from the improvement seen by teams in the control group.

Different perspectives on change—There are several additional ways to break down the results of team changes for the teams in our sample. As finer categories are drawn, however, the number of teams in each category diminishes, affecting the reliability of statistical analysis. The breakdowns in this section are intended for qualitative purposes, without regard for statistical significance.

Table 2.

Test for Significance of Team Performance Changes

Category	Winning Teams	Losing/.500 Teams
Actual Number	66	223
Control Number	57	180
Actual Mean Change	-.074	+.032
Control Mean Change	+.003	+.005
t statistic	-4.68	+1.13
Significant at p=.01 level?	YES	NO

Table 3 shows the average effects by position. The most common change under our definition is the outfield, since only three players are involved as opposed to four in the other categories. Changing the top four pitchers is the least common change, and appears to have the greatest effect for both winning (-.138 or -22 wins) and losing (+.052 or +8 wins) teams. However, a makeover in the pitching staff rarely happens alone. Often the catcher changes as well, and frequently a drastic change in pitching is part of a major team overhaul.

Table 3.

Performance Change by Position

Position	# Tms	W	Pct. Change	Change in Wins	L/.500 Tms	Pct. Change	Change in Wins
Four Pitchers	44	10	-.138	-22	34	+.052	+8
Infield	100	24	-.119	-19	76	+.046	+7
Battery	98	19	-.099	-16	79	+.026	+4
Outfield	142	28	-.091	-15	114	+.034	+5

Table 4 shows the average effects by position when only one position group is changed. This isolates the impact by position group, and changes the rankings shown in Table 3. Note that in only ten of the forty-four instances was changing the top four pitchers the only change. In the four cases involving winning teams, the effect was minor (-.012 or -2 wins). In the six cases involving losing teams, the average record declined the following year, the only instance in all the breakdowns when this occurred. According to Table 4, a total change in the infield alone has the

greatest effect for all teams, decreasing winners by -.074 or -12 wins and improving losers by +.046 or +7 wins. The infield is followed in effect by the outfield, battery and pitchers for winning and losing teams. Interestingly, the isolated infield effects are not very much different from the average changes for winning and losing teams cited in Table 1.

Table 4.

Performance Change by Isolated Position

Position	# Tms	W	Pct. Change	Change in Wins	L/.500 Tms	Pct. Change	Change in Wins
Infield Alone	59	19	-.074	-12	40	+.050	+8
Outfield Alone	96	21	-.050	-8	75	+.028	+5
Battery Alone	51	13	-.048	-8	38	+.009	+1
4 Pitchers Alone	10	4	-.012	-2	6	-.006	-1

Multiple changes have a more pronounced impact on subsequent team performance, as shown in Table 5. The increase or decrease in winning percentage is greater as changes are made in more areas. This is in accord with common sense. Note the six teams with changes in all areas: the three losing teams improved by +.116 or +19 wins, while the three winning teams dropped an amazing -.345 or -56 wins.

Table 5.

Performance Change by Number of Position Groups Changed

Position	# Tms	W	Pct. Change	Change in Wins	L/.500 Tms	Pct. Change	Change in Wins
One Group	216	57	-.055	-9	159	+.028	+4
Two Groups	57	6	-.118	-19	51	+.038	+6
Three Groups	0	0	—	—	0	—	—
All Groups	6	3	-.345	-56	3	+.116	+19

In line with this finding, there is also a bigger effect on performance for teams that release or lose all of the players involved in a position group when compared with teams that retain one or more of these players. This is the difference between a player merely losing his job and actually being traded or released. Even on the bench, a player provides a degree of continuity for the team, which doesn't exist if he is traded or otherwise leaves the team. Table 6 indicates that about two thirds of our teams retain the services of at least one player in the affected position group (noted as a partial change). The one third that make a complete change show a greater improvement or decline. Within this group of teams, those that make a complete change during the off-season show the greatest change in team record.

Table 7 shows the distribution of team changes by

league. As expected the older National League has accounted for the great number of teams meeting the criteria with 154, although since 1901, the American League has had 119 teams with significant changes and the National only 107. The magnitude of change has also been greater in the National League than in the American for both winning and losing teams. (The Federal League, included here for the sake of completeness, showed an average improvement of +23 wins for its two losing teams making massive changes.)

Table 6.

Nature of Change	# Tms	W	Pct. Change	Change in Wins	L/ .500 Tms	Pct. Change	Change in Wins
Total Change	85	20	-.099	-16	65	+.054	+9
-by season end	20	3	-.037	-6	17	+.039	+6
-at season start	65	17	-.109	-18	48	+.060	+10
Partial Change	204	46	-.063	-10	158	+.023	+4

Table 7.

Performance Change by League

League	# Tms	W	Pct. Change	Change in Wins	L/ .500 Tms	Pct. Change	Change in Wins
NL	154	40	-.088	-14	114	+.036	+6
AL	119	23	-.051	-8	96	+.019	+3
AA	14	3	-.052	-8	11	+.090	+15
FL	2	0	—	—	2	+.145	+23

The differences among leagues is explained to some extent by the eras during which they were in existence. Table 8 is a breakdown of changing teams and average change in team fortune by decade. In this analysis, a decade begins in the year ending in 0 and ends in the year ending in 9, and teams are grouped into decades based on the year prior to the changes. For example, a team that made changes between the 1949 and 1950 seasons would be included in the 1940s.

Table 8.

Performance Change by Decade

Decade	# Tms	W	Pct. Change	Change in Wins	L/ .500 Tms	Pct. Change	Change in Wins
1870s (76-79)	7	2	-.177	-29	5	+.171	+28
1880s	29	7	-.036	-6	22	+.037	+6
1890s	25	7	-.161	-26	18	+.076	+12
1900s	25	4	-.070	-11	21	+.041	+7
1910s	16	4	-.009	-1	12	+.071	+12
1920s	19	2	-.106	-17	17	+.021	+3
1930s	20	5	-.031	-5	15	+.011	+2
1940s	39	15	-.053	-9	24	+.034	+5
1950s	25	5	-.062	-10	20	+.015	+2
1960s	13	0	—	—	13	+.026	+4
1970s	29	5	-.119	-19	24	+.000	+0
1980s	30	6	-.050	-8	24	+.012	+2
1990s (90-93)	12	4	-.106	-17	8	+.025	+4

The relatively unsettled nature of baseball in the nineteenth century accounts for both the large number of changing teams prior to 1900 and the greater magnitude of resulting changes in team records. During the 1940s, a total of 39 teams made changes, many related to World War II. In 1946, for example, seven of the eight American League teams met the criteria for change in at least one position group. The advent of free agency has clearly had an impact, with the 1980s accounting for 30 teams and the 1970s for 29 teams (the 1880s also had 29 teams). This trend has continued in the four years of the 1990s, with 12 teams through 1993. On the other hand, the most stable decade was the 1960s, with only 13 teams (and no winning teams!) making changes.

In terms of the effects on team records, the 1870s were worst for winning teams (-.177 or -29 games), followed by the 1890s (-.161 or -26 games), and the 1970s (-.119 or -19 games). For losing teams, the 1870s also saw the greatest magnitude in change, +.171 or +28 games, followed by the 1890s (+.076 or +12 games) and the 1910s (+.071 or +12 games).

Finally, Tables 9 and 10 present the ten largest improvements and declines in team records for teams matching our criteria of change. Most of these top ten teams on both lists are from the nineteenth century, with the Players' League of 1890 having a big effect. For example, Pittsburgh in the National League is on both lists, with the third largest decline in 1890, and the sixth biggest increase in 1891. Notable twentieth century exceptions include the wartime New York Giants of 1942-43, the post-Black Sox-scandal Chicago White Sox, and the 1981-82 Cincinnati Reds, one of the teams that inspired this study. The biggest improvement since 1903 was the 1946 Boston Red Sox, which changed its infield and outfield as a result of the return of players from World War II and bettered its 1945 record by +.214, climbing from seventh to first.

Summary—The statistical results reveal that there actually is some truth in the saying, "We finished last with you, we can finish last without you." Losing teams, on average, improve the following year in accordance with the tendency toward the mean. Wholesale changes do not appear to boost a team's chances of adding to that improvement. Wholesale changes on a winning club, however, are a statistically significant invitation to disaster.

Table 9.

Ten Biggest Improvements Related to Major Changes in Personnel

Team		Years	Position Group[1] Changes	Type of Change[2]	Pct. Change	Standing Change
Cincinnati	NL	1877-78	I	P	+.354	6th-2nd
Detroit	NL	1885-86	I	P	+.327	6th-2nd
Brooklyn	NL	1898-99	I	C	+.310	10th-1st
New York	NL	1902-03	O	P	+.251	8th-2nd
Buffalo	NL	1880-81	O	C	+.249	7th-3rd
Pittsburgh	NL	1890-91	I,O,B,P	Mixed	+.238	8th-8th
Cleveland	NL	1879-80	O	C	+.231	6th-3rd
Pittsburgh	AA	1884-85	I,O	Mixed	+.227	11th-3rd
Baltimore	AA	1890-91	I,B,P	C	+.225	6th-4th
Milwaukee	AL	1901-02	O,B,P	Mixed	+.224	8th-2nd
St.Louis						

Position Groups: I=Infield, O=outfield, B=battery, P=four pitchers

Type of Change: C=complete, P=partial, Mixed=some position groups complete, others partial

Table 10.

Ten Biggest Declines Related to Major Changes in Personnel

Team		Years	Position Group[1] Changes	Type of Change[2]	Pct. Change	Standing Change
Cleveland	NL	1898-99	I,O,B,P	C	-.414	5th-12th
Bklyn/Balt[3]	AA	1889-90	I,O,B,P	C	-.365	1st-6/9
Pittsburgh	NL	1889-90	I,B	P	-.293	5th-8th
Cincinnati	NL	1879-80	I,O	P	-.275	5th-8th
St.Louis	AA/NL[4]	1891-92	I,O,B,P	C	-.250	2d-9/11[5]
Cincinnati	NL	1981-82	O	C	-.234	2/2[5]-6th
Chicago	AL	1920-21	I,O	P	-.220	2nd-7th
Baltimore	AA/NL[4]	1891-92	I	P	-.220	4th-12/10[5]
New York	NL	1942-43	B,P	P	-.200	3rd-8th
New York	NL	1889-90	I	C	-.178	1st-6th

1: Position Groups: I=infield, O=outfield, B=battery, P=four pitchers

2: Type of Change: C=complete, P=partial, Mixed=some position groups complete, others partial

3: AA Brooklyn and Baltimore records combined to determine percentage change in 1890, due to unique ownership situation for the two clubs.

4: St.Louis and Baltimore franchises absorbed from defunct American Association to expanded National League in 1892.

5: 1892 and 1981 were split seasons.

My Mother Called Me...

1. Mookie Blaylock   A. John
2. Mookie Wilson   B. James
3. Mickey Rivers   C. Daron
4. Catfish Hunter   D. George
5. Rube Walberg   E. William

1-C, 2-E, 3-A, 4-B, 5-D

Trivia High School

1. Marty Keough   A. Wilson (Long Beach, CA)
2. Ron Oester   B. Pomona (CA)
3. Jeff Burroughs   C. Somerset (MA)
4. Greg Gagne   D. Oakwood (IL)
5. Dusty Baker   E. Walnut Hills (Cincinnati, OH)

1-B, 2-E, 3-A, 4-C, 5-D

Trivia University

1. Kirby Puckett   A. Brigham Young
2. Cory Snyder   B. USC
3. John Olerud   C. Fresno State
4. Bret Boone   D. Bradley
5. Frenchy Bordagaray   E. Washington State

1-D, 2-A, 3-E, 4-B, 5-C

—Bob Brigham

A Reexamination of Baseball's Greatest Single-Season Records

Some surprising names

George Braungart Yancey

Before the strike that ended the season of 1994, Matt Williams and Ken Griffey, Jr. were making a run on Roger Maris' record of 61 home runs in a single season. What was the greatest home-run season in the history of major-league baseball? Was it the year Roger Maris hit 61 home runs? For many years a theoretical asterisk was placed next to Maris' record because he had 162 games in which to hit 61 home runs, while the previous owner of the record, Babe Ruth, had only 154 games to hit his 60. If people are going to qualify the records—and why shouldn't they—then they should look at more than just the length of the season. In 1927, when Babe Ruth hit 60 homers, the average player hit about six home runs. During 1961, Maris' record breaking season, the average player hit about fourteen home runs. Taken this way, Ruth's 60 homers appear much more impressive than Maris' 61.

By comparing a player's statistics to the statistics of his contemporaries, it is possible to get a much better idea of the extent to which a player dominated a statistical category during a given year. I would argue that the greatest home-run season in the history of major league baseball was 1920, the year Ruth hit 54 and nearly doubled the previous record of 29, which he had set himself the year before. Millions of fans showed up in 1920 to watch him completely rewrite

the record book. In 1920 the second highest home run total to Ruth's 54 in either league was George Sisler's 19. I believe that the second-best home-run season was 1919, the year Ruth broke the home run record of 27. That may not seem like an extraordinary number of homers by today's standards, but the second-best home run hitter that year was the National League home run champion, Gavvy Cravath, who won his sixth National League home run title that year with 12.

The support for my conclusions is in Table 1. To create Table 1, I converted all of the players' home run totals into Z-scores. To get a Z-score for home runs, I simply subtracted the average number of home runs for a given year (e.g., 6.01 in 1927) from the number of a player's home runs (e.g., 60 for Ruth in 1927). I then divided the remainder (e.g., 60 - 6.01 = 53.99) by the standard deviation for home runs for a given year (e.g., 8.49 in 1927). Ruth's Z-score for 1927 was 6.36.

When you examine all of the Z-scores for a given year, they will average zero and they will have a standard deviation of one. Thus, by converting every player's statistics to Z-scores for each year, it is possible to get an idea of how far each player performed above or below his peers for a particular year. The players have been ranked in the three tables in this article first by Z-scores and then by the conventional method of going strictly by the numbers.

George Braungart Yancey was a psychology professor before becoming a consultant for D. Hilton Associates in The Woodlands, Texas. His interest in baseball statistics began during his boyhood in Atlanta where he watched Henry Aaron overtake Babe Ruth as the all-time leader in major league home runs.

Table 1 - Home Runs

Ranked by Z-scores				Ranked by Number		
1. Ruth	8.30 (54) 1920			1. Maris	61	1961
2. Ruth	7.48 (29) 1919			2. Ruth	60	1927
3. Ruth	7.20 (59) 1921			3. Ruth	59	1921
4. Williamson	6.80 (27) 1884			4. Greenberg	58	1938
5. Ruth	6.77 (47) 1926			5. Foxx	58	1932
6. Cravath	6.67 (24) 1915			6. Wilson	56	1930
7. Freeman	6.63 (25) 1899			7. Ruth	54	1920
8. Ruth	6.36 (60) 1927			8. Ruth	54	1928
9. Pfeffer	6.25 (25) 1884			9. Kiner	54	1949
10. Ruth	6.00 (54) 1928			10. Mantle	54	1961

In examining the ten greatest batting averages in a single season, which range from .438 to .416, six of the ten occurred in the previous century and all occurred more than sixty-five years ago. Because batting averages are lower today, modern players seem to come off badly in comparisons. But according to an examination of Z-scores for batting averages in Table 2, the greatest single season for hitting for average was not by Hugh Duffy in 1894, but was by George Brett in 1980, when he batted .390. Many fans watched Brett's performance in amazement that year as he flirted with becoming the first player since Ted Williams in 1941 to bat over .400 for a season. However, his failure to reach the magic .400 level seemed to tarnish his accomplishment. But in terms of hitting for average, Brett's feat was every bit as great as Williams'. A Z-score analysis reveals that those were the two greatest batting average seasons of all time.

Table 2 -Batting Average

Ranked by Z-score				Ranked by Average		
1. Brett	3.95 (.390) 1980			1. Duffy	.438	1894
2. Williams	3.93 (.406) 1941			2. O'Neill	.435	1887
3. Carew	3.82 (.388) 1977			3. Keeler	.432	1897
4. Speaker	3.79 (.386) 1916			4. Barnes	.429	1876
5. Boggs	3.77 (.368) 1985			5. Hornsby	.424	1924
6. Hornsby	3.73 (.424) 1924			6. Burkett	.423	1895
7. O'Neill	3.72 (.435) 1887			7. Lajoie	.422	1901
8. Williams	3.68 (.388) 1957			8. Cobb	.420	1911
9. Cobb	3.60 (.410) 1912			9. Sisler	.420	1922
10. Cobb	3.50 (.383) 1917			10. Turner	.416	1894

Two more current-day players are among the Z-score list for batting average, Rod Carew and Wade Boggs. In 1977 Carew's average of .388 was 50 points higher than the next best player, NL champ Dave Parker, at .338. This remains the greatest margin of victory in the history of major league baseball. In spite of playing in modern times, Wade Boggs has one of the highest career batting averages. What kind of numbers would he have put up if he had played a century ago? In 1985 he had one of the greatest seasons of all time. Among them, Rod Carew, Wade Boggs, and George Brett have won fifteen American League batting championships—seven, five, and three, respectively. It is not surprising that in their greatest years they were able to dominate their contemporaries as Cobb, Hornsby, and Williams did on their way to winning twelve, seven, and six league batting championships, respectively. I believe that the Z-score approach to records allows us to appreciate the greatest years of the greatest players better than going strictly by the numbers. I wonder what Tony Gwynn's Z-score for batting average would have been had he been allowed to finish the 1994 season? I believe he was on a record-setting pace.

An examination of the current records for home runs and runs batted in reveals that seven of the ten greatest home run seasons occurred in the 1920s and 1930s and that all ten of the greatest RBI seasons occurred during those same two decades. In fact, three of the top RBI totals occurred during a single season, 1930, including Hack Wilson's all-time record of 190. When certain statistics are inflated during a short historical period, like batting averages in the late 1800s or RBIs in the 1930s, players from other eras may be subjected to unfair comparisons.

Players who played before the Babe Ruth era are especially hurt by home run and RBI statistics. Although Ruth is clearly the greatest home run hitter, there have been some players who have had Ruthian years. Ned Williamson's 27 homers in 1884 set a major league record that would last thirty-five years. But he was hitting balls over a fence a mere 180 feet down the left field line.

Two players who did not benefit from a short fence and who produced legitimate Ruthian years were John "Buck" Freeman, who hit 25 homers in 1899, and Gavvy Cravath who hit 24 in 1915. Freeman was a precursor to Ruth, a strong pitcher who was converted to an everyday player because of his hitting power. Cravath, as mentioned earlier, was one of the great power hitters of the early twentieth century, winning six National League home-run titles.

In the Z-score rankings for RBIs in Table 3, four pre-1920 players emerge. At the top of the list is Hall-of-Famer Adrian "Cap" Anson with his 147 RBIs for 1886. No one was close to him that year. The next best performer had only 95. Cap Anson was the top RBI producer of the nineteenthth century with 1,715.

He still ranks fourteenth for career RBIs, and in 1886 he had arguably the best RBI season in the history of the game.

Ty Cobb is also in the top five with an RBI total of only 116 for the year 1907, but his total was far superior to the average player who drove in only 43 runs that year. In fact, not only did he lead both leagues in RBIs that year, but he also led the American League in slugging percentage and total bases, while tying for second in home runs and finishing third in triples. (He also led the league in batting average and stolen bases.) Today we think of him primarily as a singles hitter, comparing him to the man who broke his record for the most career hits, Pete Rose, but he was always a great run producer.

Another great nineteenth century RBI season was Sam Thompson's 166 in 1887. That year Thompson averaged 1.31 RBIs for each game in which he played, the third best per-game average in the history of major league baseball. He also holds the records for the first and second best per-game average in a single season, 1.42 in 1894 and 1.39 in 1895. The fourth best per-game average was by Hack Wilson with 1.23 during his fabled 1930 season. Thompson had the third highest RBI total of any nineteenth century player.

Although Cy Seymour was not a Hall of Famer like Anson, Cobb, and Thompson, the 121 runs he drove in in 1905 was one of the game's ten best RBI seasons. Like Ruth and Freeman, Seymour was a pitcher at the beginning of his career.

This reexamination of single-season records provides some recognition of the prodigious accomplishments of the pre-Ruth era's top power hitters. Early players who hit for average have already found a place for themselves in the record books.

It also allows us to realize that in watching Rod Carew, Wade Boggs, and George Brett during the 1970s and the 1980s we were seeing three of the greatest single season performances in the 118-year history of major league baseball.

Finally, Z-score analysis gives us an idea of how remarkable Babe Ruth's home run feats really were. For a player today to achieve a Z-score of 8.3, as Ruth did in 1920, he would need to hit over 90 home runs. Imagine a young player who smashes Maris' record by hitting 70 home runs one year and then hits 90 to 100 the next year and continues to put up similar statistics year after year. He would become a mythical figure. That was the impact Ruth had on the game of baseball with his performances beginning in 1919.

Notes:

1. This article is limited to the major leagues discussed in Macmillan's *Baseball Encyclopedia*.

2. To compute the average number of home runs (and batting average and runs batted in) for each year, I used the eight players on each team with the most at bats for that year. I could not have completed this task without the help of Kristine Marshall, who tirelessly entered thousands of statistics from the *Baseball Encyclopedia* into the computer.

3. A standard deviation is a measure of how variable a group of scores is. If everyone hit 10 home runs one year, the standard deviation would be zero because there would be no variability, no deviation from the average of 10. The greater the differences between the scores, the greater the standard deviation will be.

References:

The Baseball Encyclopedia: The Complete and Official Record of Major League Baseball - Eighth Edition. New York: Macmillan Publishing Co. 1990.

The Ballplayers: Baseball's Ultimate Biographical Reference. Editor, Mike Shatzkin. New York: Arbor House, William Morrow 1990.

Basic Statistics: Tales of Distributions - Fifth edition. Chris Spatz. Pacific Grove, CA: Brooks/Cole Publishing Company 1993.

Table 3 - Runs Batted In

Ranked by Z-score				Ranked by Number		
1. Anson	4.14	(147)	1886	1. Wilson	190	1930
2. Ruth	4.00	(171)	1921	2. Gehrig	184	1931
3. Greenberg	3.95	(170)	1935	3. Greenberg	183	1937
4. Cobb	3.93	(116)	1907	4. Gehrig	175	1927
5. Thompson	3.91	(166)	1887	5. Foxx	175	1938
6. Gehrig	3.91	(184)	1931	6. Gehrig	174	1930
7. Anson	3.82	(114)	1885	7. Ruth	171	1921
8. Seymour	3.81	(121)	1905	8. Greenberg	170	1935
9. Gehrig	3.79	(175)	1927	9. Klein	170	1930
10. Greenberg	3.73	(183)	1937	10. Foxx	169	1932

Vada Pinson

Overshadowed and underrated

Ralph C. Moses

Only two days after what would have been Mickey Mantle's sixty-fourth birthday, the baseball world lost yet another great center fielder. Vada Pinson, who, like the Mick, could hit, hit with power, run, throw, and field with the best of his generation, died at age fifty-seven in California of a stroke.

Vada Pinson was Richie Ashburn with power, Billy Williams with speed. The 5'11", 170-pound Pinson banged out 2,757 hits, surpassing 200 hits in a single season four times. He accumulated 485 doubles, 127 triples, and 256 home runs, good enough to rank in the top 100 in all three extra-base hit categories. Pinson's speed and baserunning skill helped him to record 305 stolen bases, thus joining only Willie Mays, Andre Dawson, Bobby Bonds, Barry Bonds, Joe Morgan, and Ryne Sandberg as players who hit at least 250 home runs while stealing at least 300 bases in their careers.

Vada Edward Pinson, Jr. was born in Memphis, Tennessee on August 11, 1938. His family eventually moved to Oakland, California and he became a star outfielder for McClymonds High School, which also produced his future major league teammates Frank Robinson and Curt Flood, as well as basketball immortal Bill Russell. Legendary coach George Powles was influential in Pinson's career, helping the youngster to understand and realize his potential in becoming a professional ballplayer.

Ralph C. Moses *lives in Chicago, where he is a social worker, a teacher, and a long-suffering Cubs fan.*

Vada Pinson

Transcendental Graphics

Pinson was signed by the Cincinnati Reds before his eighteenth birthday, and he required only two minor league seasons to reach the majors. (At Wausau in the Northern League in 1956 he hit .278 in 75 games, while at Visalia in the California League in 1957 he hit .367 with 20 home runs, 97 runs batted in, and 209 hits in 135 games.) Pinson debuted with the Reds at Crosley Field on Opening Day, 1958, and recorded a single in five at bats. In his second game two day later, Pinson hit his first home run, a bases-loaded clout that lifted the Reds to a 4-1 victory over Pittsburgh at Forbes Field.

As with Mantle, Vada Pinson's initial major league season was not filled with success, and the Reds sent the slumping youngster to Seattle of the Pacific Coast League in May, where he batted a robust .343 in 124 games, thus earning a September call-up and a permanent job in center field.

In 1959, Pinson achieved a memorable first full season, batting .316, with 20 home runs, 84 runs batted in, 21 stolen bases, 205 base hits, and league-leading totals in runs scored (131), doubles (47), and outfield putouts (423). He played in the All Star Game and he earned eleven MVP votes. He did not qualify for the Rookie of the Year award, because his 96 at bats in 1958 were just beyond the cutoff of 90.

Pinson's first five full seasons in Cincinnati saw him amass 985 base hits, a total that surpassed the first five-full-year totals of Stan Musial (975), Willie Mays (954), Hank Aaron (914), and Frank Robinson (818). In those first five full years (1959 to 1963), Pinson averaged 197 hits, 108 runs scored, 37 doubles, 10 triples, 20 home runs, 88 RBIs, 26 stolen bases, and a .310 batting average.

Pinson and Frank Robinson formed a devastating lefty-righty duo that terrorized National League pitching staffs. From 1958 until 1965, Robinson (257) and Pinson (147) hit a combined 404 home runs for the Reds. Both stars reached peaks in 1961, with Robinson batting .323 with 37 home runs and 124 RBIs, while Pinson hit .343 with 16 home runs, 87 RBIs, and a league-leading 208 hits, propelling the Reds, managed by Fred Hutchinson, to their first NL pennant since 1940. Robinson won the league's MVP award, while Pinson finished third in the balloting.

In his decade as the Reds' centerfielder (1959 to 1968), Pinson hit .297 and averaged over 185 base hits, 18 home runs, 80 runs batted in, and nearly 22 stolen bases per season. Following his sensational 1961 season, Pinson's batting average dropped to .292 in 1962 as his power production increased to 23 home runs and 100 runs batted in. Then in 1963, Pinson achieved perhaps his greatest all-around season when he led the NL in hits with 204 and triples with 14, slamming 22 home runs and driving in a career-high 106 runs, while batting .313 and stealing 27 bases. After a subpar 1964 (.266, 23 hrs, 84 RBIs), he rebounded with an outstanding 1965: .305, 22 hrs, 94 RBIs, and 204 hits.

As a defensive center fielder, Pinson won one Gold Glove (1961), led NL outfielders in putouts three consecutive years (1959 to 1961), and fielding average twice (1965 and 1969). In his career he fielded .981 with an assist total of 172 and a range factor of 2.19. Seeing Pinson climb the outfield "terrace" at old Crosley Field to haul in a long drive was truly a sight to behold.

After solid seasons in 1966 and 1967 (.288 both years), Pinson's numbers began to decline in 1968 (5 home runs, 48 RBIs, .271), and the Reds traded him to the NL champion St. Louis Cardinals in exchange for Bobby Tolan and Wayne Granger. With the retirement of Roger Maris, Pinson joined ex-high school teammate Curt Flood and future Hall of Famer Lou Brock in what appeared to be a dream outfield for the Cardinals in 1969. However, Pinson's decline continued (10 hrs, 70 RBIs, .255) and after the season he was traded again, this time to Cleveland in exchange for Jose Cardenal.

Pinson spent his final six seasons in the American League with Cleveland (1970-71), California (1972-73), and Kansas City (1974-75). Although his best years were behind him, Pinson averaged 10 home runs, 48 runs batted in, a batting average of .266 and 13 stolen bases per season in the AL. Pinson's playing career came to an end in 1976 when the Milwaukee Brewers released him in spring training.

Pinson became an outstanding coach and hitting instructor for Seattle, the Chicago White Sox, Detroit, and Florida from 1977 until 1994. His death came only one year after his retirement from the coaching ranks.

Pinson ranks in the top 100 lifetime in the following categories: games played (2,469), at bats (9,,645), runs (1,366), hits (2,757), doubles (485), triples (127), and home runs (256). He also had 1,170 runs batted in, a .286 lifetime batting average, a .442 slugging average, and a .330 on-base percentage.

He ranks in the top ten in the following 1960s categories: games (1,516), at bats (6,086), runs (885), hits (1,776), doubles (310), triples (93), and stolen bases (202). For the decade, he hit .292 with 175 home runs, 792 runs batted in, and a .460 slugging average. A durable player, Pinson played in 508 consecutive games between 1958 and 1962. He hit eight career grand slam home runs, and both his 1,000th and 2,000th lifetime hits were home runs.

An outstanding all-around big league ballplayer over a long career, Pinson was always underrated and overshadowed.

Triple Milestone Pitchers

Are they extinct?

Bill Gilbert

Just as the top hitters strive for the triple milestones of 30 home runs, 100 runs batted in and a batting average of .300, the top starting pitchers strive for 20 wins, 200 strikeouts and an earned run average below 3.00. These milestones define a dominant power pitcher.

Hitters have achieved triple milestones a total of 220 times by ninety-five different players beginning in 1920. Triple milestones for pitchers have been more rare: a total of 182 times, by 102 different pitchers, beginning in 1879. Triple milestone seasons were fairly common in the nineteenth century when the pitching distance was 50 feet and the top starters typically logged over 500 innings. In the twentieth century, triple milestones have been achieved only 108 times by 58 different pitchers. Since 1920 when hitters began achieving triple milestones, there have been only 68 triple milestone seasons by 39 different pitchers.

The first pitchers to achieve triple milestones were Monte Ward and Will White in 1879. The first twentieth century pitchers to accomplish this feat were Bill Donovan, Noodles Hahn, and Christy Mathewson in 1901. The pitchers who did it the most are Walter Johnson (7), Juan Marichal (6), Tim Keefe (5), and Christy Mathewson (5). Johnson did it seven years in succession (1910-1916). The youngest to do

it was Amos Rusie (1890) at 19, two months younger than Ward (1879). Three twentieth century pitchers did it at age 20, Dwight Gooden (1985), Bob Feller (1939) and Christy Mathewson (1901). Gooden was the youngest by two weeks. The oldest to do it was Dazzy Vance (1928) who, at 37, was one month older than Cy Young (1904). This was the only time Young ever achieved triple milestones.

Pitching Cycles—Pitching has run through three well defined cycles over the last 115 years. The first was from 1879 through 1892, when the pitching distance was only 50 feet and ERAs may not be totally accurate. During this fourteen year period, triple milestones were reached 74 times by 44 different pitchers. In all but one of these instances, the pitcher worked at least 380 innings, a level that hasn't been reached since Pete Alexander worked 388 in 1917. The most prominent were Tim Keefe (5) and John Clarkson (4), but the list also includes names like Dupee Shaw, Lady Baldwin, Toad Ramsey, Jersey Bakely, Icebox Chamberlain, and Egyptian Healy.

When the pitching distance was increased from 50 feet to 60 feet, six inches in 1893, there were no triple milestone pitchers for eight years. The next cycle began in 1901. From 1901 through 1917, triple milestones were reached 40 times by 19 different pitchers. This was an era of some of the all-time greats; Johnson (7), Mathewson (5), Pete Alexander (4) and Ed Walsh (4).

The next period, from 1918 through 1938, was a

Bill Gilbert is retired after a 35-year career with Exxon. A lifelong baseball fan, he spent fourteen years in Little League as a coach and administrator. Living thirty miles from the Astrodome, he attends about twenty games a year and spends part of his time writing for various baseball publications.

heyday for hitters. In this twenty-one-year period, there were only three triple milestone seasons for pitchers, two by Dazzy Vance and one by Lefty Grove. During these same twenty-one years, hitters achieved triple milestones 72 times! In the eight year period from 1939 through 1946, which included the war years, Bob Feller (3) and Hal Newhouser (2) accounted for all five of the triple milestone seasons.

In the next eight years, from 1947 through 1954, no major league pitchers recorded 200 strikeouts in a season. Herb Score and Bob Turley broke that string in 1955 and Score followed with a triple milestone season in 1956. Sam Jones reached triple milestones in 1959 and Don Drysdale did it in 1962, before the third cycle of dominant pitchers began in 1963. In the thirteen years from 1963 through 1975, triple milestones were achieved a total of 46 times by 25 different pitchers. Six Hall of Famers dominated this era, Juan Marichal (6), Ferguson Jenkins (4), Tom Seaver (4), Sandy Koufax (3), Bob Gibson (3) and Gaylord Perry (3).

Changes made in the late 1960s to put more offense in the game coupled with the trend toward five-man rotations have threatened the triple milestone pitcher with extinction. In the fifteen years from 1976 through 1990, pitchers achieved only eleven triple milestone seasons. Roger Clemens did it three times and eight other pitchers did it once.

During 1991-1995, no pitchers reached triple milestones and only seven pitchers recorded 260 or more innings in a season. Of the 182 triple milestone seasons achieved by pitchers, there have been only twelve occasions when a pitcher did it with fewer than 260 innings pitched.

Triple Milestones And the Hall of Fame—Thirteen twentieth century pitchers have recorded three or more triple milestone seasons. All are in the Hall of Fame except the still-active Clemens. Ten twentieth century pitchers have two triple milestone seasons. Five are in the Hall of Fame: Eddie Plank, Vance, Newhouser, Drysdale and Steve Carlton. The other five are Joe Wood, Jim Maloney, Dean Chance, Mickey Lolich and Nolan Ryan.

Twenty-six Hall of Fame pitchers never achieved a triple milestone season. Whitey Ford and Jim Bunning are the only ones who had as many as 200 strikeouts in a season. Ford did it in 1961), when his ERA was 3.21, well above his career mark of 2.74. Bunning had three straight seasons (1964-1966) with ERAs under 3.00 and more than 200 strikeouts, but he fell one win short of 20 each year. Dizzy Dean and Warren Spahn each led the National League in strikeouts four straight years, but neither ever recorded 200 strikeouts in a season. Other prominent Hall of Fame pitchers who never struck out 200 batters in a season include Lefty Gomez, Carl Hubbell, Catfish Hunter, Bob Lemon, Jim Palmer and Robin Roberts. Ted Lyons' top strikeout year was 74. Current Hall of Fame candidates Phil Niekro and Don Sutton never had a triple milestone season.

Triple Milestone Trivia—The last pitchers to reach triple milestones were Clemens and Ramon Martinez in 1990. Martinez is the only twentieth century triple milestone pitcher who has reached each of the milestones only once in his career.

In 1994, Greg Maddux and Bret Saberhagen were on target for their first triple milestone seasons when the season was interrupted by the strike. In 1995, both Maddux and Randy Johnson would have had a shot if the season had been 162 games instead of 144.

Babe Ruth achieved triple milestones as a hitter a record twelve times. He came reasonably close as a pitcher in 1916 with 23 wins, an ERA of 1.75 and 170 strikeouts. A remarkable minor league achievement was recorded by Roy Sanner playing for Houma in the Evangeline League in 1948 when he reached triple milestones in both hitting (.386, 34, 126) and pitching (21-2, 251, 2.58).

Triple Milestones in the Future—The next cycle of dominant pitchers frequently reaching triple milestones is nowhere in sight. A number of things would have to happen for it to occur.
- A return to full 162-game seasons.
- Calling the strike zone as it is defined in the rule book.
- At least a partial return to four man rotations.
- Pitchers working on their craft as hard as hitters work on theirs.

Pitchers Triple Milestones (20 Wins, 200 Strikeouts, ERA less than 3.00)

First—Monte Ward and Will White (1879).

First (20th Century)—Bill Donovan, Noodles Hahn and C. Mathewson (1901).

Most times—W. Johnson (7), J. Marichal (6), T. Keefe (5), C. Mathewson (5).

Consecutive seasons—Johnson 7 (1910-1916).

Youngest—Amos Rusie (1890) and Monte Ward (1879)–19.

Youngest (20th Century)—D. Gooden (1985), B. Feller (1939), and C. Mathewson (1901)–20.

Oldest—Dazzy Vance (1928) and Cy Young (1904)–37.

Pitchers Triple Milestone Cycles

	No.	Avg. IP	Avg. K/9	
1879-92	74	518	4.9	T. Keefe (5), J. Clarkson (4)
1893-1900	0			(Change from 50 ft to 60 ft, 6 in.)
1901-17	40	360	5.9	W. Johnson (7), C. Mathewson (5), P. Alexander (4), E. Walsh (4)
1918-38	3	293	6.9	D. Vance (2), L. Grove (1)
1939-46	5	319	7.6	B. Feller (3), H. Newhouser (2)
1947-55	0			(No pitchers with 200 strikeouts)
1956-62	3	278	7.6	H. Score, S. Jones, D. Drysdale
1963-75	46	302	7.5	J. Marichal (6), F. Jenkins (4), T. Seaver (4), S. Koufax (3), B. Gibson (3), G. Perry (3)
1976-90	11	260	8.0	R. Clemens (3), 8 others (1)
1991-95	0			(Only 6 seasons over 260 IP)

Three or more triple mile-stone seasons (twentieth century).

Pitcher	Seasons	HOF	Years
Walter Johnson	7	Yes	1910-16
Juan Marichal	6	Yes	1963-66, 68-69
Christy Mathewson	5	Yes	1901, 03-05, 08
Rube Waddell	4	Yes	1902-05
Ed Walsh	4	Yes	1907-08, 11-12
Pete Alexander	4	Yes	1911, 14-15, 17
Ferguson Jenkins	4	Yes	1967-68, 71, 74
Tom Seaver	4	Yes	1969, 71-72, 75
Bob Feller	3	Yes	1939-40, 46
Sandy Koufax	3	Yes	1963, 65-66
Bob Gibson	3	Yes	1966, 68-69
Gaylord Perry	3	Yes	1966, 72, 74
Roger Clemens	3	Active	1986-87, 90

Two triple milestone seasons (twentieth century).

Pitcher	Seasons	HOF	Years
Eddie Plank	2	Yes	1904-05
Joe Wood	2	No	1911-12
Dazzy Vance	2	Yes	1924, 28
Hal Newhouser	2	Yes	1945-46
Don Drysdale	2	Yes	1962, 65
Jim Maloney	2	No	1963, 65
Dean Chance	2	No	1964, 67
Mickey Lolich	2	No	1971-72
Steve Carlton	2	Yes	1972, 80
Nolan Ryan	2	Inelig	1973-74

Hall of Fame Pitchers without a Triple Milestone Season

	Debut Year	Most Ks	Years Led League	20 Win Seasons
Joe McGinnity	1899	171	0	7
Addie Joss	1902	132	0	4
Chief Bender	1903	159	0	2
Mordecai Brown	1903	172	0	6
Stan Coveleskie	1912	133	1	5
Herb Pennock	1912	101	0	2
Eppa Rixey	1912	134	0	4
Red Faber	1914	182	0	4
Burleigh Grimes	1916	136	1	5
Jesse Haines	1918	120	0	3
Waite Hoyt	1918	105	0	2
Ted Lyons	1923	74	0	3
Red Ruffing	1924	190	1	4
Carl Hubbell	1928	159	1	5
Dizzy Dean	1930	199	4	4
Lefty Gomez	1930	194	3	4
Early Wynn	1939	184	2	5
Warren Spahn	1942	191	4	13
Bob Lemon	1946	170	1	7
Robin Roberts	1948	198	2	6
Whitey Ford	1950	209	0	2
Hoyt Wilhelm	1952	139	0	0
Catfish Hunter	1965	196	0	5
Rollie Fingers	1968	115	0	0
Jim Palmer	1970	199	0	8

Last Pitchers to Reach Triple Milestones

Roger Clemens, (1990), 21-6, 209 strikeouts, 1.93 ERA

Ramon Martinez (1990), 20-6, 223 strikeouts, 2.92 ERA

Only 20th Century Pitcher to Hit Each Milestone Only Once

Ramon Martinez (1990)

Pitchers Who Were on Target for Triple Milestones in 1994

	ACTUAL			PROJECTED		
	W	SO	ERA	W	SO	ERA
Greg Maddux	16	156	1.56	22	221	1.56
Bret Saberhagen	14	143	2.74	20	205	2.74

Pitchers Who Were on Target for Triple Milestones in 1995

	W	SO	ERA	W	SO	ERA
Greg Maddux	19	181	1.63	21	203	1.63
Randy Johnson	18	294	2.48	20	328	2.48

Minor League Achievement

Roy Sanner - Houma, Evangeline League (Class D), 1948

Hitting   .386, 34, 126

Pitching   21-2, 251, 2.58

Matty and His Fadeaway

The origins of a legend examined

Dick Thompson

Christy Mathewson and his fadeaway. Baseball's most heroic figure and his fabled weapon. The game's greatest celebrity, pitching for its most visible team and playing for its most colorful manager. Three-hundred and seventy-three wins and a charter inductee to the Hall of Fame. Every SABR member knows the story, right? Well, not exactly.

Today the fadeaway is known as the screwball, which seems fitting, for as the fadeaway it remains synonymous with just one man: the great Matty. He wasn't the first to throw it, but he was the first to master it to legendary perfection. In Lee Allen's, *The National League Story*, American League umpire Jack Sheridan, who worked the 1905 Series, said, "That fadeaway ball of Matty's is the greatest thing I ever saw. It had the lefthanded hitters ducking away just as badly as the righthanders."

Determining the origin of Mathewson's fadeaway should be a simple task, but, like countless other elements of baseball lore, just where Matty first learned the pitch remains shadowy. Scanning the reference works on Mathewson for its origin will get you three different theories.

Theory one—The first is that a teammate named Williams, no first name known, taught it to Mathewson while they were pitching for the Taunton,

Massachusetts, team in 1899. This theory, in book form, can to traced back to 1947. There are at least six publications adhering to it. In 1987, authors John Thorn and John Holway, in *The Pitcher*, said Williams's first name was Dave, and that he was a teammate of Mathewson at both Taunton in 1899 and Honesdale, Pennsylvania, in 1898, where Matty pitched for a semipro team.

Theory two—*The Crooked Pitch*, written by Martin Quigley and published in 1984, said that Rube Foster taught Mathewson the pitch sometime around 1902. Holway, in his 1981, *Rube Foster: The Father of Black Baseball*, and later in 1988's *Blackball Stars*, said it was Foster in 1903. Ken Burns also went with this theory in his film version of the game, and then went a step further when *Shadow Ball: The History of the Negro Leagues*, was published in 1994. Authors Burns, Geoffrey Ward, and Jim O'Connor stated, "[John] McGraw knew there was no chance of slipping Foster into the big leagues. Instead, he paid Rube to teach Christy Mathewson his fadeaway."

Theory three—The latest theory cropped up in 1988 when Noel Hynd wrote, in *The Giants of the Polo Grounds*, that pitcher Virgil Garvin taught Matty the pitch when they were teammates at Taunton in 1899. Two subsequent biographies of Mathewson, both published in 1993, *Christy Mathewson*, and *Matty, An American Hero*, also opted for this theory, although the latter waffled between both the Williams and the

Dick Thompson would like to thank Art Ahrens, Dick Clark, Kerry Keene, Bob Lindsay, Hank Martyniak, Ron Mayer, Ray Nemec, John Pardon, Bob Richardson, Jim Riley, Ray Robinson, and John Thorn for assistance with this article.

Garvin theories.

Taunton—We'll pick up the century old trail in Taunton, Massachusetts, a small city located halfway between Boston and Providence, Rhode Island. Mathewson joined the Taunton club in late July, 1899. It was his professional debut. The New England League that year was an organization in turmoil. It started out as a conventional eight-team circuit, with two teams dropping out in June, and two more in early August, just two weeks after Matty joined the league. The four surviving teams played on until Labor Day.

The league, like many other nineteenth century minor leagues, left no known existing statistics. In 1994, I completed an eighteen-month project to collect these statistics. For many years Mathewson's 1899 Taunton record, as provided by *The Sporting News*, was thought to be five wins and two losses, but in fact Matty won just twice against *thirteen* losses. He had the worst winning percentage in the league for any pitcher involved in more than six decisions. Mathewson pitched well at times, but he was unable to overcome the caliber of his mates. Interestingly enough, the Taunton club's home field of 1899 is still in use as a baseball field today, and a plaque now hangs there commemorating the fact that Matty played on that field.

Let's tackle the Virgil Garvin theory first. Mathewson is remembered as a tragic hero dying young from lung disease. Garvin's story is much more grim. He died at age 34 from tuberculosis. His wife died just a few years later from the same disease. Their only child died as an infant. Garvin was from Navasota, Texas, where some of his scrapbooks still exist at the public library and with relatives of his wife. None of the information obtained from the Navasota library mentioned Mathewson or the fadeaway. Garvin's file at the Hall of Fame is empty.

The Garvin theory is the easiest to debunk. Not only was Garvin not on the 1899 Taunton team, but he did not pitch in the New England League at all that year. Garvin pitched seven seasons in the big leagues and a quick glance at his *Baseball Encyclopedia* or *Total Baseball* record shows that he pitched nearly 200 innings for Chicago in the National League in 1899. A review of the Chicago papers indicates that Garvin spent the entire season with the major league club.

Where did the Garvin theory originate? Probably from Hall of Famer Johnny Evers' 1910 book, *Touching Second*. On page 108, Evers stated,

Yet before Mathewson learned the trick of pitching his 'fader', there was one who pitched the same ball in even more wonderful style. Virgil Garvin; a tall, slender young Texan, with extraordinarily long fingers, pitched the ball before Mathewson, but he did not understand its use or worth.

At no point does Evers link Garvin to teaching Matty the pitch, but this apparently is the root of this legend.

Now to the Williams theory. No one named Williams pitched for Taunton in 1899. There was, however, a third baseman named Williams who played seventeen games with Taunton that year, and his time with the team corresponded with Mathewson's. Could he have been Matty's teacher?

The Taunton paper never gave a first name to Williams and but for a lucky break this lead would surely have ended here, but the nearby Brockton (Massachusetts) *Times*, on August 31, 1899, published this small item in its baseball column: "Williams, who is playing third base for Taunton, proves to be McAndrew, the old Dartmouth fullback." Dartmouth alumni records confirm that David Carr McAndrew, Class of 1898, was the Taunton player who called himself Dave Williams.

McAndrew's reputation was as a football player and coach. Newspaper stories in his Dartmouth file show that he played minor league baseball, placing him with Taunton in the New England League and later in the Pacific Coast League (no confirmation can be found of Williams/McAndrew playing in the PCL). There are many documented examples of players using assumed names during that time period. Why McAndrew, who died in Braintree, Massachusetts, in 1937, chose to do so is unknown. No evidence can be found linking him to the fadeaway.

Honesdale—The paper trail now shifts to the May, 1912, issue of *St. Nicholas Magazine* which printed an article, authored by Mathewson, titled, *How I Became a Big League Pitcher*. This article contained many little-known facts on Matty's early life and career, which independent research later verified. Matty, in discussing where he learned the fadeaway, wrote:

In Honesdale, there was a lefthanded pitcher named Williams who could throw an out-curve to a righthanded batter. Williams exhibited this curve as a sort of 'freak delivery' in practice, over which he had no control. He showed the ball to me, and told me how to throw it.

Mathewson also said that Williams, whom he never gave a first name to, "once played a few games in one of the big leagues."

Mathewson's Hall of Fame file is made up of hundreds of newspaper stories and clippings. It can take all day to read. Included in the file are several pieces of the fadeaway puzzle. An obituary of Frank Scheurholz, the last surviving member of the 1898 Honesdale team (he died in 1974), describes Williams as "Dave Williams, a lefty from Scranton."

The late Keith Sutton, one of the founding members of SABR, and a longtime resident of Honesdale, published in 1973 a book titled *Wayne County Sports History* (Honesdale is in Wayne County), which included a picture of that 1898 Honesdale team. Mathewson is in the picture, as is Dave Williams, as is "Mac" McAndrew. Is the Honesdale player of 1898 named McAndrew the same man who played in Taunton in 1899 as Dave Williams? It's probable, but not certain. But if the Taunton Dave Williams is really the Honesdale "Mac" McAndrew, who the heck is the Honesdale Dave Williams? Sutton answers this question by saying,

> Two pitchers of this Honesdale team, Mathewson and Davey Williams, went on to pitch in the big leagues. Mathewson for the New York Giants and Williams, a left-handed pitcher, for the Boston Red Sox in 1902.

The 1898 Honesdale Dave Williams and the 1899 Taunton Dave Williams were clearly two different people.

All of the baseball encyclopedias show Williams as David Owen Williams. He was born in Scranton, Pennsylvania in 1881, and died in Hot Springs, Arkansas in 1918. He is listed as a left-handed pitcher who appeared in three games for the Red Sox in 1902. The Boston papers indicated that Williams, although pitching infrequently, was with the team for most of that season. He was a protege of Boston slugger and fellow Pennsylvanian Buck Freeman. Williams's death date and location were unknown until about ten years ago when SABR researcher Ray Nemec ran across mention of his death while doing Western League research.

Williams's Hall of Fame file is empty except for his death certificate and a small item from a Scranton

paper. That item mentioned that at the time of this death Williams was a captain in a Minnesota National Guard unit that had originated in Duluth, Minnesota. The Duluth paper said that Williams became sick while stationed in Arizona. He was transferred to a military hospital in Hot Springs, where he died from kidney failure. For the ten years prior to his death he had been living in Hibbing, Minnesota.

Williams had wandered the country as a baseball nomad, good enough to keep getting minor league jobs, but unable to establish himself in the majors. He eventually settled in Hibbing where he became a big fish in a little pond. He was a member of the police force, the town's probation officer, and the star of the local baseball team. Hibbing had an official day of mourning over his passing.

Williams's obituary in the Hibbing *Daily Tribune* of April 25, 1918, was lengthy. When describing his early baseball days in Pennsylvania it stated:

> It was here that Williams taught Christy Mathewson, now manager of the Cincinnati nine, the 'fade-away,' one of the freaks of the pitching art, and which returned the famous Mathewson many a victory.

Now, Hibbing, Minnesota, in 1918 was clearly not on the main street of the city of baseball. If such a direct link to Williams teaching Matty the fadeaway appeared in that Hibbing paper, it was because Williams had made that claim himself. He probably drank a lot of free beer telling listeners how he taught the great Mathewson the finer points of pitching.

Rube Foster—There is still the last theory to discuss. Did Rube Foster have any role in the development of Matty's fadeaway? No, he didn't. Foster's role is nothing more than a fable. Every author who has made the claim that Foster taught Matty the pitch has done so without offering original research. That's because no such link exists. Both Quigley and Holway, like most of the authors regarding the Williams and Garvin theories, pointed out that the Foster theory was based on legend. Only the Burns group unequivocally named Foster as Matty's teacher.

Proponents of the Foster theory argue that Mathewson's statistics improved dramatically from 1902 to 1903, supposedly when Foster tutored Matty. Untrue. His won-lost record did go from 14-17 to 30-13, but that can be attributed to the arrival of McGraw and his restructuring of the team. The Giants went from last place in 1902 to second place in 1903. Matty's improvement was just a combination of playing for a better team and his own natural progression. Tom Seaver's career course from 1967-1969 is very similar to Mathewson's 1901-1903 seasons.

Foster was a true pioneer of baseball and his spot in the Hall of Fame is well-deserved. He was a great pitcher who was known to throw a screwball. Did Mathewson and Foster ever get together and discuss pitching, and if they did, did they discuss the fadeaway? It's a moot point. Did Babe Ruth and Ted Williams ever get together and discuss hitting, and if they did, did they discuss hitting home runs? Does anyone believe Babe Ruth is responsible for teaching Ted Williams how to hit home runs?

Foster was not a grizzled old veteran teaching a young Mathewson. Foster was born in Texas in 1879,

Matty in Pennsylvania less than a year later. When Matty first saw the pitch as an 18-year-old teenager in Honesdale, Foster was a 19-year-old who had probably never been been out of the state of Texas.

At this point I would interject, in jest, that since Garvin and Foster were both from the state of Texas, maybe Garvin taught the pitch to Foster. But on second thought, someone might read this and years from now the "Garvin taught Foster" theory might make it into print.

Forget Virgil Garvin and Rube Foster. The Dave Williams who played for Boston in 1902 taught Christy Mathewson the fadeaway at Honesdale, Pennsylvania in 1898. Matty said so, so did Williams. Fact must always remain more important than fascinating legend to true historians.

Mathewson at Taunton, 1899

Date	Opposition	W/L	S/R	CG	IP	Hits	BB	K	Runs	Comment
July 21	Manchester	L	S	Y	8	9	1	3	6	
July 24	Brockton	L	S	Y	8	16	3	4	13	
July 27	Portland	W	S	Y	8	5	0	4	3	8-inning game
July 29	Pawtucket	L	s	Y	9	12	4	7	6	
August 1	Brockton	L	S	Y	8	16	2	4	8	
August 3	Manchester	L	S	Y	8	8	4	2	8	
August 5	Portland	L	S	Y	7	7	3	1	5	8-inning game
August 8	Newport	ND	R	N	6	7	2	2	5	
August 14	Portland	L	S	Y	8	7	1	1	4	
August 17	Manchester	L	S	Y	8	13	0	2	5	
August 21	Manchester	L	S	Y	9	13	3	6	11	
August 23	Portland	L	S	Y	9	24	2	2	19	
August 26	Portland	L	S	Y	8	9	2	1	5	
August 29	Portland	W	S	Y	9	3	0	7	1	
September 1	Manchester	L	S	Y	5	5	1	1	3	5-inning game
September 2	Newport	ND	R	N	3	4	0	3	2	
September 4	Newport	L	S	Y	9	10	5	2	4	
Totals	17 games	2-13		15	130	168	33	52	106	

On August 8, Kerrins, the starting pitcher for Taunton, gave up eight runs to Newport before being relieved by Mathewson. Tanuton came back to tie the game before Matty gave up the winning runs. By today's standards, Mathewson would receive credit for the loss. However, based on data provided by Frank Willians in the premiere edition of *The National Pastime*, it's safe to say that the loss, in 1899, would commonly have gone to the starter.

Mid-summer Vacations

The best ever who never made an All Star team

Carl Isackson

Consider the following group of major leaguers: Dave Stenhouse, Biff Pocoroba, Ted Gray, Matt Keough, Lee Walls, Bob Schmidt, Jerry Walker, Dean Stone, Toby Atwell, Thurman Tucker, Duane Josephson, Randy Gumpert, Bruce Edwards, and Joe Haynes.

What do these players have in common? Other than a heavy dose of mediocrity, each could tell his grandchildren that he was once invited to participate in baseball's showcase, the annual All Star Game.

Now consider this group: Ellie Rodriguez, Walt Masterson, Hal Smith, Jim Finigan, Johnny Wyrostek, Craig Reynolds, Hal Wagner, and Burgess Whitehead.

What's the common thread for this group? Well, for reasons difficult to fathom, these players were *twice* chosen to appear in the midsummer classic. Even the most trusting grandchild of these players may find that story hard to swallow.

Any knowledgeable baseball fan knows that the All Star selection process is a combination of talent, politics, and luck. And commonly, talent is not the prime consideration. Nearly every summer, there is a public outcry in some major league city about a hometown favorite who deserved to make the All Star team but did not.

Most often, this is the result of baseball's "quota system"—the fact that each team must have an All Star representative. To meet this requirement, less deserving players from poor teams may get an All Star nod over more worthy candidates from talent-laden ballclubs. It's safe to assume that many of the players mentioned above were beneficiaries of this practice.

But this isn't about obscure players and their brief, shining moments in the midsummer sun. This is about the more accomplished players who, despite distinguished careers, were *never* chosen to play in an All Star Game.

Now, there are many reasons as to how this can happen. The aforementioned quota system is one. Politics comes into play if a player happens to be unpopular with whoever is in a position to do the choosing—be it the All Star manager, fellow players, or the fickle fans. A player may be victimized by having his best seasons when other players at his given position have been even more impressive. It's possible, too, that certain players have a history as "slow-starters" or "warm-weather" performers and consequently have not produced impressive stats by All Star time.

Here then is a roster of some very fine ballplayers who managed somehow to escape official All Star recognition for an entire career. (Obviously, inclusion is limited to players who had their best seasons after the All Star Game was instituted in 1933.)

Catcher—Because there are so few great catchers, it's rare that even a merely above-average receiver will escape All Star recognition for an entire career. It's likely there have been more mediocre catchers on All

Carl Isackson is a contractor residing in the San Francisco Bay area. He has been an avid Giants fan since 1965.

Star squads than at any other position. Consequently, there are no glaring injustices to report. The most notable of those catchers never chosen are Joe Ferguson, Cliff Johnson, Mike Heath, Alan Ashby, Rick Dempsey, and Brian Harper.

First Base—Former Cleveland Indian great Hal Trosky is quite possibly the best player *ever* to never receive anointment as an All Star. In a seven-year stretch from 1934 to 1940, Trosky's *average* season consisted of 29 homers, 121 RBIs, and a .314 batting average. But it was Trosky's misfortune to play first base during the heyday of Lou Gehrig, Jimmie Foxx, and Hank Greenberg. That considered, Hal's yearly omission from the All Star ranks does become a bit more palatable. But no other player has ever put up such awesome statistics without All Star recognition at some point in his career.

Honorable mention at First Base goes to Donn Clendenon, Wes Parker, and Joe Kuhel. Kuhel had to compete not only against Gehrig, Foxx, and Greenberg, but Trosky as well.

Second Base and Shortstop—As with catchers, there are no striking omissions here. That is, until you consider some of the Punch-and-Judys who *have* played in All Star Games: Billy Hunter, Dick Howser, and Billy Moran to name a few. Given that, it's surprising that the likes of Jim Gantner, Gerry Priddy, Ted Sizemore, Bill Doran, Woodie Held, and Wayne Causey never earned a single All Star berth.

Third Base—Longtime baseball man Bobby Bragan once referred to Clete Boyer as the "most underrated player ever." Many other contemporaries will attest that Boyer was every bit as good a fielder as the legendary Brooks Robinson. And Clete was no slouch with the bat, either. Nine times he reached double figures in home runs. Still, he was never selected to an All Star team, victimized by both Brooksie and the plethora of Yankee teammates on the All Star squads of that period. Other fine hot corner performers who never made the All Star grade are Billy Werber, Bob Bailey, Doug Rader, Aurelio Rodriguez, Richie Hebner, Ken McMullen, and Billy Cox.

Outfield—In 1953, Milwaukee Braves rookie outfielder Bill Bruton led the National League in stolen bases. During a distinguished twelve-year career, Bruton won two more stolen-base crowns, twice topped the league in triples, and once led in runs scored. He was a fine fielder, too. Unfortunately,

Bruton was up against the likes of Willie Mays, Frank Robinson, Hank Aaron, Duke Snider, and Richie Ashburn for All Star recognition. More recently, Kevin McReynolds had a five-year run from 1986 to 1990 in which he averaged 25 homers and 90 RBIs. Overshadowed by his more glamorous teammates, Kevin's only reward was a three-day vacation each July. And perhaps most surprisingly, flychaser-supreme Garry Maddox could not parlay his eight consecutive Gold Gloves and six postseason appearances into even a single All Star invitation.

Recently retired is a player who may rival Hal Trosky for the honor of "Greatest-Ever Non-All Star". That is the injury-plagued Kirk Gibson. No doubt Kirk's many injuries contributed to his yearly non-selection. But even in his MVP season of 1988, Gibson was overlooked for the NL squad* (although it's somewhat understandable as his MVP numbers are among the least impressive ever). Still, he retired as the all-time home run leader for a non-All Star.

Other excellent outfielders who were never selected as All Stars are Wally Post, Jose Cardenal, Cesar Tovar, Bill Virdon, Jim Northrup, and Dwayne Murphy.

Pitchers—The Red Sox Ellis Kinder gets the nod as the best pitcher ever who never made an All Star team. Kinder can quite accurately be considered the Dennis Eckersley of his day. As a starter in the fabled 1949 American League pennant race, Kinder fashioned a record of 23-6, leading the league in both winning percentage and shutouts. By 1951, Ellis was in the bullpen and topping the majors in saves—a feat he would duplicate in 1953. When Kinder retired in 1957, he was only the second pitcher ever—Firpo Marberry being the first—to notch both 100 wins and 100 saves. But Kinder was the *first* pitcher ever to notch both 20-win and 20-save seasons.

The much-traveled Mike Torrez has registered the most wins ever (185) for a pitcher who was never an All Star. Seven times Torrez won at least 15 games without a single All Star nod.

Royals great Dennis Leonard has the distinction of being the only *3-time* 20-game winner who never made an All Star team, being overlooked in 1977, 1978, and 1980. This was during an impressive run of eight consecutive winning seasons in which Leonard won at least ten games per season.

Other successful starting pitchers who were never All Stars include Bill Gullickson (11 double-digit win seasons), Bob Forsch (11), Paul Splittorff (10), Elden Auker (9), Charlie Leibrandt (8), Rudy May (8), and

Earl Wilson (8). John Denny (7) is unique in that he once topped the NL in both ERA (1976) and Wins (1983) and yet was never an All Star.

Historically, it has not been unusual for relief specialists to be overlooked for All Star consideration. Many an All Star pitching staff has been composed solely of starting pitchers and only recently has it become commonplace to have more than one stopper selected. So it's hardly surprising that there is a pretty fair crop of relievers who have never been All Stars. Leading the way is Gene Garber with 218 career saves—good enough for thirteenth place on the all-time list heading into the 1995 season. Other neglected bullpen aces of note are Ted Abernathy (148 career saves, 2 save crowns), Terry Forster (127, 1), Jack Aker (123, 1), Al Worthington (110, 1),

Frank Linzy (110, 0), Ron Kline (108, 1), Al Brazle (60, 2), and Hugh Casey (55, 2).

So, there you have it. No All Star stories for these players to tell, but still plenty of baseball heroics with which to impress their grandkids.

*Seven times in history, players who have failed to make the All Star team went on to win that year's league MVP award. In addition to Gibson, they are Hank Greenberg (1935), Don Newcombe (1956), Dave Parker (1978), Willie Stargell (1979), Robin Yount (1989), and Terry Pendleton (1991). For those curious, sixteen pitchers have failed to be All-Stars in the year they won the Cy Young Award—starting with the very first recipient, Don Newcombe (1956). Most recently, Braves ace Greg Maddux was somehow ignored in 1993. Jim Palmer (1973 and 1976) and Bret Saberhagen (1985 and 1989) have twice been bypassed as All-Stars in their Cy Young seasons.

Mike Piazza:
Best-Hitting Catcher Ever?

He's off to baseball's best career start

Tomas Rubalcava

A batting average over .300, 30 home runs, and 100 RBIs by a rookie catcher? Preposterous. Bench, Berra, Cochrane—none of them ever did it. A catcher topping .340 while hitting over 30 home runs—in 112 games? Ridiculous. Neither Cochrane nor Dickey ever hit 30 home runs in a season. Three consecutive .300 seasons by a catcher in this day and age? Impossible. Bench never hit .300. Ridiculous, impossible, and preposterous, but Mike Piazza accomplished all of those feats in his first three seasons.

An undrafted first baseman after high school, Piazza enrolled at Miami-Dade Community to learn how to catch. A year later, he was still such a nonentity to the scouting community that the Los Angeles Dodgers drafted him only as a favor to a certain Piazza family friend named Lasorda.[1] Piazza ultimately forced his way into the Dodger plans when he hit 29 homers and drove in 80 runs at Bakersfield in 1991.

After the Dodgers' horrible 1992 season, the brass decided to give their Minor League Player of the Year every chance to win a regular job. That year, the team produced the only last-place finish by a Dodger team in 87 years. It ranked last in the National League in home runs, runs and slugging percentage; the catchers combined to hit .234 with seven homers and 48 RBIs in 590 at-bats. Additionally, the years of squatting behind the plate caught up with incumbent Mike Scioscia, as he finished up with a career-low .282 slugging average while driving in only 24 runs. The

decision to release Scioscia was made a bit easier as Piazza hit .350 with 23 home runs and 90 RBIs.

The unanimous choice for National League Rookie of the Year honors led the Dodgers and all big league catchers with 35 homers, 112 RBIs, a .318 average, a .561 slugging average, 174 hits, 81 runs, and 307 total bases.[2] Table 1 shows how his freshman totals compare with those of other outstanding rookie catchers. Table 2 shows how rare for catchers is his .300-30-100. Table 3 lists catchers who hit 35 home runs. In setting an LA record for home runs, Piazza also set franchise marks for home runs and RBIs by a rookie, and major league standards for HR, RBIs, slugging percentage, hits, and total bases by a rookie catcher.

In strike-shortened 1994, Piazza's .319 average 24 home runs and 92 RBIs again topped the Dodgers, and all big league catchers, in the triple crown categories. He also became the first National League receiver to hit over .300 in consecutive seasons since Ted Simmons did it in 1972 and 1973. His .86 RBI per game ranks second in LA history only to Tommy Davis' .94. He was on a pace to equal or better his rookie statistics in every offensive department before play ended prematurely.

Even the shortened 1995 season did not prevent Piazza from producing a Hall of Fame-caliber year (.346, 32, 93). At no time during the season did his batting average fall below .344 (on July 29). His average was just .00016 off the LA record, while his .606 slugging average bettered the previous LA mark by 29

Thomas Rubalcava is hanging out in East Los Angeles.

points.[3] In becoming the first catcher to hit 30 homers and bat over .340, Piazza produced the fourth best home run ratio by a catcher (1 HR/13.6 AB).[4] Table 4 points out that the other catchers who topped .600 all did so with teams which had more potent lineups than the 1995 Dodgers, in years when the league's batters punished the pitchers much more than National League hitters did in 1995. To top it all off, Piazza won the catchers' Triple Crown yet again.

Piazza's numbers compare favorably with those of any active player, any player in Dodger franchise history, or anybody who has ever strapped on the catching gear. Besides Piazza, only Frank Thomas has hit over .300, hit 20 homers, and driven in 90 runs each of the last three years. Table 5 lists where Piazza ranks among all major leaguers in batting, slugging, RBIs produced per at bat. Over the three years 1993-94-95, Piazza ranked eleventh in HR, eighth in RBI, third in BA, and eighth in SA. Among National Leaguers, only Dante Bichette and Barry Bonds had more RBIs over those three seasons, while only Tony Gwynn had a higher batting average. Table 6 shows how Piazza compared to other National Leaguers over those three seasons. Every player who ranks ahead of him in these categories plays either first base or in the outfield.

No LA Dodger has ever strung together three seasons as explosive as Piazza has in his first three "full" seasons. His .327 batting average, .569 slugging average and 91 homers are the best three-year totals by an LA player. Only Steve Garvey and Tommy Davis had more RBIs in a three-year span, but they each had many more opportunities. Garvey drove in 41 more runs than Piazza in 547 more times at bat, while Davis produced two more RBIs in 295 more at bats. Needless to say, no LA catcher comes close to matching Piazza's production. From 1984 to 1992, LA catchers combined to hit .241 with 95 homers and a .343 slugging average (Piazza already had 92 home runs at the end of 1995). Piazza's .322 average ranked fourth in franchise history. No Dodger player, whether Angeleno or Brooklynite, has a higher slugging average (.557), home run ratio (15.8 AB/HR), or RBI per game ratio (.78).[5] Making Piazza's accomplishments even more remarkable is the fact that he plays half his games in pitcher-friendly Dodger Stadium, whereas players like Babe Herman, Duke Snider, Gil Hodges, and Roy Campanella played their home games in cozy Ebbets Field.

Table 7 shows that no active catcher can match Piazza's offensive prowess. In his first three seasons, Piazza led all catchers in games, at bats, runs, hits, to-

tal bases, home runs, RBIs, batting and slugging. Table 8 demonstrates that Piazza's statistics during his first three years were more impressive than those produced by any Hall of Fame catcher. Only Johnny Bench had more RBIs after three full seasons as a regular catcher (22 more RBIs in 342 more at bats). Only Bill Dickey had a higher average (.328 to .322). No third-year catcher has ever had as many home runs or had a higher slugging average.

To put things in perspective, Hall of Fame catchers averaged .289 with 17 home runs, and a .452 slugging average per 530 at bats. The average Hall of Famer hit .303 with 19 homers and 93 RBI for a .480 slugging average per 576 at bats. Piazza averages .322 with 31 HR, 101 RBI for a .557 slugging average per 452 at bats.[6] While it is premature to lobby for Piazza's entrance into Cooperstown (after all he is only 27 years old), Piazza has already produced some monumental feats. Fans are calling Piazza the best-hitting catcher since Bench. Maybe someday they'll call Bench the best hitting catcher before Piazza. It might happen any year now.

Table 1.

Outstanding seasons by rookie catchers[7]

Player	Year	Team	BA	HR	RBI	GCaught
Mickey Cochrane	1925	PhA	.331	6	55	133
Bill Dickey	1929	NYA	.324	10	65	127
Johnny Bench	1968	Cin	.275	15	82	154
Carlton Fisk	1971	Bos	.293	22	61	131
Matt Nokes	1987	Det	.289	32	87	109
Mike Piazza	1993	LA	.318	35	112	147

Table 2.

35HR/100 Games Caught

	HR	Year	Team	GC
Gabby Hartnett	37	1930	ChN	136
Walker Cooper	35	1947	NYN	132
Roy Campanella	41	1953	Bkn	140
Joe Torre	36	1966	Atl	114
Johnny Bench	45	1970	Cin	139
Johnny Bench	40	1972	Cin	129
Carlton Fisk	37	1985	ChA	130
Mike Piazza	35	1993	LA	147

Table 3.

.300-30-100 Seasons by Players Catching Over 50 Games

	BA	HR	RBI	Year	Team
Gabby Hartnett	.339	37	122	1930	ChN
Rudy York	.307	35	103	1937	Det
Walker Cooper	.305	35	122	1947	NYN
Roy Campanella	.325	33	108	1951	Bkn

Roy Campanella	.312	41	142	1953	Bkn
Roy Campanella	.318	32	107	1955	Bkn
Joe Torre	.315	36	101	1966	Atl
Mike Piazza	.318	35	112	1993	LA

Table 4.

.600 Slugging Percentages/100 Games Caught

	SA	Year	Team	TmSA	LgSA
Gabby Hartnett	.630	1930	ChN	.481	.448
Bill Dickey	.617	1936	NYA	.483	.421
Roy Campanella	.611	1953	Bkn	.474	.411
Mike Piazza	.606	1995	LA	.400	.408

Table 5.

Active Leaders

RBI/100 AB		BA		SA	
Frank Thomas	21.5	Tony Gwynn	.336	Frank Thomas	.593
Albert Belle	21.2	Wade Boggs	.334	Albert Belle	.571
Mike Piazza	20.9	Frank Thomas	.323	Mike Piazza	.557
Mark McGwire	20.4	Mike Piazza	.322	Tim Salmon	.541
Jose Canseco	20.2	Kirby Puckett	.318	Barry Bonds	.541

Table 6.

Top National League Performances, 1993-1995

HR		RBI		BA	
Barry Bonds	116	Dante Bichette	312	Tony Gwynn	.372
Matt Williams	104	Barry Bonds	308	Mike Piazza	.327
Fred McGriff	98	Mike Piazza	297	Greg Jefferies	.325
Sammy Sosa	94	Jeff Bagwell	291	Jeff Bagwell	.324
Mike Piazza	91	Andres Galarraga	289	Andres Galarraga	.321
SA		AB/RBI		AB/HR	
Barry Bonds	.634	Matt Williams	4.60	Matt Williams	12.0
Matt Williams	.624	Barry Bonds	4.66	Barry Bonds	12.4
Jeff Bagwell	.577	Mike Piazza	4.67	Mike Piazza	15.2
Mike Piazza	.569	Jeff Bagwell	4.75	Fred McGriff	15.4
Dante Bichette	.567	Andres Galarraga	4.98	Sammy Sosa	16.9

Table 7.

Selected Offensive Performances by Catchers (1993-1995)

	G	AB	R	H	2B	3B	HR	RBI	BA	SA
Mike Piazza	368	1386	227	453	59	2	91	297	.327	.569
Mike Stanley	330	1112	187	323	66	2	61	224	.290	.518
Chris Hoiles	339	1103	178	300	53	1	67	193	.272	.504
Sandy Alomar Jr.	210	710	100	203	28	2	30	110	.286	.458
Ivan Rodriguez	346	1328	168	386	79	7	38	190	.291	.447
Terry Steinbach	321	1164	141	329	66	4	36	165	.283	.439
Darren Daulton	314	1109	177	293	71	8	48	216	.264	.472
Rick Wilkens	301	961	152	247	51	3	44	131	.257	.454
Don Slaught	227	729	68	215	32	2	12	89	.295	.394

Table 8:.

Hall of Fame Catchers—Totals After Three Seasons[8]

	G	AB	R	H	2B	3B	HR	RBI	BA	SA
Roy Campanella 1948-50	339	1152	168	323	52	8	62	216	.280	.501
Gabby Hartnett 1922-25	344	1055	149	337	58	13	48	177	.319	.521
Mickey Cochrane 1925-27	380	1222	199	386	49	20	26	182	.316	.453
Bill Dickey 1928-31	379	1305	181	428	73	24	21	210	.328	.468
Yogi Berra 1947-49	331	1199	173	348	60	15	47	247	.290	.483
Al Lopez 1928,30- 2	368	1197	142	338	51	14	7	140	.282	.366
Ray Schalk 1912-15	423	1269	121	332	44	11	2	136	.262	.318
Johnny Bench 1967-70	486	1787	254	502	101	8	87	326	.281	.492
Rick Ferrell 1929-32	408	1282	178	373	84	14	6	183	.291	.392
Ernie Lombardi 1931-33	298	945	93	278	50	11	19	138	.294	.431

Piazza's career totals (1992-95):

G	AB	R	H	2B	3B	HR	RBI	BA	SA
389	1455	232	469	74	2	92	304	.322	.566

Notes

1. Of all the players drafted ahead of Piazza by the Dodgers, only #3 Billy Ashley, #6 Eric Karros, #7 Jeff Hartsock, #9 Jim Poole, and #16 Brian Traxler, reached the majors, with only Karros making significant contributions.

2. Before Piazza, Wally Berger was the only NL rookie to bat .300, hit 30 HR, and drive in 100 runs (.310, 38, 119) in 1930, when the league as a whole hit .303. When Piazza topped .300-30-100, the league hit .264.

3. Piazza's .346 average was the highest average by a catcher since Elston Howard's .348 in 1961, highest by an NL catcher since Smoky Burgess' .354 in 1954, and highest by a Dodger catcher since Babe Phelps' .367 in 1936.

4. Johnny Bench (13.4 in 1970 and 13.5 in 1972), and Roy Campanella (12.7 in 1953) are the only players to top Piazza's 1995 HR ratio while catching over 100 games.

5. In franchise history, only Willie Keeler's .358 career average, Babe Herman's .339, and Jack Fournier's .337 rank ahead of Piazza's .322. From Dodgers: The Complete Record of Dodgers Baseball, (New York: Collier Books, 1986), 12-13.

6. "Measures of Greatness," Topps Company Inc., 1995 baseball cards #601-608.

7. Rudy York's 1937 season (.307, 35, 103) and Earl Williams' 1971 season (.260, 33, 87) are not included because York only caught 54 games and Williams only caught 72 games.

8. Listings for Hall of Fame catchers after the first three seasons in which they appeared in over 50 games. Part of the list appears in "Dodger Catcher Hits on a Higher Level," John Romano, Baseball Digest, Jan. 1996, 41. Roger Bresnahan is not included in this list because he played regularly at other positions before becoming a full-time catcher.

Pittsburgh: June 1903

Pirates pitching allows no runs for a record 56 innings

Joe Elinich

The Pittsburgh Pirates were the first baseball dynasty of the twentieth century. From 1901 to 1903 they won the NL flag by margins of 7.5, 27.5 and 6.5 games over their closest rivals. After their 1901 and 1902 titles, the Pirates were not picked to repeat in 1903, because they had lost pitchers Jack Chesbro and Jesse Tannehill to the raiding American League. It was this season, though, during the week of June 3–10, that Pirate pitchers set a major league record that stands to this day.

For 56 consecutive innings, including six complete ball games, Pirate pitchers did not allow a run. This streak was the keystone of a nine-game winning streak that sent the Pirates surging ahead of Chicago and New York. On June 3, the third-place Pirates whitewashed the second-place Giants, 7-0. Deacon Phillippe allowed eight hits over nine innings while walking one and fanning eight, highlighted by striking out the side in the fifth inning. Honus Wagner served as acting manager that day, a duty he frequently assumed during his career, as Fred Clarke was ill and ordered to stay away from the park by his physician. The Pirates held a 1-0 lead until the fifth, when the Buccos, inspired by Phillippe's pitching in the Giants' half of the inning, rallied for five runs to seal the win. Giant catcher Frank Bowerman, must not have enjoyed the spectacle of Corsairs crossing home plate before him as he argued with umpire Jim

Johnstone, and was ejected from the game. It was the second time that Bowerman was tossed by rookie Johnstone that year. Honus Wagner was the batting star of the game: 3 for 5 and a run scored. However, catcher Eddie Phelps was noted by the Pittsburgh *Press* for his fine play as he tallied a brace of singles and called a fine game behind the dish.

June 4 saw the Pirates blank the Giants, 5-0, behind the pitching of Sam Leever. The "Goshen Schoolmaster" showed "old time form" during the game in what may have been a veiled reference to the sore arm he developed during the season and which would keep him out of the World Series.

For the second day, only one Giant reached third base as manager Fred Clarke returned to the bench but not to the field. Claude Ritchey tallied four hits in four tries off Iron Man Joe McGinnity, who pitched poorly but was saved by some fine defensive play by the Giants. The highlights of the game were Ginger Beaumont's long home run to deep centerfield in the fifth inning and the successful double steal by Ritchey and Otto Krueger, subbing for Clarke in leftfield, which resulted in Ritchey's steal of home for the first Pirate tally.

Christy Mathewson was tossed from this game in the fifth inning by umpire Johnstone, and the *Press* admonished Matty to be more discreet, as his "kicking" was clearly distinguished from the other Giants because his voice was "like that of a girl."

On June 5, the Beaneaters from Boston came to town. Mired in sixth place, their final resting place in

Joe Elinich is a member of SABR's Forbes Field Chapter. He charts games for the Baseball Workshop at Three Rivers Stadium and works for the federal government. He has been married for twenty years and has a daughter.

the standings, the Beaneaters had the worst offense in the league and proved to be easy pickings for Pirate pitchers.

Irving "Kaiser" Wilhelm, a 29-year-old rookie, allowed only five hits while walking none as he allowed only one runner to reach third base, and led the Pirates to a 5-0 victory. This would be the only shutout on Wilhelm's 5-3 record, which in turn would be the only winning season he posted in his nine-year, 56-105, major league career.

Manager Fred Clarke returned to the lineup and made two hits in four tries while scoring a run. Honus Wagner and Ed Phelps were again cited by the *Press's* reporter (probably Ralph S. Davis) for their defensive play.

On June 6, the Pirates smashed Togie Pittinger and the Beaneaters for 17 hits and an easy 9-0 victory behind the solid pitching of Ed Doheny. Doheny allowed seven hits and walked one. Pirate misplays allowed two men to reach third, but Doheny worked his way out of trouble.

Fred Clarke was outstanding, with a diving catch in left field and a perfect five-for-five day at the plate. Ginger Beaumont posted four hits in five tries including his second homer of the week (he would hit seven that season). Rightfielder Jimmy Sebring and first baseman Kitty Bransfield teamed up for a double play. On the down side, Claude Ritchey, who made a pair of errors and was caught off base during the game, struck out for the third time that season in an era when strikeouts were not kept as an official stat for hitters. It was apparent that someone was keeping track, at least on the local level.

This fourth victory broke the major league record for consecutive shutouts. The Pirates extended their mark with another Phillippe whitewash on June 7, 4-0. This was a 5-1/2 inning rain-shortened game as it began to drizzle almost from the start. Umpire Hank O'Day kept the troops going and even scolded Boston first baseman Fred Tenney who tried the ritualistic delaying tactics in the top of the fifth as the rain's intensity increased. The game ended on a Honus Wagner triple to open the bottom of the sixth (it stands in the record book according to the rules of the day).

While the Deacon was not at his best, allowing seven hits in the six innings he pitched, the Beaneaters were the ones who had the greater difficulty with the elements as they made three errors in the five innings they played, allowing the Bucs to score their four runs on only four hits.

The Phillies followed the rain to town on June 8.

The inclement weather continued as the teams were not able to play until June 9. Sam Leever pitched his second shutout of the streak. (He would lead the league with seven.) The Pirates won, 2-0, as the Quakers' Tully Sparks hurled a fine game in his own right.

Honus Wagner was the star of the game, with two hits in three tries. He scored a run, stole a base, and had a sacrifice hit, all while batting cleanup. However, he saved his best for last, literally, as the Phillies posted runners on second and third in the ninth inning with two out, threatening to tie the score. Bill "Klondike" Douglass was sent to pinch hit for Sparks with runners in scoring position. He "landed on one of Leever's slants" and ripped a liner toward left which Wagner speared with a leaping catch to end the game.

The Pirate's record now stood at 53 scoreless innings, as they had ended the game previous to the streak with a pair of scoreless innings. They had also now shut the opposition out for six straight games and articles were being written in the Pittsburgh papers demanding the authorities undertake a search for home plate at Exposition Park.

Kaiser Wilhelm took the mound for the Pirates on June 10 against the Phils and he held the Quakers scoreless for the first three innings to raise the Bucco mark to 56 innings, while the Pirates built a 6-0 lead off Phillie hurler "Frosty Bill" Duggleby. In the fourth, the streak ended. Wilhelm walked Roy Thomas, one of six passes he issued that day, and the Phillies leadoff hitter was advanced around to score on an out. The Pirates would build the lead to 7-3 as they entered the bottom of the ninth. Wilhelm loaded the bases with one out, but a fine running catch of a foul fly by third baseman Tommy Leach relieved the pressure and the Kaiser rallied to finish the game. Clarke, Sebring, Wagner, and Leach each had two hits.

Although the scoreless streak had ended, the Pirates were far from finished. On June 11, they hosted the Brooklyn Superbas and Deacon Phillippe posted his third successive shutout in an impressive 9-0 win. Phillippe was the master hurler during this streak, posting three of his four shutouts for the season. The Deacon allowed but three hits, one a scratch single, while walking only one and whiffing seven. Catcher Ed Phelps was noted for the fine game he called and was a perfect three for three at the plate while scoring a run and stealing a base.

Phelps was repeatedly singled out for his fine play during this streak and throughout the season. Eddie was in his second year with the Pirates and would post his second best career batting mark (.282) while playing 81 games. While former Pirate catcher and now Phillie manager, Chief Zimmer, would call him the "best catcher in the league" and a "coming star," he would play only 633 games in eleven big league seasons and finish with a career batting mark of .251.

The Pirates led the league with sixteen shutouts in 1903 and finished with the second best ERA (2.91) to Chicago (2.77).

As has been a Pirate trademark down to the present day, this early dynasty had a formidable offense. It led all major league teams with 793 runs scored. It was second in batting to Cincinnati (.288) with a .286 mark and led the league in slugging percentage (.393), triples (110) and home runs (34). Despite all this firepower, it was the depleted Pirates pitching staff that posted a mark that the *Press* claimed would stand for all time. And it has.

Sunday Best

In 1898, Utica, New York, returned to the ranks of professional baseball, and in doing so became the only team in the New York State League to play home games on Sundays. This home field advantage on Sunday paid great dividends. Utica compiled an 11-4 record in its games on the Sabbath. Perhaps the 30,400 fans Utica drew to the fifteen Sunday games—nearly the same total it drew to the remaining forty-five home games.—gave the team incentive. The chief beneficiary was pitcher "Wild Bill" Settley, who had a 4-1 Sunday record.

In 1899, Rome joined its neighbor in the NYSL, and became the second team to host Sunday ball. In June, several Rome players were arrested for playing on Sunday, but all were acquitted. A month later, a group in Utica began pushing for the elimination of Sunday ballplaying. This lead to the arrest of manager Howard Earl and his players by Sheriff Reese on July 30. A week later, the jury deliberated for fifteen minutes before returning with a "not guilty" verdict, based on the fact that the game was played on private, not public, grounds.

Utica fans would not have supported a ban on Sunday games, because once again the team was very successful, compiling an 11-2 record and drawing 20,500 on the Sabbath. Pitchers John Malarkey (21-37 in six major league seasons) and Utican Wee Willie Mills (21-14 for Utica in 1899) both posted 3-0 Sunday records.

In 1900, Utica won the NYSL championship, and its Sunday play once again contributed. The team went 13-3 and drew 27,000 fans, again nearly half the total season's attendance. Willie Mills (26-12) lead Utica with a 4-1 Sunday record. Ironically, Johnny Dobbs, Utica's best player and the league's leading hitter at .366, hit only .246 on Sundays.

Utica's Sunday dominance reached its peak in 1901, when the team went 14-2 (.875) and drew nearly 20,000 fans to its Sunday games. George Merritt (23-8) pitched most of the Sunday games, posting an extraordinary 11-0 record with four shutouts, allowing only two earned runs in the eleven games.

In its first four seasons in the NYSL, Utica went 49-11 (.817) on Sundays, and 209-166 (.557) the rest of the week. At a time when a crowd of 500 was considered good for a weekday game, Utica averaged over 1,600 fans on Sundays. Perhaps driven by Utica's on success on Sundays, most NYSL teams began playing on the Sabbath in 1902.

—Scott Fiesthumel

Manager for a Day

A complete record and some interesting stories

Steven G. LoBello

Accounts of the brief major league careers of "one-game wonders" have made for interesting historical reading.[1] Similarly, twenty-eight men have served as manager for a single game in a season. The table that accompanies this paper provides information about single-game managers from 1876 to 1989. Many of these men only managed one game in their entire baseball careers. Often, they were coaches who served as interim managers when the skipper was fired. Others were one-game managers as part of a longer career as a manager. Often, the single-game managers were bit players who are barely remembered. In several cases, however, an interesting story surrounds these brief stays in the major league spotlight.

Eddie Stanky is remembered for his single game appearance as manager of the Texas Rangers in 1977.[2] Stanky took over the fourth-place Rangers from Frank Lucchesi, who had apparently lost the respect of his players after he got into a fist fight with second baseman Lenny Randle.[3] The day after his team defeated the Twins, Stanky resigned as manager because he was "lonesome and homesick."[4] His professional managerial career came to a bizarre end that saw four different men hold the Texas job one week.[5]

Eddie Sawyer, manager of the Philadelphia Phillies, made an abrupt departure after the first game of the 1960 season. After the Phillies lost their opening game, 9-4, to the Reds, Sawyer announced his resig-

nation. The reason he gave for quitting was that he "just didn't want to manage."[6] Coach Andy Cohen managed the Phillies to a win in the second game of the day. Sawyer holds the record for quitting or being fired at the earliest point in a season.[7] His replacement was Gene Mauch, then skipper of the American Association team in Minneapolis.

When Mauch was fired in 1968, coach George Myatt managed the Phillies for one game. However, it was not Mauch's dismissal that gave Myatt his opportunity. Mauch was on hand to manage the first game of a home doubleheader against the Dodgers, but had to leave for Los Angeles to be with his wife, who was to undergo surgery.[8] Myatt took charge of the team for the second game. While in Los Angeles with his wife, Mauch received a phone call from management informing him of his dismissal.[9] Mauch was replaced by Bob Skinner, who became a one-game manager himself in 1977, when he piloted the San Diego Padres between the tenures of John McNamara and Alvin Dark.

McKechnie, Southworth, and Street—After the St. Louis Cardinals lost the 1928 World Series to the New York Yankees, Cardinals manager Bill McKechnie was demoted to manager of Rochester in the International League.[10] His replacement in St. Louis was Billy Southworth, then manager of the same Rochester team, which had won the IL pennant in 1928.[11]

After management broke up the team in the off-

Steven G. LoBello is an associate professor of psychology at Auburn University at Montgomery.

season, Southworth's 1929 Cardinals were no better than a .500 ball club. In July, with the team at 43-45, Southworth was sent back to Rochester to replace McKechnie, who was then brought back to take over the Cardinals.[12] During this second job switch between McKechnie and Southworth, the Cardinals faced the Philadelphia Phillies with coach Gabby Street acting as manager. The Cardinals, apparently happy about McKechnie's return, beat the Phillies, 8-2, with Grover Cleveland Alexander going the distance on the mound.[13]

With McKechnie in charge, the Cardinals fared only slightly better than they had with Southworth. The team finished with a 78-74 record for a fourth-place standing for the season.[14] Soon after returning to manage the Cardinals, McKechnie spoke to reporters at Forbes Field in Pittsburgh and announced that he would forsake baseball to run for tax collector in Wilkinsburg, Pennsylvania, his home town. Whether he was serious about the race is not known, but McKechnie wanted to repay management for his demotion by holding off on signing a contract.[15]

After the season McKechnie signed a four-year contract to manage the Boston Braves, refusing a one-year deal offered by the Cardinals.[16] He managed the Cincinnati Reds to a World Series title in 1940, and was inducted into the Hall of Fame in 1962. Gabby Street replaced McKechnie as manager of the Cardinals in 1930.[17] Street managed St. Louis through part of the 1933 season, winning the pennant in 1930 and the World Series in 1931. Billy Southworth returned to manage the Cardinals in 1940 and took them to the World Series during the war years of 1942, 1943, and 1944. His teams won the '42 and '44 series, and he later managed the Boston Braves in the '48 series, which the team lost.

O'Farrell and Shotten—In 1934 the Cincinnati Reds had been in the lower division for many seasons and general manager Larry MacPhail was hoping that a managerial change would improve prospects. Rumors were swirling that former Philadelphia manager Burt Shotten would be coming to take over the Reds.[18] However, MacPhail hired Bob O'Farrell, catcher for the St. Louis Cardinals, who had managed that team to within a half-game of the 1927 National League pennant.[19] As manager of the Reds, O'Farrell was the fourth member of the 1933 Cardinals to manage a major league team during the 1934 season.[20] O'Farrell picked Shotton to be a coach about ten days after signing with the Reds.[21] But O'Farrell could not pull the Reds out of the cellar and his brief tenure was punctuated by reports that he was about to be fired.[22]

O'Farrell was fired in July and replaced by Chuck Dressen, then managing the Southern Association team in Nashville.[23] Dressen could not make the next game against the Chicago and coach Burt Shotton was again, briefly, the manager of a major league team, leading the Reds to an 11-2 rout of the Cubs.[24]

Dressen also could not bring the Reds into contention and he was dismissed near the end of the 1937 season. For both Dressen and Shotton, their Cincinnati service was a prelude to better days. Each man later managed the Brooklyn Dodgers, and each took the team to the World Series twice (all losses) during the 1940s and 1950s. Bob O'Farrell briefly returned as an active player, but never managed again in the major leagues.

Dykes and Gordon—In 1960, Jimmy Dykes of Detroit and Joe Gordon of Cleveland swapped jobs in an unprecedented trade of managers. What began as a joke between the general managers turned into reality when both teams were slumping.[25] As the two men left for their new teams, Detroit's regularly scheduled game was managed by Billy Hitchcock, while Cleveland's game was managed by Jo-Jo White. Both interim managers guided their teams to wins. White never managed again, but Hitchcock went on to manage Baltimore and Atlanta in the 1960's. Dykes was fired before the last game of the 1961 season, which created an opportunity for Mel Harder to manage a single game. Gordon was dismissed after the 1960 season, but later managed in Kansas City.

The twenty-eight men listed in the table had a combined record of 18-10 in their single-game opportunities, for a respectable .643 win percentage. Many factors could account for this high mark. Any change at the top may lead a team to play better for a brief time. Or games against weak opponents may be responsible for the quality of play under the one-game managers, a hypothesis that would not be difficult to investigate. More likely, it is a statistical artifact of a small sample. One fact is certain: we can draw no conclusions about the managerial acumen of fourteen of these men because they only managed this single major league game in their careers. The other half of this group had opportunities beyond the one-game appearances. The combined career won-lost records of these men was 3,159-3,132, for a .502 win percentage. While this seems a mediocre mark, keep in mind that the group includes five World Series managers: Howser, Kuenn, Shotton, Sawyer, and Street. But it also includes Chris Van Der Ahe, who could only manage three wins against fourteen losses, and others with career losing records, such as Bob Skinner (93-123) and Cal Ripken, Sr. (68-101).

Considering that baseball has such a long history, and that managers come and go with regularity, it is surprising that there are so few men who only managed a single game. There are several topics about managers of brief tenure that could be explored. For instance, who was Bickerson, manager of one game for Washington in 1884, and whatever became of him after his single-game appearance?

Notes:

1. Leon Uzarowski, "A Short Cup of Coffee," in L. Robert Davids, ed., *Insider's Baseball* (New York: Charles Scribner's Sons), pp. 257-260.

2. New York *Times*, June 24, 1977, p. A17, p. A20.

3. New York *Times*, March 29, 1977, p. 21, p. 23.

4. New York *Times*, June 24, 1977, p. A17.

5. New York *Times*, June 28, 1977, p. 25.

The four managers were Lucchesi, Stanky, Connie Ryan as interim manager, and Billy Hunter as Stanky's permanent replacement.

6. New York *Times*, April 15, 1960, p.16.

7. Ibid.

8. New York *Times*, June 15, 1968, p. 42.

9. New York *Times*, June 16, 1968, Sec. V, p.1, p. 2.

10. New York *Times*, November 22, 1928, p. 32.

11. Ibid.

12. New York *Times*, July 24, 1929, p. 18.

13. Ibid.

14. *The Baseball Encyclopedia, 8th Edition*, p. 256.

15. New York *Times*, August 8, 1929.

16. New York *Times*, October 8, 1929, p. 25.

17. New York *Times*, October 31, 1929, p. 23.

18. New York *Times*, January 3, 1934, p. 25.

19. New York *Times*, January 6, 1934, p. 21.

20. The others were Frankie Frisch (St. Louis - NL), Rogers Hornsby (St. Louis - AL), and Jimmie Wilson (Philadelphia - NL).

21. New York *Times*, January 23, 1934, p. 23.

22. New York *Times*, May 16, 1934, p. 25.

23. New York *Times*, July 28, 1934, p. 9.

24. New York *Times*, July 29, 1934, Sec. III, p. 6.

25. New York *Times*, August 4, 1960, p. 18

One-Game Managers

Date	Team	Manager	Replaced	Date	Team	Manager	Replaced
1879	Syracuse (N)	Bill Holbert	Mike Dorgan	8/26/72	Houston (N)	Salty Parker**	Harry Walker
1884	Washington (AA)	Bickerson	Holly Hollingshead	9/30/73	Boston (A)	Eddie Popowski**	Eddie Kasko
1895	St. Louis (N)	Chris Von Der Ahe*	Al Buckenberger	9/7/73	Texas (A)	Del Wilber	Whitey Herzog
7/28/29	St. Louis (N)	Gabby Street*	Billy Southworth	9/28/75	Milwaukee (A)	Harvey Kuenn**	Del Crandall
6/10/33	Cleveland (A)	Bibb Falk	Roger Peckinpaugh	5/22/77	San Diego (N)	Bob Skinner**	John McNamara
7/28/34	Cincinnati (N)	Burt Shotton#	Bob O'Farrell	5/11/77	Atlanta (N)	Ted Turner	Dave Bristol
5/3/44	Chicago (N)	Roy Johnson	Jimmie Wilson	5/12/77	Atlanta (N)	Vern Benson	Ted Turner
7/15/48	Brooklyn (N)	Ray Blades	Leo Durocher	6/23/77	Texas (A)	Eddie Stanky**	Frank Lucchesi
7/2/59	Boston (A)	Rudy York	Pinky Higgins	7/24/78	New York (A)	Dick Howser*	Billy Martin
4/14/60	Philadelphia (N)	Eddie Sawyer*	—	6/8/80	St. Louis (N)	Jack Kroll**	Ken Boyer
4/14/60	Philadelphia (N)	Andy Cohen	Eddie Sawyer	7/13/85	Baltimore (A)	Cal Ripken, Sr.*	Joe Altobelli
8/3/60	Detroit (A)	Billy Hitchcock*	Jimmy Dykes	5/8/86	Seattle (A)	Orlando Martinez	Chuck Cottier
8/3/60	Cleveland (A)	Jo-Jo White	Joe Gordon				
10/1/61	Cleveland (A)	Mel Harder	Jimmy Dykes		* had a later managing stint		
5/22/63	Washington (A)	Eddie Yost	Mickey Vernon		** had an earlier managing stint		
6/15/68	Philadelphia (N)	George Myatt*	Gene Mauch		# had prior and subsequent managing experience		

Knowing When to Hang 'Em Up

Career-ending World Series winners

John Sasman

The aging superstar announces his retirement, collects his 3,000th hit, completes his farewell tour around the league, and guides his team to its first world championship in twenty years.

That's the way it's supposed to happen.

The reality is that few players have ever ended their major league careers playing on a World Series winner. Of those that did, few were regulars, let alone stars. Even fewer contributed in any significant degree to their teams during the season or in the Series.

Including 1993 world champions Alfredo Griffin and Willie Canate (who is still playing in AAA, and at 24 has an excellent chance of returning to the majors), forty-two position players and fourteen pitchers made their final major league appearance as members of a winning World Series team. Included in this group are three Hall of Famers: Joe DiMaggio, Eddie Mathews, and Johnny Mize. Also included are such lesser lights as Billy Bates, Creepy Crespi, and Karl Spooner.

The Careers—First, let's examine the careers of these players. Of the forty-two position players, only twenty-one spent at least five years in the majors. Only twelve of these logged five years as regulars (400 plate appearances or 100 games). Likewise, only seven of the fourteen pitchers spent at least five years in the majors. In fact, most of the players who ended their careers on World Series winners were marginal play-

ers who were lucky to make a major league roster.

There were exceptions, however. Along with the three Hall of Famers, several members of this elite group had distinguished careers. Sherry Magee played sixteen seasons and led the National League four times in RBIs in the dead ball era before hanging it up with the Reds in 1919. Roy Smalley Jr. lasted thirteen seasons, several as a top-notch shortstop before bowing out with the 1987 Twins. Wally Moon hit .289 over a twelve-year career that ended in 1965 with the world champion Dodgers. Spud Chandler won the 1943 American League MVP and finished with a 109-43 career mark in eleven seasons. Joe Horlen posted a league-leading 2.06 ERA in 1967 and won in double figures seven of twelve years. Don Mincher, Dick Green, Ron Oester, John Wathan, Paul Lindblad, and George Frazier also had decent careers.

The Final Seasons—Few of the players that ended their careers as World Series winners had remarkable careers. Fewer distinguished themselves in their final season. Only nine of the nonpitchers registered more than 300 plate appearances. (Only three had more than 400.) Only one pitcher, Jim Tobin, won more than nine games.

The best final season clearly belongs to Joe DiMaggio. He hit only .263, with 12 homers, but still drove in 71 runs in only 415 at bats. All the other members of this group combined for 48 homers. Roy Smalley accounted for eight of those, and managed a .275 batting average as a designated hitter in 1987.

John Sasman lives in Fort Collins, Colorado. He is most interested in exposing the myths created by bandboxes such as Coors Field.

1945 at 13-19. Spud Chandler (9-5 with a 2.46 ERA at the age of 40 in 1947), and Russ Christopher (17 saves and a 2.90 ERA for the '48 Indians) had the only other final seasons of note.

The Final Series—Coming into the World Series, few of these players were poised for a final, dramatic swan song. As a whole, they hit .213 in the Series with one homer and a .277 slugging average in 157 at bats. Only three players had more than two hits in the Series. The pitchers posted a 6.39 ERA and walked 20 batters in 31 innings. Bill Bevens, of course, pitched magnificently in 1947, but nobody else managed more than four innings.

No player ended his career in true storybook fashion. No pitcher who pitched more than four years and appeared in at least thirty games or fifty innings in his final season pitched in more than one game or for more than three innings in the Series. Only one position player who played at least five years and amassed 300 plate appearances in his final season collected more than one hit in the Series. In 1951, Joe D went 6 for 23, with a home run, two doubles, and five RBI. His final performance stands alone.

Bill Bevins in the 1947 World Series.

Two other players whose fortunes were dramatically affected by World War II had at least solid final campaigns. Johnny Sturm spent his only major league season as the Yankees regular first baseman in 1941 before heading off for the war. He hit .239 and scored 58 runs. Bob Maier also only spent one year in the majors. He was Detroit's regular third baseman in 1945 and managed a .263 average. He was one of eight Tigers, however, who played in the 1945 Series, but never again once the veterans returned home.

Jim Tobin was one of those teammates. He finished

The Managers—While there have been relatively few players who ended their careers as world champions, there have been no managers smart enough to retire as champs. In fact, no manager has ever retired (or been forced into retirement) after winning a division title. The closest anyone has come is second place. Danny Murtaugh can claim the most successful final season as a manager with his 92-70 record for the 1976 Pirates. (Casey Stengel went on to the Mets after the Yankees canned him when New York lost the 1960 Series to Pittsburgh in seven games.)

Players who played their final games as World Series winners

Position Players	Year	Team
Jack O'Brien	1903	Boston A
Babe Towne	1906	Chicago A
Bill O'Neill	1906	Chicago A
Josh Devore	1914	Boston N
Bill Carrigan	1916	Boston A
George Whiteman	1918	Boston A
Sherry Magee	1919	Cincinnati
Harry Lunte	1920	Cleveland
Lee King	1922	New York N
Hinkey Haines	1923	NewYork A
Tommy Taylor	1924	Washington
Ralph Miller	1924	Washington
Walter French	1929	Philadelphia A
Pat Crawford	1934	St. Louis N
Johnny Sturm	1941	New York A
Creepy Crespi	1942	St. Louis N
Red Borom	1945	Detroit
Bob Maier	1945	Detroit
Hub Walker	1945	Detroit
Chuck Hostetler	1945	Detroit
Joe Hoover	1945	Detroit

Position Players	Year	Team
Joe DiMaggio	1951	New York A
Johnny Mize	1953	New York A
George Shuba	1955	Brooklyn N
George Wilson	1956	New York A
Nippy Jones	1957	Milwaukee N
Wally Moon	1965	Los Angeles N

	Year	Team
Don LeJohn	1965	Los Angeles N
Eddie Bressoud	1967	St. Louis N
Eddie Mathews	1968	Detroit
Ed Charles	1969	New York N
Don Mincher	1972	Oakland
Mike Andrews	1973	Oakland
Billy Conigliaro	1973	Oakland
Dick Green	1974	Oakland
John Wathan	1985	Kansas City
Roy Smalley	1987	Minnesota
Ron Oester	1990	Cincinnati
Billy Bates	1990	Cincinnati
Pat Tabler	1992	Toronto
Alfredo Griffin	1993	Toronto
Willie Canate	1993	Toronto

Pitchers	Year	Team
Joe Martina	1924	Washington
Jim Mooney	1934	St. Louis N
Jim Tobin	1945	Detroit
Les Mueller	1945	Detroit
Zeb Eaton	1945	Detroit
Spud Chandler	1947	New York A
Bill Bevens	1947	New York A

Pitchers	Year	Team
Russ Christopher	1948	Cleveland
Karl Spooner	1955	Brooklyn N
Chuck Churn	1959	Los Angeles N
Hal Woodeshick	1967	St. Louis N
Joe Horlen	1972	Oakland
Paul Lindblad	1978	New York A
George Frazier	1987	Minnesota

Hooks Dauss's 1911 Season

Coming into his own with Winona of the Minnesota-Wisconsin League

Terry Bohn

Hooks Dauss

In 1911, while pitching for the Winona (MN) Pirates, Hooks Dauss compiled a 21-11 season that never made the record books.

What you can find in *Daguerreotypes* is that he pitched for the Duluth White Sox of the Minnesota-Wisconsin—the Minny—League in 1909 and 1910, and had a 1-1 record in three games for the St. Paul Saints in 1911.

The mystery is easily solved. Duluth's official scorer, irked that he was not paid, refused to send the team's stats to the league office at season's end. Therefore, the league could compile no complete records for publication. Dauss's 21-11, and the statistics of every player in the league, fell into baseball's black hole.

Following is a brief summary of Dauss's minor league career in Minnesota with emphasis on his previously unknown season in Winona.

Duluth manager Al Kuehnow, who was a native of Cleveland, annually gathered his team in that city for training. In the spring of 1909, the White Sox played a series of exhibition games in the Indiana and Ohio area, and in early April played the South Bend team of the Central League. George Dauss pitched for South Bend that day and defeated Duluth, 5-3. Impressed and needing pitching help, Kuehnow purchased Dauss from South Bend. He returned to Minnesota with his new team for the Minny League season. Dauss had a record of 19-10 in 33 games with

the pennant-winning White Sox and established himself as one of the league's brightest young pitching prospects.

While pitching for Duluth in 1910, Dauss's season ended prematurely due to illness. His record stood at 7-7 after a 6-5 loss to Rochester on Independence Day, his last appearance of the season. The Duluth *News-Tribune* reported on July 12 that Dauss was sick in bed, and three days later that he was in the hospital. However, it was implied that the mysterious medical problem was not too severe because it was reported on both July 18 and 26 that he "should be ready soon." Nothing was added concerning Dauss's

Terry Bohn *works in systems development with the North Dakota Department of Human Services.*

condition until a September 10 article that said he "...is getting back into shape and will be ready to play ball next spring."

The Winona *Republican-Herald*, in an article on March 11, 1911, reported that Dauss "was forced to undergo an operation a short time ago." Nonetheless, the Duluth club received an offer from Mike Kelley, manager of the St. Paul Saints, for the use of Dauss for the 1911 season. He became the property of St. Paul, but Duluth had the option of using him for the season provided he was returned to the Saints after the Minny League schedule. Duluth was apparently not sure if Dauss was going to be able to play effectively and the team decided not to offer him a spot on their roster.

Dauss went to spring training with the Saints in Excelsior Springs, Missouri. After only a few days, on March 29, Dauss's services were sold to Winona for $100, although he technically remained the property of St. Paul. The *Republican-Herald* reported Dauss "nearly made good with the Saints and may be re-called by Kelley before the season is over if needed." After his first practice with his new club on April 22, Winona officials were "convinced that he is in perfect condition and has...lost none of his former ability." The next day Dauss pitched five strong innings in his first exhibition start.

Dauss had a banner year in 1911 with his new team and showed no lingering effects from his illness. He got off to a good start when he pitched 5.2 innings of no-hit ball in relief in his team's opener against Eau Claire on May 9. He was placed in the starting rotation and won his next three starts with complete games, including back-to-back shutouts against Superior and Wausau on May 18 and 24. After a no-decision, Dauss won three more starts in a row. After a 4-2 win over his former Duluth teammates on June 8, his record stood at a perfect 7-0.

The Winona ace continued his winning ways during the month of June. He did not pitch as brilliantly as in the first month of the season, but the Winona batters supplied him with 39 runs in his seven June starts. He went 5-2 during the month to run his record to 12-2 and was soon regarded as the dominant pitcher in the circuit.

In the early part of the season, Dauss's batting skill contributed to several of his victories. In the 1-0 victory over Wausau on May 24, his RBI double supplied the game's only run. He homered in a 9-2 win over Rochester on May 31, and again in the bottom of the ninth inning for a 7-6 Winona win on June 15, also over Rochester. On June 26 he homered and tripled

in a 16-7 route of Red Wing, and rapped two more hits in a relief win on June 29. By the end of June, he was 21 for 51 (.412).

Dauss continued his pitching dominance in July. He lost his first decision of the month to LaCrosse on July 3, but then won his next six decisions to run his record to a remarkable 18-3. Dauss gave up just ten runs in those six decisions and struck out 59 batters, including 12 in three consecutive games. This streak also began a series of nine straight complete games.

Dauss then tailed off and lost eight of his last eleven decisions, although he continued to pitch well. He gave up more than three runs just once and in his eight losses his teammates scored more than one run just twice. For example, in a 3-1 loss to Duluth on August 11, Dauss struck out 15 and walked no one.

Despite the drop off in his record, Dauss was attracting major league attention. R. J. Gilkes, a Cleveland scout who is credited with signing Joe Jackson, said, "That man Dauss of your Winona club is a good man. I saw him work but Pittsburgh had already gotten to him. That little fellow has the requirements of a good moundsman, and if I'm not mistaken, he will make a valuable man in time for the Pirates." Dauss was, in fact, purchased by Pittsburgh, but was immediately released back to St. Paul. He joined the Saints for the balance of the 1911 season and had a 1-1 record in three games.

The Winona Pirates, under manager Joe Killian, led the league from opening day until mid-August when their offense slumped and they were overtaken by Superior. They ended the season in second place, 5.5 games behind Superior. Based on box scores printed in the Winona *Republican-Herald*, Dauss pitched in 35 games in 1911, 29 of them starts. He also appeared in ten other games as an outfielder and pinch-hitter. According to modern rules in determining won-lost records, Dauss finished with a mark of 21-11. He gave up just 193 hits in 266.2 innings pitched and struck out 254 while walking only 84. Earned runs were not recorded at that time but the most accurate estimate is that he was charged with 79 runs for an ERA of 2.67.

During this previously unknown season, Dauss proved he had recovered from his physical problems and gained the experience necessary to pitch at a more competitive level. He was clearly the best pitcher in the league and the 1911 campaign in Winona served as a springboard to the American Association and a stellar major league career in which he won 222 games.

Twenty-Year Men

An elite group

Warren N. Wilbert

Well into a second century of play, baseball at the major league level sports a listing of more than 14,000 players. Some have played in only a game or two, pitched in one inning, or had but a single at bat, like Bob Lipski of the Cleveland Indians, who appeared in two 1963 games and, unfortunately, whiffed in his only time up there; or George Lowe of the 1920 Cincinnati Reds, who pitched two innings in a single game. These and others who made it to the bigs for that proverbial cup of coffee far outnumber the players whose careers stretched to ten, fifteen, or twenty years. While the Lipskis and Lowes would make an interesting study, our focus here is on the twenty-year men, an elite group of worthies that includes both superstars and lesser lights.

To put the twenty-year men into perspective, keep in mind that the average major league career lasts three to five seasons. Out of 14,166 player entries in the 1995 edition of *Total Baseball*, 104 logged twenty or more seasons. That amounts to about seven players out of every 1,000, a minuscule .0073 percent. Working upward toward the twenty-year plateau, we find a gradually diminishing number of players. The list, with five examples from each year bracket beginning with the fifteen year mark, looks like this:

Years	No. of Players	Representative Names
15	187	Madlock, Carty, Geronimo, Hiller, Stieb
16	123	Shantz, Tekulve, Marichal, Oberkfell, Rojas
17	116	Moses, Bresnahan, Medwick, Root, Bunning
18	88	Marquard, McMahon, Burgess, Hodges, Schalk
19	58	Wheat, Monday, Jenkins, Koosman, Grimes
20	32	Rice, Downing, Yount, Alexander, Seaver
21-24	66	Gossage, Quinn, Sutton, Dahlen, Rose
25-27	7	Hough, Kaat, Ryan, John, Collins (Eddie), Wallace, and McGuire.

Almost half of the twenty-year men (forty-six of the 104 listed) are Hall of Famers. Thirty-two are position players and fourteen are pitchers. The Old Fox, Clark Griffith, a twenty-year pitcher-manager and longtime owner of the Senators, was elected to the Hall as an executive. Of the players, some of whom are destined soon to make the induction ceremonies at Cooperstown (George Brett, Nolan Ryan, and Robin Yount), twenty-two are pitchers and thirty-six are position players.

Yount and Brett might just be two of a dying breed who played out their careers with one ball club. Of the twenty-year men, the one-team list includes:

Position players:

Luke Appling	20 years, White Sox
George Brett	21 years, Royals
Fred Clarke	21 years, Louisville-Pittsburgh franchise
Al Kaline	22 years, Tigers
Stan Musial	22 years, Cardinals

Warren Wilbert, hopelessly faithful to his White Sox, gamely keeps alive his hope that someday, maybe in the next millenium, his boys will bring home a blue ribbon. Meanwhile, he keeps right on working on his next book on great individual seasons.

Mel Ott	22 years, Giants	
Brooks Robinson	23 years, Orioles	
Willie Stargell	21 years, Pirates	
Hans Wagner	21 years, Louisville-Pittsburgh franchise	
Carl Yastrzemski	23 years, Red Sox	
Robin Yount	20 years, Brewers	

Pitchers:

Urban "Red" Faber	20 years, White Sox
Mel Harder	20 year, Indians
Walter Johnson	21 years, Senators
Ted Lyons	20 years, White Sox

This distinguished group of fifteen has no fewer than thirteen Hall of Famers in its number. (Too bad there isn't a catcher in the bunch—what a ball club you could put together!)

Among ball players still in the game during 1995, two head the list from the standpoint of longevity. They are Andre Dawson and Dave Winfield. Dawson hit the twenty-year club in 1995, while Winfield rounded out campaign number twenty-two. The fol-

lowing list indicates the number of seasons completed through 1995. An asterisk (*) marks those most likely to hit the twenty-year mark.

	No. of Players	Representative Names
Completing 15th year in 1995:	8	Cal Ripken*, Brett Butler*, Fernando Valenzuela
Completing 16th year in 1995:	6	Jay Howell, Lee Smith, Jesse Orosco, Harold Baines
Completing 17th year in 1995:	2	Tim Raines, Rickey Henderson
Completing 18th year in 1995:	5	Paul Molitor*, Bob Welch, Ozzie Smith, S. Sanderson
Completing 19th year in 1995:	4	Eddie Murray*, Rick Honeycutt, A. Trammell*, Lou Whitaker

It's no easy deal, this twenty-year business. For fifty-eight players (sixty-two counting those who complete number nineteen in 1995) that one more time just wasn't in the cards. The men who made it are listed below, pitchers first.

Pitchers with Twenty or More Seasons in the Majors

B=First and last season, total seasons.

C=Number of seasons at least 30 innings pitched.

D=Number of teams played for, team most seasons.

E=HOF induction year.

F=Career innings pitched and career strikeouts.

G=Total Pitching Index.

Pitcher	B	C	D	E	F	G
Alexander, G	1911-30 (20)	18	3, CHI-NL (9)	1938	5190- 2198	64.9
Blyleven, B	1970-92 (22)	21	5, MN-AL (11)		4970-3701	30.9
Carlton, S	1965-88 (24)	22	6, PHL-NL (15)	1994	5217- 3136	33.2
Eckersley, D#	1975- (20)	20	4, OAK-AL (8)		3082- 2245	28.8
Faber, U	1914-33 (20)	20	1, CHI-AL (20)	1964	4086-1471	27
Gossage, R	1972-94 (22)	22	9, NY-AL (6)		1809-1502	30.2
Griffith, C	1891-14 (20)	14	7, CHI-NL (8)	1964	385-955	29.7
Harder, M	1928-47 (20)	19	1, CLV-AL (20)		3426-1160	20
Hough, C	1970-94 (25)	22	4, LA & TX (11)		3801-2362	15
Hoyt, W	1918-38 (21)	19	7, NY-AL (10)		3762-1206	14.4
John, T	1963-89 (26)	25	6, NY-AL (8)		4710-2245	25
Johnson, W	1907-27 (21)	21	1, WAS-AL (21)	1936	5914- 3509	90.5
Jones, S	1914-35 (22)	19	6, BOS-AL (6)		3883-1223	8.4
Kaat, J	1959-83 (25)	24	5, WAS/MN (15)		4530-2461	19
Leonard, D	1933-53 (20)	20	4, WAS-AL (15)		3218-1170	25.8
Luque, A	1914-35 (20)	17	4, CIN-NL (12)		3220-1130	26.3
Lyons, T	1923-46 (21)	20	1, CHI-AL (21)	1955	4161-1073	36.7
McDaniel, L	1955-75 (21)	20	5, STL-NL (8)		2139-1361	14.8
Newsom, B	1929-53 (20)	17	9, WAS-AL (7)		3759-2082	3.9
Niekro, J	1967-88 (22)	20	7, HOU-NL (11)		3584-1747	-5.4
Niekro, P	1964-87 (24)	23	4, MIL-AT (19)		5404-3342	35.4
Pennock, H	1912-34 (22)	22	3, NY-AL (11)	1948	3571- 1227	6.8
Perry, G	1962-83 (22)	22	8, SF-NL (10)	1991	5350-3534	34.4
Quinn, J	1909-33 (23)	22	8, NY-AL (7)		3920-1329	23.6
Reuss, J	1969-90 (22)	20	8, LA-NL (9)		3669-1907	2.1
Rixey, E	1912-33 (21)	21	2, CIN-NL (13)		4494-1350	25.9
Ruffing, R	1924-47 (22)	21	3, NY-AL (15)	1967	4344- 1987	26.9
Ryan, N	1966-93 (27)	26	4, HOU-NL (9)		5386-5714	20.8
Seaver, T	1967-86 (20)	20	5, NY-NL (12)	1992	4782- 3640	48.2
Simmons, C	1947-67 (20)	18	4, PHL-NL (13)		3348-1697	12.6
Spahn, W	1942-65 (21)	20	3, BOS/MIL (20)	1973	5243- 2583	47
Sutton, D	1966-88 (23)	23	5, LA-NL (16)		5282-3574	13.6
Tanana, F	1973-93 (21)	20	6, CAL&DET (8)		4188-2773	13.3
Wilhelm, H	1952-72 (21)	19	9, CHI-AL (6)	1985	2254- 1610	40
Wynn, E	1939-63 (23)	22	3, CLV-AL (9)	1972	4564-2334	16.6

#Eckersley's career statistics through 1994

Position Players with Twenty or More Seasons in the Majors.

B=First and last season, total seasons.

C=Number of seasons at least 40 at bats

D=Number of teams played for, team most seasons.

E=HOF induction year.

F=Career runs scored, career RBIs.

G=Total Player Rating (Thorn and Palmer Sabrmetric Rating).

Player	B	C	D	E	F	G
Aaron, H	1954-76 (23)	23	2,MIL/ATL(21)	1982	2174-2297	89.8
Anson, A	1871-94 (22)	22	3,CHI-NL(22)	1939	1719-1879	29.9
Appling, L	1930-50 (20)	19	1,CHI-AL (20)	1964	1319-1116	40.7
Beckley, J	1888-07 (20)	20	4,PIT-NL (9)	1971	1600- 1575	22.7
Brett, G	1973-93 (21)	21	1,KC-AL (21)		1583-1595	39
Buckner, W	1969-90 (22)	21	5, CHI-NL (8)		1077-1208	-2.2
Carey, M	1910-29 (20)	18	2,PIT-NL (16)	1961	1545-1040	23
Cavarretta, P	1934-55 (22)	19	2,CHI-NL (20)		990-920	5.6
Clarke, F	1894-15 (21)	18	1,LOU/PIT (21)	1945	1619- 1015	28.6
Cobb, T	1905-28 (24)	24	2,DET-AL (22)	1936	2246-1937	91.2
Collins, E	1906-30 (25)	20	2,PHL-AL (13)	1939	1821- 1300	69.7
Cooney, J	1921-44 (20)	13	3,BOS-NL (15)		408-209	- 10.1
Cramer, D	1929-48 (20)	18	4,PHL&DET (7)		1357-842	- 28.4
Cronin, J	1926-45 (20)	18	3,BOS-AL (11)	1956	1233- 1424	39.4
Cross, Lave	1887-07 (21)	21	9,PHL-NL (6)		1333-1345	14.5
Dahlen, W	1891-11 (21)	21	4,CHI-NL (8)		1589-1233	51.4
Davis, G	1890-09 (20)	19	3, NY-NL (10)		1539-1437	50
Davis, H	1895-17 (22)	15	6,PHL-AL (16)		1001-951	11
Dawson, A#	1976- (20)	20	4, MTL-NL (11)		1337-1540	31.1
Dempsey, R	1969-92 (24)	20	6,BLT-AL (12)		525-471	4.2
Downing, B	1973-92 (20)	20	3,CAL-AL (13)		1188-1073	18.6
Dykes, J	1918-39 (22)	21	2,PHL-AL (15)		1108-1071	9.3
Evans, Darrell	1969-89 (21)	20	3,ATL-NL (9)		1344- 1354	34.6
Evans, Dwight	1972-91 (20)	20	2,BOS-AL (19)		1470- 1384	30.4
Fairly, R	1958-78 (21)	20	6,LA-NL (12)		931-1044	- 0.6
Fisk, C	1969-93 (24)	23	2,CHI-AL (13)		1276-1330	24
Gleason, K	1888-12 (22)	20	6,PHL-NL (10)		1020-823	- 10.9
Grimm, C	1916-36 (20)	18	4,CHI-NL (12)		908-1078	-20.9
Hartnett, G	1922-41 (20)	19	2,CHI-NL (19)	1955	867- 1179	40.1
Hornsby, R	1915-37 (21)	21	5,STL-NL (13)	1942	1579- 1584	81.8
Jackson, R	1967-87 (21)	21	5,OAK-AL (9)	1993	1551- 1702	42.8
Johnstone, J	1966-85 (20)	17	8,CAL&PHL-NL(5)		578- 429	-8.4
Judge, J	1915-34 (20)	18	3,WAS-AL (17)		1184-1034	6.1
Kaline, A	1953-74 (22)	21	1,DET-AL(22)	1980	1622- 1583	44.6
Killebrew, H	1954-75 (22)	19	2,WAS/MN (21)	1984	1283- 1584	26.4
Lajoie, N	1896-16 (21)	21	3,CLV-AL (13)	1937	1504- 1599	94.3
Maranville, R	1912-35 (23)	21	5,BOS-NL (15)	1954	1255-844	13.1
Mays, W	1951-80 (22)	22	2,NY/SF-NL (20)	1979	2062- 1903	92.2
McCarver, T	1959-80 (21)	18	3,STL-NL (12)		590-645	6.2
McCovey, W	1959-80 (22)	22	3,SF-NL (18)	1986	1229- 1555	36.5
McGuire, D	1884-12 (26)	22	11,WAS-NL (8)		770-787	12.6
Morgan, J	1963-84 (22)	19	5,HOU-NL (10)	1990	1650- 1133	56.3
Mota, M	1962-83 (20)	16	4,LA-NL (13)		496-438	-8.4
Musial, S	1941-63 (22)	22	1,STL-NL (22)	1969	1949- 1951	70.5
Nettles, G	1967-88 (22)	21	6,NY-AL (11)		1193-1314	21.4
O'Connor, J	1887-10 (21)	20	7,CLV-NL (7)		713-671	- 9.3
O'Farrell, R	1915-35 (21)	17	4,CHI-NL (12)		517-549	6.1
Ott, M	1926-47 (22)	21	1,NY-NL (22)	1951	1859-1860	62.7
Perez, T	1964-86 (23)	22	4,CIN-NL (16)		1272-1652	9.9
Rice, S	1915-34 (20)	18	2,WAS-A (19)	1963	1514-1078	9.1
Robinson, B	1955-77 (23)	22	1,BAL-AL (23)	1983	1232- 1357	19.8
Robinson, F	1956-76 (21)	21	5,CIN-NL (10)	1982	1829- 1812	69
Rose, P	1963-86 (24)	24	3,CIN-NL (19)		2165-1314	20
Sewell, L	1921-42 (20)	16	4,CLV-AL (13)		653-696	- 9.4
Simmons, A	1924-44 (20)	18	7,PHL-AL (12)	1953	1507- 1827	25.6
Simmons, T	1968-88 (21)	19	2,STL-NL (13)		1074-1389	16.8
Speaker, T	1907-28 (22)	21	4,CLV-AL (11)	1936	1882- 1529	86.5
Stargell, W	1962-82 (21)	20	1,PIT-NL (21)	1988	1195- 1540	32.8
Staub, R	1963-85 (23)	23	6,NY-NL (9)		1189-1466	27.6
Valo, E	1940-61 (20)	18	8,PHL-AL (13)		768-601	6.5
Vernon, M	1939-60 (20)	18	5,WAS-AL (14)		1196-1311	3.7
Wagner, H	1897-17 (21)	21	1,LOU/PIT (21)	1936	1736-1732	81.3
Wallace, B	1894-18 (25)	21	3,STL-AL (15)	1953	1057- 1121	36.9
Waner, P	1926-45 (20)	19	4,PIT-NL (15)	1952	1627-1309	36.1
Winfield, D##	1973- (22)	22	6,NY-AL (9)		1658- 1829	39.7
Yastrzemski, C	1961-83 (23)	23	1,BOS-AL (23)	1989	1816-1844	45.5
Yount, R	1974-93 (20)	20	1,MIL-AL (20)		1632-1406	43.1

#Dawson's career statistics through 1994

##Winfield's career statistics through 1994

[1] All data and player statistics taken from Total Baseball, 1995 edition.

An Analysis of the First Round of Baseball's Amateur Draft

How have teams done?

David C. Thomas

How has the success or failure of first-round draft picks affected the postseason performance of major league teams? How do first-round draft choices compare, on average, with the rest of an organization's draft choices? This analysis will provide those answers as well as provide a compendium of other facts relating to the amateur draft's first-round draft choices from 1965 through the 1994 draft. (All statistics include player and team results through the 1994 season.)

With the onset of free agency in the mid-1970's came the partial dismantling of the "build from within" mode of operation of all major league baseball teams that involved the amateur draft and player trades. The draft, however, still remains an integral part of all baseball organizations and with the escalation of payrolls, teams are looking to their minor league affiliates for talented and affordable players that can get them to postseason play.

Much like the overall amateur draft analysis published in last year's *Baseball Research Journal*, I've compared statistical rankings of each team's 1965-1994 first-round players making it to the major leagues. I've then compared these rankings with the updated postseason performance of each team.

The analysis provides a balanced statistical weighting between career major league batting and pitching statistics that combines longevity (at bats and innings pitched) with performance (home runs, RBIs, batting

David Thomas is a product manager for AMP Incorporated in Greensboro, North Carolina.

average, wins, won-loss percentage, ERA). Each of the eight statistical categories (four batting and four pitching) are then ranked based on the number of teams. These eight categorical rankings are then added together, by team, to determine a final ranking point total. Last, this point total is ranked to determine each team's overall statistical performance.

Having determined the statistical rankings, we now want to analyze actual team postseason performances. Let's assume a team's post-season participation, based on a point system, is a more accurate measure of a team's performance than a cumulative won-loss record. Given that the draft began in 1965 and that it usually takes a few years for players to develop before advancing to the majors, we can conveniently track drafted players' performances from the beginning of divisional playoffs in 1969 through the 1994 season (or 1993, given the strike). By setting up a point system that awards one point for divisional champions, three points for league champions, and five points for World Series winners, we are able to calculate and rank a team's postseason performance that can then be compared with the previously determined statistical rankings.

The results in Table 1 indicates the Orioles, Blue Jays, Twins, and Pirates have fared poorly relative to the success of their first rounders in the majors, yet they have done well in postseason. Since the "all rounds" rankings of the Blue Jays and Orioles are less than exemplary, we could conclude that trades or, more likely, free agency led to their postseason success. Yet with the Twins and Pirates, their "all rounds" rankings are in the upper half of all teams, suggesting possibly good scouting, drafting, and development of organization players in the other rounds contributed more to their postseason success.

Conversely, let's look at the White Sox, Brewers, Red Sox, Angels, and Expos. Each of these teams has been in the upper half of first-round rankings with four of the five in the top six overall. Yet their post-season results are abysmal. Granted the White Sox have had outstanding drafts in the 1990s and without a strike in 1994 might have made it into, or even won, the World Series. But as things stand, they are still the "underperformer" leader of the first-round versus postseason comparison.

If we look for the teams that are the models of consistency we see the Mets, Reds, and Yankees have had relatively good drafts (first and all rounds) and good postseason results. Despite the fact that these statistical results are based on signed and unsigned draft picks, it is these three teams that positively stand out in the analysis.

The overall first-round percentage of players to make it to the majors is 57.6 percent, or 430 out of 746 players. Table 2 shows a breakdown of each team's percentage and rank. It should be noted these ranks were not used in Table 1 since the statistics of individual players, by team, making to the majors are better indicators of team performance. However, it is interesting to see how a team's overall percentage ranked with this overall team drafting average. Also included on Table 2 is the number of first-round choices that never made it out of Class A ball or never pro ball at all.

Table 1

	1st Rnd vs. Postseason			1st Rnd vs. All Rnds		
	1st Rnd Rnk	Post Season Rnk	1st vs Post Diff	1st Rnd Rnk	All Rnds Rnk	1st vs All Rnd Diff
Angels	6	19	-13	6	8	-2
Athletics	9	1	+8	9	15	-6
Blue Jays	26	8	+18	26	24	+2
Brewers	3	17	-14	3	22	-19
Indians	14	24	-10	14	21	-7
Mariners	18	24	-6	18	26	-8
Orioles	23	3	+20	23	14	+9
Rangers	17	24	-7	17	16	+1
Red Sox	2	15	-13	2	5	-3
Royals	15	12	+3	15	8	+7
Tigers	21	14	+7	21	17	+4
Twins	25	11	+14	25	11	+14
White Sox	3	20	-17	3	20	-17
Yankees	15	5	+10	15	8	+7
Astros	20	20	0	20	25	-5
Braves	12	14	-2	12	17	-5
Cardinals	5	12	-7	5	2	+3
Cubs	24	20	+4	24	13	+11
Dodgers	11	3	+8	11	1	+10
Expos	10	23	-13	10	12	-2
Giants	8	16	-8	8	7	+1
Mets	1	7	-6	1	4	-3
Padres	7	17	-10	7	23	-16
Phillies	19	9	+10	19	19	0
Pirates	22	9	+13	22	6	+16
Reds	13	2	+11	13	2	+11

Table 2

	#Choices	Class A only	Majors	Pct	Rank
Angels	31	2	24	.774	1
Athletics	31	2	19	.613	10
Blue Jays	19	3	9	.474	24
Brewers	25	2	16	.640	7
Indians	30	4	17	.567	15
Mariners	20	0	15	.750	2
Orioles	26	5	15	.577	13
Rangers	28	5	21	.750	2
Red Sox	29	3	14	.483	21
Royals	26	0	16	.615	9
Tigers	30	4	15	.500	19
Twins	31	2	17	.548	16
White Sox	31	3	21	.677	5
Yankees	22	0	13	.591	11
Astros	29	1	14	.483	21
Braves	29	3	17	.586	12
Cardinals	34	4	17	.500	19
Cubs	34	3	18	.529	17
Dodgers	29	3	14	.483	21
Expos	27	2	14	.519	18
Giants	31	0	20	.645	6
Mets	35	0	22	.629	8
Padres	26	0	19	.731	4
Phillies	28	4	16	.571	14
Pirates	30	9	13	.433	26
Reds	29	4	13	.448	25

In comparing Table 1 with Table 2 some interesting facts can be inferred. Although many teams' percentage ranking of draft choices to the majors are similar to the batting/pitching statistical rankings, there are some anomalies. The Reds, Dodgers, Cardinals, and

Red Sox may not have had many players reaching the majors, but their choices had longer careers, while the Mariners, Rangers, Orioles, and Twins had more players with shorter careers.

I've also analyzed the origins of the first-round draftees. Of the 716 first-round picks since 1965, 288 or roughly 39 percent came from the college ranks. Over the last twelve years, though, 57 percent were college players. Since it typically takes a high-school player a few more years to mature, I will use 1989 as the cutoff year to analyze the percentage of high school versus college players making it the majors. From the period of 1965 through 1989 for first-round draftees, only 58 percent of high-school players made "The Show" compared with 76 percent of college players. This underscores the mid-1980s shift of drafting more first-round college players than high schoolers since these players should be ready to make it to the majors sooner to fill the voids created by free agency or jettisoned high salary players.

Another area of research highlighted in Table 3 is how first-round choices one through ten have fared, statistically, from 1965 through 1994 relative to their performances in the majors. I expected number one choices, with all the pressure on them, to perform at a level closer to a lower top ten pick. Interestingly not only were number one choices third overall, but the statistical pattern of the top ten choices, for the most part, mirror their drafting order. Even though the third pick overall came out on top statistically, there wasn't much difference in the statistical rating points between the average first, second or third overall draft picks.

Table 3 (P = Rating points, R = Rank)

	AB	HR	RBI	BA	IP	W	Pct	ERA	P	R
1st	57,849	1,903	7,980	.266	6,451	512	.491	5.50	29	3
2nd	38,568	1,368	5,491	.2641	10,902	595	.486	3.91	27	2
3rd	42,111	1,032	5,018	.275	10,027	562	.497	4.02	25	1
4th	35,246	1,134	4,997	.272	9,207	491	.481	3.73	34	4
5th	13,910	471	1,850	.2643	6,459	401	.555	3.69	39	5
6th	47,785	1,430	6,208	.2596	932	46	.484	4.04	44	6
7th	15,729	387	1,861	.2600	2,974	158	.459	4.40	56	7
8th	13,002	381	1,599	.2496	5,599	323	.494	4.08	58	9
9th	9,280	233	1,139	.2494	5,258	294	.508	3.61	56	7
10th	34,186	1,003	4,774	.2629	725	26	.394	4.61	63	10

The last category I would like to cover is the first round career minor leaguers. In the first twenty-five years of the draft, 216 out of 610 (35 percent) of the draftees never made it the major leagues. Some of the players from the mid- to late 1980s may still make it,

but if not, I would at least like to recognize the top ten, first round, career minor league statistical performers (see Table 4).

Table 4

First round career minor league statistical leaders.

AB		RBI		W	
Alan Cockrell	4048	Alan Cockrell	658	Brian Ryder	56
Juan Bustabad	3245	Tim Glass	440	Rich O'Keefe	51
Neil Rasmussen	3070	Dan Haynes	377	Grady Hall	50
Les Filkins	3024	Les Filkins	374	Johnny Ard	49
Ed Kurpiel	2892	Tito Nanni	372	Mike Martin	48
Tito Nanni	2775	Kevin Garner	366	Jeff Bumgarner	48
Tim Glass	2707	Scott Bryant	363	Tim Cole	48
Kevin Burrell	2679	Otis Foster	361	Joe Kucharski	47
Mark Merchant	2620	Greg David	357	Sam Welborn	46
Greg David	2601	Alan Zinter	357	Doug Heinhold	45
		Robert Robinson	357	Joe DiFabio	45

H		BA (1000 AB min)		L	
Alan Cockrell	1104				
Les Filkins	813	Derek Jeter	.302	Jeff Bumgarner	71
Juan Bustabad	802	Joe Vitiello	.296	Tim Cole	64
Neil Rasmussen	748	Jeff Pyburn	.295	Joe Kucharski	62
Ed Kurpiel	730	Glenn Franklin	.289	Ricky Barlow	58
Tito Nanni	701	Dmitri Young	.288	Dave Masters	56
Mark Merchant	678	Robert Weaver	.286	Rod Boxberger	55
Glenn Franklin	667	Scott Bryant	.285	Dean Burk	54
Tim Glass	662	Craig Landis	.284	Jackie Davidson	54
Mike Ondina	628	Brian Rosinski	.283	Brian Bickerton	53
Hugh Walker	628	Mike White	.277	Rich O'Keefe	51

HR		IP		ERA (300 IP min)	
Tim Glass	131	Rich O'Keefe	940	Doug Heihold	2.83
Alan Cockrell	115	Grady Hall	898	Brien Taylor	3.02
Kevin Garner	92	Tim Cole	883	Chris Roberts	3.02
Scott Bryant	88	Joe Kucharski	857	Joe DiFabio	3.17
Robert Robinson	86	Dave Masters	854	Dave Proctor	3.18
Paul Croft	84	Brian Ryder	848	Jim Browning	3.22
Alan Zinter	82	Jeff Bumgarner	839	Lew Olsen	3.25
Dan Haynes	76	Sam Welborn	820	Steve Reed	3.35
Shane Andrews	73	Jackie Davidson	820	Mike Poehl	3.39
Greg David	67	Larry Payne	773	John Ericks	3.44

Supplemental to Table 5, albeit on the opposite side of the spectrum, are the first-round, career minor leaguers with the lowest career batting averages and ERA's. This table lists the "below-the-Mendoza line" players and introduces for the first the "above-the-Huffman line" players, named for the pitcher, Phil Huffman (Toronto '79 and Baltimore '85), who pitched 178 career innings in the majors yet had an ERA over 6.00 (6.03).

Table 5

"Mendoza Line" Team

Player	Draft Team	Draft Year	AB	HR	RBI	BA
Bruce Compton	Indians	1977	342	2	34	.143
Ken Thomas	Orioles	1972	257	1	25	.148
John Jones	Senators/Rangers	1967	426	1	27	.150
Kevin Brandt	Twins	1979	142	1	9	.155
Billy Simpson	Rangers	1976	575	0	51	.177
Ken Plasha	White Sox	1965	592	3	53	.186
Jay Roberts	Braves	1981	732	9	68	.187
Noel Jenke	Red Sox	1969	475	5	49	.192
Chris Schwab	Expos	1993*	628	7	64	.193
Gary Polczyski	Reds	1970	1174	9	113	.194
John Hibner	Rangers	1977	1219	30	151	.194
Al Shirley	Mets	1991*	1096	37	123	.197

"Huffman Line" Team

Player	Draft Team	Draft Year	IP	W	L	ERA
Jacob Shumate	Braves	1994*	31.2	0	4	8.24
Mark Snyder	Indians	1982	35	0	5	7.20
Pete Janicki	Angels	1992*	83.2	3	8	6.99
Robbie Beckett	Padres	1990*	443.1	13	38	6.37
Erik Sonberg	Dodgers	1983	379.2	16	33	6.14
Rick Greene	Tigers	1992*	122.1	5	10	6.03

* Player still active in 1994

A couple of footnotes to Table 5: Six of the players are still playing so my guess is that most, if not all, will disappear from the lists before their careers are complete. Also, despite the Senators/Rangers excellent percentage of first-round draft choices making it the majors, after two poor first-round draft picks in 1976 and 1977, the Rangers replaced their farm director, beefed up their scouting department from seven to ten scouts; and then proceeded to forego their 1978 first-round pick as compensation for signing Mike Jorgenson. Jorgenson proceeding to hit a resounding .205 over the next two years for the Rangers before he moved on to a new city. However, it did not end there for the Rangers since their 1979 through 1981 first-round picks ended up playing only 182 total major league games collectively.

The Rangers' consecutive years of poor drafting is certainly one of futility, but they are not alone. The Mets will probally never live down the fact that the only first pick overall never to make it to the majors was their 1966 first-round pick, Steve Chilcott.

Clearly this analysis indicates the winners and losers in first-round drafting. I'm not sure, though, that any one team has found the secret to successful drafting year in and year out. There are just too many variables to take into consideration. We'll continue, however, anaylyzing the data and maybe we can spot the trends that will suggest a pattern for successful drafting in the future.

Sources:

The Baseball Draft: The First 25 Years ; 1965-1989, 1990. Baseball America

Baseball Almanac; 1991, 1992, 1993, 1994, 1995. Baseball America

Major League Handbook; 1995. Stats, Inc.

Minor League Handbook; 1992, 1993, 1994, 1995. Stats, Inc.

The Baseball Encyclopedia 9th Edition; 1993. Macmillan Publishing Company

Baseball Guide; 1966 through 1994. The Sporting News

Official Baseball Register; 1966 through 1994. The Sporting News

The First Replacement Players

The "Tigers" of May 18, 1912

Joe Naiman

P rior to the 1995 preseason, baseball had used replacement players only once, on the well-known occasion when the Detroit Tigers went on strike to protest the suspension of their teammate, Ty Cobb. Cobb had gone into New York's Highlander Park stands after a heckler. The incident was witnessed by American League president Ban Johnson, who fined Cobb and issued a ten-day suspension.

Although Cobb had few friends on his team, the Tigers felt players should be better protected from unruly fans. They staged a sympathy strike, and they had support throughout the American League.

The strike was set for May 18, a road game in Philadelphia. The Tigers management knew that a forfeit would bring a $5,000 fine, which in 1912 was more than many players made in a year. The penalties for a forfeited game could also include loss of the franchise, and Tigers management rounded up anyone it could to ensure that a game would be played.

The players were recruited on short notice from the Tigers coaching and scouting staff and from the amateur, semipro, and retired players available in the Philadelphia area. Eight of the players never appeared in another major league game, three (all from the Tigers staff) came out of retirement to play, and one made his debut in the game and appeared in one more major league game four years later.

The comeback kids—Tiger manager Hughie Jennings (who would play in another game in 1918) came out of retirement to pinch hit in the ninth. Hall of Famer Jennings had made his mark as a player with the Baltimore Orioles in the 1890s, and managed the Tigers from 1907 to 1920.

Joe Sugden, a Philadelphia native who scouted for Detroit and had played big league ball from 1893 to 1905, started at first base and made the game's final out. Including his 1-for-4 performance (with a walk) on this day, he batted .255 in 835 games as a major leaguer. Sugden's run in the game brought his career total to 303.

Catcher Deacon McGuire already held the record for most major league seasons played, at twenty-five, beginning in 1884. This would give him twenty six, a record that would not be tied until 1989, and that wouldn't be broken until 1993. (If you count the National Association, Cap Anson appeared in twenty-seven big league seasons).

At the age of 48, coach McGuire was the oldest player on the field. His career was stretched to 1,781 games with this appearance. He went one for two to run his career hits total to 1,749 hits and his batting average to .278. He also scored his 770th run.

The others—McGuire was replaced in the lineup by Jack Smith, the only Tiger replacement who used an alias. Smith, whose real name was John Joseph Coffey, was hit by a pitch in his only plate appearance.

Joe Naiman, the local contact for the Ted Williams Chapter of SABR, works full-time for a high-tech firm and part-time as a writer for various publications. He lives in Lakeside, California.

Deacon McGuire

Jim McGarr, the leadoff hitter and second baseman, was hitless in four at bats. Billy Maharg, who later played in one game for the 1916 Phillies, and who would gain notoriety as the intermediary between Chicago Black Sox players and gamblers, started at third base before being relieved by Ed Irvin. Maharg, who stood only 5' 4-1/2", was hitless in one at bat.

Irvin, who replaced Maharg at third base, switched over to catcher in the seventh inning. Irvin, who died in February, 1916, after being thrown from a saloon window, had two triples (in the fourth and ninth innings) in three at bats, but did not score. His participation was a controversy in itself, because he had allegedly signed a National League contract with the Phillies.

Pitcher Al Travers was 6'1" and weighed 180 pounds. In eight innings (Philadelphia had no need for the bottom of the ninth), Travers gave up 24 runs on 26 hits, walking seven and striking out one. He was hitless in three at bats before manager Jennings batted for him in the ninth. Travers, whose previous baseball experience with an organized team was as equipment manager for the St. Joseph's collegiate team, was paid $50 for pitching after showing the best deliveries during the pitching tryouts.

Transcendental Graphics

Dan McGarvey played left field for the Tigers. McGarvey was hitless in three at bats, although he walked and stole a base. The center fielder was Bill Leinhauser, who stood 5'10" but weighed only 150 pounds. He was hitless in four trips to the plate.

Shortstop Pat Meaney, who was hitless in two at bats, but reached as a hit batsman, had played professionally in the Pacific Coast League, but was making his major league debut at the age of 40. This is a record that lasted until Satchel Paige came to Cleveland in 1948 at the age of 42. (Harry Wright, who played in the National Association from 1871 to 1875, played in the National League's inaugural 1876 season at age 41.)

Facts and figures—Other than McGuire only one of the twelve players was not born in Pennsylvania. Hap Ward (given name Joseph) was born in Leesburg, New Jersey, and died in Elmer, New Jersey. Ward, the right fielder, was hitless in two plate appearances and drew a walk. His most prominent contribution was a one-handed catch of Jack Barry's long drive to right field in the second inning. (Barry would reciprocate with a one-handed leaping catch off a Sugden line drive in the seventh.)

Most of the players were born and died in Philadelphia. McGarr died in Miami, Florida, and Smith, who was born in Oswayo, Pennsylvania, died in New York City. Leinhauser died in Elkins Park, Pennsylvania. Jennings was born in Pittston, Pennsylvania, and died in Scranton.

Two of the replacement players, both of whom were appearing in their only game, are on the list of former players who lived to be at least 90 years old. Hap Ward lived 93 years and 292 days and Jim McGarr lived 92 years and 254 days. The average lifespan of the replacement players was 70 years, 4 months, and 7 days. (The exact date of birth in 1882 for Ed Irvin is unknown and I calculated his lifespan at exactly 34 years. The exact date of birth in July, 1871, for Pat Meaney is also unknown and I calculated his lifespan at 51 years and 90 days.) The median age of death of these players exceeds that figure, falling between 70 years and 364 days for the player living the seventh-longest and 75 years and 349 days for the player living the sixth-longest. (The players were born between November, 1863 and November, 1893. The dates of their deaths range from February, 1916 to July, 1981.)

The game—The "real" Tigers went to the park, put on their uniforms, participated in a short practice, and then changed uniforms with the replacement players. Philadelphia manager Connie Mack, who suggested that Jennings should resign because of his inability to handle the Tigers players, started all of his regulars except for outfielders Bris Lord and Rube Oldring, who were replaced by Harl Maggert and Amos Strunk, respectively, although Mack only let his pitchers throw three innings each.

The Saturday game drew a crowd of about 20,000 people, including the striking Tigers. A number of Philadelphia fans demanded their money back, but when their demand was refused all returned to their seats peacefully, and there was no disorder at the end of the game.

Jack Coombs struck out three batters in his three innings, allowing no hits and one walk. Meanwhile, Philadelphia had scored three times in the bottom of the first and three times in the bottom of the third. Coombs was the only player among the eleven Athletics who played who didn't get a base hit.

Boardwalk Brown relieved Coombs to start the fourth. He struck out five and hit one. Although he allowed two Detroit runs in the top of the fifth, he also scored two runs and had two hits at the plate.

In the bottom of the fifth inning the Athletics scored eight runs. They scored four more in the sixth, giving Brown an 18-2 lead when he left the game.

Pennock relieved Brown, walking two, hitting one, and striking out seven. Philadelphia scored four more times in the seventh and twice in the eighth, giving Pennock a 24-2 lead to hold in the top of the ninth.

Philadelphia was led offensively by Eddie Collins, who scored four runs on five hits and stole four bases; Danny Murphy, who scored four runs and had one of the team's eight stolen bases, and Amos Strunk, who had four hits in six at-bats. The Athletics were also helped by seven Detroit errors: two wild throws by McGuire, a wild throw by Irvin, dropped thrown balls by McGarr and Meaney, and botched fielding attempts by McGarvey and Sugden.

Following the game Cobb himself urged his teammates to end the strike. After Sunday off because of Pennsylvania laws prohibiting play on the Sabbath, the regular Tigers returned to the field for the game of May 20, leaving the twelve replacement players their footnote in history.

Rewriting the Record Book

Pre- and post-integration career records

Michael J. Haupert

The topic of comparative records before and after the integration of the top professional leagues has never been broached. Prior to 1947, no league existed in which all of the best players competed against one another. Neither the Negro Leagues nor the major leagues were playing against the best talent in the country. Each was playing against the best talent of a particular color.

I believe that equal weight should not be given to records set by white players competing against only whites, or black players competing against only blacks. Josh Gibson's league leading .440 batting average in 1938 does not appear among the all-time major league best averages, because it was set against the inferior talent level of the Negro Leagues. This does not explain, however, why Rogers Hornsby's .424 average is not demeaned for also being set against an inferior talent level, consisting of only white players. Records set against all white or all black competition are inflated in the same way minor league records are inflated, by being set against other than the best talent available.

We would have a hard time arguing that the quality of play was the same prior to integration as it was afterward. After all, by 1957, 56 fellow Negro League players had joined Jackie Robinson on major league rosters. That means that, about 15 percent of roster spots were occupied by players who had been barred from the game just a decade earlier. And by this time,

former Negro Leaguers had captured seven MVP awards, one Cy Young award, and six Rookie of the Year awards.

It is obvious that segregated baseball is not the highest quality baseball. I think that there should be separate sections of the record book for pre- and post-integration records. This article represents a first step in that direction by examining a selection of career hitting and pitching records, and separating them into two categories. First, the current, accepted major league records (from 1901-92), set by a mixture of players who played against the best available white competition (i.e., those playing before 1947) and those who played against the best overall competition (from 1947 onward). Second, I have compiled what I argue are the true major league records, representing the more significant achievements made by players competing exclusively against the best available competition, regardless of color. These records include only the years 1947-92, after the integration of professional baseball began.

In composing the tables below, I used the Bill James Electronic Baseball Encyclopedia (1992). For players whose careers spanned the pre- and post-integration eras, I included only the relevant portion of their career in the post-integration records. For example, Stan Musial is third on the all-time doubles chart with 725. When, however, the major league career record holders are tabulated from 1947 onward, Musial slips to sixth, with 540 doubles, the number he accumulated in his post-integration career.

Michael J. Haupert is an associate professor of economics at the University of Wisconsin at LaCrosse.

The tables compare selected career hitting and pitching records as they currently stand in the record books with the way they should be rewritten to reflect the higher level of competition since integration. I think it is time to recognize that only those players who played after the integration process began can truly be considered to have played against the best the game had to offer. Those who played before 1947 never faced the best available competition, no matter what league they played in. The record books should recognize this by putting emphasis on the greater of the achievements: records set against the best available competition.

Career Runs Scored Leaders

1901-1992		1947-1992	
Ty Cobb	2,245	Hank Aaron	2,174
Hank Aaron	2,174	Pete Rose	2,165
Babe Ruth	2,174	Willie Mays	2,062
Pete Rose	2,165	Frank Robinson	1,829
Willie Mays	2,062	Carl Yastrzemski	1,816
Stan Musial	1,949	Mickey Mantle	1,677
Lou Gehrig	1,888	Joe Morgan	1,650
Tris Speaker	1,882	Al Kaline	1,622
Met Ott	1,859	Lou Brock	1,610
Frank Robinson	1,829	Robin Yount	1,570

Career Runs Batted In Leaders

1901-1992		1947-1992	
Hank Aaron	2,297	Hank Aaron	2,297
Babe Ruth	2,211	Willie Mays	1,903
Lou Gehrig	1,990	Carl Yastrzemski	1,844
Stan Musial	1,951	Frank Robinson	1,812
Ty Cobb	1,933	Dave Winfield	1,710
Jimmie Foxx	1,921	Reggie Jackson	1,702
Willie Mays	1,903	Tony Perez	1,652
Mel Ott	1,860	Ernie Banks	1,636
Carl Yastrzemski	1,844	Mike Schmidt	1,595
Ted Williams	1,839	Stan Musial	1,594

Career Doubles Leaders

1901-1992		1947-1992	
Tris Speaker	792	Pete Rose	746
Pete Rose	746	Carl Yastrzemski	646
Stan Musial	725	George Brett	634
Ty Cobb	725	Hank Aaron	624
Carl Yastrzemski	646	Robin Yount	558
George Brett	634	Stan Musial	540
Hank Aaron	624	Al Oliver	529
Paul Waner	603	Frank Robinson	528
Charlie Gehringer	574	Dave Parker	526
Robin Yount	558	Willie Mays	523

Career Hits Leaders

1901-1992		1947-1992	
Pete Rose	4,256	Pete Rose	4,256
Ty Cobb	4,190	Hank Aaron	3,771
Hank Aaron	3,771	Carl Yastrzemski	3,419
Stan Musial	3,630	Willie Mays	3,283
Tris Speaker	3,515	Rod Carew	3,053
Carl Yastrzemski	3,419	Robin Yount	3,025
Eddie Collins	3,310	Lou Brock	3,023
Willie Mays	3,283	Al Kaline	3,007
Paul Waner	3,152	George Brett	3,005
Rod Carew	3,053	Roberto Clemente	3,000

Career Home Run Leaders

1901-1992		1947-1992	
Hank Aaron	755	Hank Aaron	755
Babe Ruth	714	Willie Mays	660
Willie Mays	660	Frank Robinson	586
Frank Robinson	586	Harmon Killebrew	573
Harmon Killebrew	573	Reggie Jackson	563
Reggie Jackson	563	Mike Schmidt	548
Mike Schmidt	548	Mickey Mantle	536
Mickey Mantle	536	Willie McCovey	521
Jimmie Foxx	534	Ernie Banks	512
Willie McCovey	521	Eddie Mathews	512

Career Batting Average Leaders

1901-1992		1947-1992	
Ty Cobb	.366	Ted Williams	.340
Rogers Hornsby	.358	Wade Boggs	.338
Tris Speaker	.345	Rod Carew	.328
Ted Williams	.344	Tony Gwynn	.327
Babe Ruth	.342	Stan Musial	.326
Harry Heilman	.342	Kirby Puckett	.321
Bill Terry	.341	Roberto Clemente	.317
George Sisler	.340	George Kell	.313
Lou Gehrig	.340	Don Mattingly	.311
Wade Boggs	.338	Richie Ashburn	.308

Career Stolen Base Leaders

1901-1992		1947-1992	
Rickey Henderson	1042	Rickey Henderson	1042
Lou Brock	938	Lou Brock	938
Ty Cobb	892	Tim Raines	730
Eddie Collins	745	Joe Morgan	689
Max Carey	738	Willie Wilson	660
Tim Raines	730	Bert Campeneris	649
Joe Morgan	689	Vince Coleman	610
Willie Wilson	660	Maury Wills	586
Bert Campaneris	649	Davey Lopes	557
Vince Coleman	610	Cesar Cedeno	550

Career Shutout Leaders

1901-1992		1947-1992	
Walter Johnson	110	Warren Spahn	63
Grover Alexander	90	Tom Seaver	61
Christy Mathewson	79	Nolan Ryan	61
Eddie Plank	69	Bert Blyleven	60
Warren Spahn	63	Don Sutton	58
Tom Seaver	61	Bob Gibson	56
Nolan Ryan	61	Steve Carlton	55
Bert Blyleven	60	Gaylord Perry	53
Don Sutton	58	Jim Palmer	53
Ed Walsh	57	Juan Marichal	52

Career Earned Run Average Leaders

1901-1992		1947-1992	
Ed Walsh	1.82	Hoyt Wilhelm	2.52
Addie Joss	1.89	Whitey Ford	2.74
Mordecai Brown	2.06	Sandy Koufax	2.76
Christy Mathewson	2.11	Roger Clemens	2.80
Rube Waddell	2.11	Jim Palmer	2.86
Cy Young	2.12	Tom Seaver	2.86
Walter Johnson	2.16	Orel Hershiser	2.87
Eddie Plank	2.35	Juan Marichal	2.89
Eddie Cicotte	2.37	Rollie Fingers	2.90
Doc White	2.39	Bob Gibson	2.91

Career Complete Games Leaders

1901-1992		1947-1992	
Walter Johnson	531	Warren Spahn	373
Grover Alexander	438	Robin Roberts	305
Christy Mathewson	433	Gaylord Perry	303
Eddie Plank	410	Ferguson Jenkins	267
Warren Spahn	382	Bob Gibson	255
Ted Lyons	356	Steve Carlton	254
George Mullin	353	Phil Niekro	245
Red Ruffing	335	Juan Marichal	244
Cy Young	331	Bert Blyleven	242
Burleigh Grimes	314	Early Wynn	235

Career Strikeout Leaders

1901-1992		1947-1992	
Nolan Ryan	5,668	Nolan Ryan	5,668
Steve Carlton	4,136	Steve Carlton	4,136
Bert Blyleven	3,701	Bert Blyleven	3,701
Tom Seaver	3,640	Tom Seaver	3,640
Don Sutton	3,574	Don Sutton	3,574
Gaylord Perry	3,534	Gaylord Perry	3,534
Walter Johnson	3,509	Phil Niekro	3,342
Ferguson Jenkins	3,192	Bob Gibson	3,117
Bob Gibson	3,117	Jim Bunning	2,855

Career Wins Leaders

1901-1992		1947-1992	
Walter Johnson	417	Warren Spahn	355
Grover Alexander	373	Steve Carlton	329
Christy Mathewson	373	Don Sutton	324
Warren Spahn	363	Nolan Ryan	319
Steve Carlton	329	Phil Niekro	318
Eddie Plank	326	Gaylord Perry	314
Don Sutton	324	Tom Seaver	311
Nolan Ryan	319	Tommy John	288
Phil Niekro	318	Bert Blyleven	287
Gaylord Perry	314	Robin Roberts	286

Career Winning Percentage Leaders

1901-1992		1947-1992	
Whitey Ford	.690	Whitey Ford	.690
Dwight Gooden	.683	Dwight Gooden	.683
Lefty Grove	.680	Roger Clemens	.679
Roger Clemens	.679	Sandy Koufax	.655
Christy Mathewson	.668	Ron Guidry	.651
Sandy Koufax	.655	Jim Palmer	.638
Deacon Phillippe	.652	Ed Lopat	.635
Ron Guidry	.651	Juan Marichal	.631
Lefty Gomez	.649	Don Newcombe	.623
Mordecai Brown	.649	Bob Lemon	.623

Dazzy Vance in 1930

One of the game's ten best seasons

Joseph Cardello

A bad back and a bad cold—not exactly the best way for a pitcher to start a new season. Especially a 39-year-old pitcher. And more especially, a 39-year-old pitcher coming off a poor, injury-plagued campaign the year before.

But that's the situation Dazzy Vance faced at the opening of the 1930 season. Nineteen-twenty-nine had been a miserable year for Vance. His record had dropped to 14-13, while his earned run average had ballooned to 3.89. Except for 1926—a year of persistent arm trouble—these were his worst statistics for ten years. He had also given up more hits than innings pitched, threw only one shutout, and, most revealing of all for the man who had led the league in strikeouts seven consecutive seasons, he had the lowest number of K's since he became a regular major league pitcher in 1922.

Brooklyn fans had every reason to wonder: Was the Ol' Dazzler finished? Could their good-natured, hard-throwing stalwart bounce back at age 39?

The prospects for Vance looked grim after his first start against Boston on April 19. In the very first inning, the Braves put up four runs on four hits and two walks. They led off the second inning in much the same vein with a hit and a walk. At this point, manager Wilbert Robinson brought in Johnny Morrison to take over. Dazzy was charged with six runs in one inning pitched.

Six days later, after a few rain-outs, Vance made his

second start of the year. Once again he faced the Braves. But that would be the only similarity between this game and his first appearance. Vance spoiled the Braves' home opener with a three-hitter, winning 5-1. The only Boston run came in the first, when Jimmy Welsh singled, and Rabbit Maranville hit a grounder to first baseman Del Bissonette, who fielded it cleanly but threw past Jake Flowers at second base. With runners on second and third, Gene Robertson drove in an unearned run with a sacrifice fly.

This game on April 25 began a two-month stretch for Vance that has to rank among the most impressive in the history of major league pitching.

This was, of course, the legendary "Year of the Hitter," when not just individuals, but entire leagues and teams hit .300—when runs came in avalanches, and buried the ERAs of almost every pitcher. That's what makes Vance's accomplishment so remarkable. From April 25 to June 26 Vance started thirteen games, completed nine of them, and compiled an ERA of 1.68. If you exclude his one poor performance in this stretch—when he yielded seven runs in six innings on June 6—his ERA is an astounding 1.16. Considering that the ERA for all National League pitchers in 1930 was an astronomical 4.97, Vance's ERA for these two months looks more like Bob Gibson in 1968—the "Year of the Pitcher"—than anything you'd expect in the Big Bang Era of 1930.

In these thirteen games Vance recorded only one shutout. But he could easily have had two or three others with decent support in the field. Still, despite

Joseph Cardello is a statistical analyst for Beyer Associates. He lives in Columbia, Maryland, and specializes in Brooklyn baseball.

his heroic efforts, his record stood at only 8-6 at the end of June. Why?

On May 6 he pitched well but lost to Chicago, 3-1.

On May 31 he left the game for a pinch hitter against Philadelphia, behind 2-1. Brooklyn lost, 3-1.

On June 15 he was victimized by five errors and a variety of other misplays against the Cardinals. He gave up seven runs, only one earned. He did not pitch particularly well that day, but with flawless support he would have won.

On June 20 he lost to Cincinnati, 2-1. In the sixth inning, with Brooklyn ahead, 1-0, Joe Stripp of the Reds bunted, catcher Hank DeBerry scooped it up and promptly tossed it into right field. With Stripp on second, Harry Heilmann tapped an easy grounder to Flowers, who let it go through him into right field, scoring Stripp. George Kelly then lined a double into right-center to give Cincinnati a 2-1 "victory."

Vance could easily have sported an 11-3 or 10-4 record at the end of June. But with only 8 wins and 6 losses to show for his extraordinary pitching, his achievement has not only escaped the notice of baseball historians, it also totally escaped the notice of contemporary sportswriters, who wrote about how Vance was not the star he used to be, and how he was struggling just to keep above a .500 percentage. And this after he had given up more than two earned runs only once in thirteen starts! And while his pitching colleagues were getting clobbered!

On the Fourth of July, Vance pitched the morning game of a doubleheader against the Giants. After six innings he had a 4-0 lead, but he couldn't hold it and the Robins lost, 5-4, in the eleventh inning. He rebounded five days later with a 3-hit shutout, but then suffered through his toughest two weeks of the season.

July 14: Pitching with a 12-3 lead over Pittsburgh, Vance—as he sometimes did when he had a big cushion—figured he could coast the rest of the way, so he let up visibly and started lobbing the ball somewhat lackadaisically. He still won the complete game, but damaged his record by giving up 12 hits and 7 runs over the last four innings. Manager Robinson apparently saw no reason to take him out since he was clearly not putting much strain on his arm.

Overuse—July 17: Uncle Robbie called on Vance to relieve for the first time that year, and with only two days' rest. He came in with none out in the ninth inning and held the Cubs in check with the aid of two fine catches by Bissonette at first. But with one out in the thirteenth, Footsie Blair singled, followed by Woody English, whose ground ball hit the second-

base bag and ricocheted into center field. Kiki Cuyler then hit a line drive to Gink Hendrick at first base, who leaped but could not hold it. Riggs Stephenson followed with a hard grounder right at Glenn Wright, but the Robins' shortstop let it pass on into the outfield. Chicago won the game, 6-3.

July 19: With the surprising Robins in the midst of a pennant race, Robinson sent Vance out to start after he pitched five innings of relief only two days before. Vance left the game trailing, 3-1, to Chicago, with two on and no one out in the eighth. Ray Phelps came in to relieve, walked Hack Wilson to load the bases, and then got Stephenson on a grounder to first that forced English at home plate. Charlie Grimm then bounced one back to Phelps, who threw to DeBerry at the plate for one out. It looked like an easy double play. Unfortunately, DeBerry threw the ball twenty feet over Bissonette's head at first base, two runs scored, and the Cubs took a 5-1 lead. The Robins came back with three runs in the bottom of the eighth, but fell short, 5-4. Vance took the loss.

Vance lasted only 1-2/3 innings in his next start, then relieved for two innings just two days later, and started again three days after that, yielding three runs in seven innings without a decision. At the end of July, Vance had a 10-10 record with an ERA of 2.92— mighty fine by 1930 standards. More to the point, manager Robinson had violated the practice he himself had developed, and which had made Vance a star. The principle was simple: Vance needed more rest between starts than most other pitchers. But Uncle Robbie got caught up in the heat of the race, and began to overuse his mainstay. The team, and Vance's record, paid the price for Robbie's poor judgment.

But in late summer Vance again showed the resilience of his aging arm. In his next five appearances he pitched 43-1/3 innings, gave up only five earned runs, and threw two shutouts—a 5-0 victory over Pittsburgh and a 1-0 triumph over Carl Hubbell, who walked in the winning run in the bottom of the ninth. Vance also had one victory in a seven-inning relief stint, and one blown save in this stretch—and still he picked up two more losses. How?

A few defensive lapses—On August 12, in front of 40,000 fans in Chicago, Vance pitched courageously against the league champions, but once again his defense let him down. Blair led off the Cubs' first inning with a ground ball straight to Flowers at second base. Flowers kicked it out to right field, where Johnny Frederick added his own special touch, and Blair ended up on second. English then beat out a slow grounder to Flowers, and Cuyler followed with a sacrifice fly, scoring Blair from third. Hack Wilson then tested Flowers again, who failed again. Stephenson then drove in English from second with a clean hit.

Trailing 2-0 right from the break, Vance pitched out of trouble inning after inning. He walked four Cubs, gave up fourteen hits, and left a total of sixteen runners on base. The game went into extra innings, the Cubs finally winning it in the eleventh. With the bases full and the infield drawn in, Stephenson bounced one down the third base line and off the glove of Wally Gilbert. Vance lost, 3-2.

Brooklyn had many chances to win it in the ninth and tenth innings, when they loaded the bases. But they failed to score. It was the Brooklyn eighth that offered one of those legendary examples of Robins' baserunning magic that so astounded fans, players, and sportswriters alike. A triple by Babe Herman, a walk to Bissonette, and a single by Al Lopez produced...absolutely nothing. Herman was caught off third on a fielder's choice, and Bissonette was thrown out at the plate trying to score from second on Lopez's single.

Dazzy Vance

After shutting out Pittsburgh in his next start, Vance faced the Reds on August 22. Behind 2-1 in the eighth, Vance gave up a single to Tony Cuccinello. Heilmann grounded straight to Mickey Finn, who tossed to Wright at second, who dropped the ball. A sacrifice advanced the runners to second and third. An intentional pass loaded the bases. Then Red Lucas hit an easy fly to short left field. Hendrick came in. Hendrick went back. Then Hendrick came in again. He dropped it. Two runs scored, and Vance lost 4-1.

Vance won a rare 8-7 game against the Giants on August 28, when his teammates battered the great

Carl Hubbell with seven runs in the sixth inning and saved Vance's win. But business returned to normal when Vance next took the mound in Boston. He gave up four hits and three runs in six innings and left for a pinch hitter in the seventh. The Braves scored those three runs in the first inning: one infield hit, one base on balls, one sacrifice bunt attempt that went for a hit, one strikeout that the catcher let through for a passed ball, one pop fly caught by Finn who temporarily lost consciousness as he casually began to return the ball to Vance on the mound, whereupon Maranville broke from third base, scoring on Finn's wild throw to the plate—followed by

Johnny Neun, who stole home after breaking from third on Vance's windup and scoring easily when catcher Lopez dropped the pitch. Three runs without a ball leaving the infield. Boston went on to an easy win, 6-0.

Vance followed this tragicomedy with three brilliant complete games. First, a 5-2 victory over the Giants when he was actually *helped* by good support in the field, although even in this game one of the runs scored on a Bill Terry single in the ninth, an uncontested "steal" of second, a balk by Vance, and a groundout. Next, a 2-1 win over Chicago, with Vance striking out thirteen Cubs—the highest single game total by any pitcher in 1930. Finally, a crushing ten-inning loss to St. Louis, 1-0, on September 16. This demoralizing result stopped an eleven-game Brooklyn winning streak, and sent the Robins reeling out of first place. They never recovered and finished a fast-fading fourth. Vance had two more starts—a win and a loss—that ended one of the most impressive, neglected seasons ever by any pitcher.

At first glance it's hard to understand how anyone with a 17-15 record could be compared with Ron Guidry in 1978, Walter Johnson in 1912, Grover Cleveland Alexander in 1915, Lefty Grove in 1931, Dazzy Vance himself in 1924, Bob Gibson in 1968, or any other legendary season you'd care to mention. But the statistics are revealing, if well-hidden.

1. Vance's ERA in 1930 was 2.61. Carl Hubbell finished a distant second in the Na-tional League with 3.87. That discrepancy of 1.26 between the top two ERA leaders is the largest gap *ever* in either league.

2. The National League ERA for all pitchers in 1930 was 4.97. The gap of 2.36 runs between Vance's ERA and the overall league ERA is also the largest in history—except for Ernie Bonham of the Yankees in 1940, who appeared in only twelve games and pitched only 99 innings, and Greg Maddux in 1994, who shattered Vance's long-standing mark.

3. Even using the New Age stats in *Total Baseball*, the results are impressive. Vance's Adjusted Starter Runs is 29.9 points higher than his nearest 1930 competitor. Only seven pitchers ever recorded a wider gap: Cy Young in 1901, Walter Johnson in 1913, Grover Alexander in 1915, Dolf Luque in 1923, Vance in 1924, and Lefty Grove in 1931 and 1932. The record is equally strong with Adjusted ERA.

Compare below the records of Lefty Grove and Dazzy Vance in 1930. Remember that Grove, one of the great pitchers of all time, was pitching for one of the great teams of all time—the Philadelphia A's. Alas, the Ol' Dazzler pitched for the Brooklyn Robins—decidedly *not* one of the great teams of all time.

1930:
How Grove and Vance fared in "The Year of the Hitter"

	Grove	Vance
Opp. B.A.	.247 (AL .288)	.246 (NL .303)
Opp. OBP	.284 (AL .351)	.284 (NL .360)
ERA	2.54	2.61
Hits per 9 innings	8.44	8.39
K's per 9 innings	6.46	6.02
Shutouts	2	4
Starter Runs	68.3	68.0
Adj. Starter Runs	62.7	65.9
Adjusted ERA	176	188
W-L	28-5	17-15
Age	29	39

A Tale of Two Players

A Foxx–Mantle comparison

Steve Krevisky

Jimmie Foxx

Imagine two players, born a generation apart. One was a legend in his time, who graced the covers of countless magazines, was, and remains the idol of millions of Americans. The other, just as much a giant in his era, never got the publicity that he deserved, and is hardly remembered by the casual fan, but his accomplishments are truly staggering. The two players, Mickey Mantle and Jimmie Foxx have an astounding number of things in common, from the mundane to the glorious.

Both athletes were born in small towns, and their birthdays are but two days apart. Mickey Charles Mantle was born in Spavinaw, Oklahoma on Oct. 20, 1931. James Emory Foxx was born on Oct. 22, 1907 in Sudlersville, Maryland.

Their home run totals were also two apart: 536 for Mantle, 534 for Foxx. Both have a 6.6 home run percentage. Foxx' Slugging Average, .609, is the highest ever for a righthanded batter, and fourth all-time. Mantle's SA of .557 is the highest ever for a switch-hitter.

Both men won three MVP Awards, doing so in exactly the same pattern and at just about the same ages. Foxx, the first player to win three, took home his awards in 1932, 1933, and 1938. This is a tremendous achievement, especially when you consider his competition throughout the 1930s: Ruth, Gehrig, Greenberg, Gehringer, Grove, Simmons, Averill, Trosky, DiMaggio, Williams. Foxx won these awards at the ages of 25, 26, and 31.

Mantle garnered his three MVPs in 1956, 1957, and 1962. Mantle's competition included Berra, Maris, Ford, Howard, Kaline, Colavito, Killebrew, Jensen, Fox...and Williams. Mantle, too, won his MVP awards at the ages of 25, 26, and 31.

Foxx and Mantle both won Triple Crowns in the same year that they won an MVP. Foxx's Triple Crown occurred in 1933 (see my article on this sub-

Steve Krevisky is an associate professor of mathematics at Middlesex Community-Technical College in Middletown, Connecticut. He has given presentations at numerous SABR regional meetings and national conventions. He is especially interested in Foxx and other "unsung" greats of the pre-expansion era.

ject in TNP, 1993), while Mantle's came in 1956. By today's rules, Jimmie would have also won the Triple Crown in 1932, since Dale Alexander, the batting title winner, had fewer than 400 at bats. *(Total Baseball* gives Foxx the crown for 1932. If you agree with their doing so, you consider him the only player in major league history to win it two years in a row.) Mantle's 1956, like Foxx' 1932, marked his emergence as a true superstar.

Foxx and Mantle are among the very few players in the major league history to hit 50 home runs in two different seasons. They are the *only* two players in major league history to blast 50 homers in a season and win a batting title. Foxx did it in 1932 and 1938. Mantle did it in 1956.

They are also the only two players in major league history to hit 50 home runs in a season and *not* lead the league. This happened to Foxx in 1938, when he belted 50 round trippers, but Hank Greenberg drilled 58. Mantle blasted 54 in 1961, only to be runner-up to Maris' 61.

Both led the AL in HR four times, Foxx in 1932, 1933, 1935 (a tie with Hank Greenberg—see my *TNP*, 1995 article), and 1939 (even though he missed twenty-five games); Mantle in 1955, 1956, 1958, and 1960.

Both Foxx and Mantle led the league in on-base percentage three times. Foxx did it in 1929, 1938, and 1939; Mickey in 1955, 1962, and 1964. Again, we have comparable patterns.

Foxx led the league in slugging average five times to Mantle's four.

Foxx and Mantle shared many similarities. But Mickey's death was national news for days. Jimmie's was obscure. Mantle played in New York, with all that implies. He led great teams, and seemed to be in the World Series every year. And he seems to have been the boyhood hero of every network anchor and executive in America.

Foxx performed in Philadelphia and Boston in an earlier age. Although he played for one of the great teams of all time in the 1929-1931 A's and was acknowledged as one of the great players of his era, he didn't cut the national figure he probably would have if he'd been a Yankee or if he had played today. Fans who love the Mick should take another look at Jimmie Foxx.

Mickey Mantle

Earned-Base Average

How efficient is a hitter?

Lawrence Tenbarge

A couple of years ago I conceived of the idea of somehow combining slugging and on-base percentage as a means of determining maximum efficiency. The system I settled upon is basic. I refer to it as "Earned-Base Average."

Suppose a player has ten official at bats and gets three hits. His regular batting average, of course, is .300. Now suppose one of those hits was a homer. He thus had six total bases, a .600 slugging average. But what if he also drew two walks? How should these be figured in? I simply treat them as two more at bats, earning one of the possible four bases.

So the hypothetical player came up to the plate twelve times (ten at bats plus two walks) and "earned" eight bases (six total bases plus two walks). He therefore had an "earned-base average" of .667.

By combining slugging and on-base percentage in this method, the strengths of both tend to cover the weaknesses of each.

Total Baseball uses a statistic called "Production," that on the face of it looks similar but is really quite different. It simply combines the two numerators which, of course, contain some common elements, since hits are calculated for slugging average and on-base percentage. Retaining only the base 1.00 denominator gives a distorted picture. "Production" is an abstraction. Earned-Base Average represents something the player actually did.

Consider for a moment: using the same example,

the player actually "earned" two bases for every three times he came to the plate. If a player has a .500 slugging average and a .400 on-base average, by the stack-up method he had a "Production" of .900. A .300 batting average means that a player hit safely in 30 percent of his regular at bats. A .900 "Production" represents 90 percent of what?

Now consider a quick example of my method. In 1961 Mickey Mantle had 514 at bats and collected 353 total bases for a .687 slugging average. He also drew 126 walks. Thus, he had 640 plate appearances and "earned" 479 bases, an EBA of .748, just a hair behind Ruth's career mark of .751 (see the charts below).

I compiled two separate EBA lists. I used a cut-off point of 4,500 plate appearances. This accounts for some current players, such as Cecil Fielder and Frank Thomas not being included. With more seasons, both of them will make an updated list. One shows what players actually did, and the other shows how each compared to his contemporaries. To do this I computed the EBA for each league for each season since the turn of the century, then averaged them for the years of each players' career. By dividing each players' career EBA by the average of the league-years in which he played, we arrive at REBA, the Relative Earned-Base Average. This is the best possible comparison, since it normalizes eras over time and allows a much fairer estimate of a player's actual ability, as differences in playing conditions over time are accounted for.

Lawrence Tenbarge is a freelance writer specializing in science, science fiction, and baseball history.

Of course, the Law of Diminishing Returns is in operation here. The better one gets, the harder it is to improve. Suppose a player has been up to the plate ten times and has earned eight bases, an EBA of .800. If he then draws two walks, he improves only 33 points to .833 (10 for12). Another player has been up ten times also but has earned only two bases (.200).

He also then draws two walks. His mark will then improve 133 points to .333 (4 for12). This may appease those who feel uncomfortable giving walks the same status as a single. In the general picture of a batter versus the pitcher and defense, however, a base is a base.

Earned-Base Average Absolute Scale

1	Babe Ruth	.751	39	Al Rosen	.564	76	Bobby Bonilla	.538	113	Riggs Stephenson	.525
2	Ted Williams	.710	40	Joe Jackson	.563	77	Greg Luzinski	.538	114	George Foster	.525
3	Lou Gehrig	.691	41	Larry Doby	.562	78	Ernie Banks	.537	115	Wally Post	.524
4	Jimmie Foxx	.668	42	Jeff Heath	.561	79	Eddie Murray	.537	116	Alvin Davis	.524
5	Hank Greenberg	.661	43	Chick Hafey	.561	80	George Brett	.536	117	Jim Wynn	.524
6	Mickey Mantle	.635	44	Ty Cobb	.561	81	Ted Kluszewski	.536	118	Joe Morgan	.523
7	Rogers Hornsby	.624	45	Tris Speaker	.560	82	Bill Dickey	.536	119	KIrk Gibson	.522
8	Joe Dimaggio	.623	46	Tommy Henrich	.559	83	Roy Sievers	.536	120	Don Mincher	.522
9	Ralph Kiner	.621	47	Wally Berger	.559	84	Jack Fournier	.536	121	Dave Kingman	.521
10	Stan Musial	.615	48	Norm Cash	.557	85	Roger Maris	.536	122	Jesse Barfield	.521
11	John Mize	.613	49	Jack Clark	.557	86	Sid Gordon	.534	123	Arky Vaughan	.521
12	Barry Bonds	.613	50	Roy Campanella	.556	87	Roy Cullenbine	.534	124	Ken Singleton	.521
13	Willie Mays	.610	51	Rocky Colavito	.554	88	Orlando Cepeda	.534	125	Jason Thompson	.520
14	Mel Ott	.605	52	Will Clark	.554	89	Gene Tenace	.533	126	Rico Carty	.519
15	Hack Wilson	.601	53	Frank Howard	.553	90	Joe Cronin	.533	127	Minnie Minoso	.519
16	Fred McGriff	.601	54	Reggie Jackson	.552	91	Carl Yastrzemski	.533	128	Kiki Cuyler	.519
17	Mike Schmidt	.601	55	Mickey Cochrane	.552	92	Vic Wertz	.533	129	Earle Combs	.518
18	Charlie Keller	.600	56	Goose Goslin	.549	93	Pedro Guerrero	.533	130	John Mayberry	.517
19	Hank Aaron	.600	57	Hank Sauer	.549	94	Boog Powell	.532	131	Bobby Doerr	.516
20	Duke Snider	.595	58	Gil Hodges	.547	95	Bobby Bonds	.532	132	Richie Zisk	.516
21	Frank Robinson	.595	59	Reggie Smith	.546	96	Joe Medwick	.531	133	Rick Monday	.516
22	Dick Allen	.591	60	Rudy York	.544	97	Tony Lazzeri	.531	134	Enos Slaughter	.515
23	Harmon Killebrew	.587	61	Bill Terry	.544	98	Rickey Henderson	.531	135	Mike Greenwell	.514
24	Earl Averill	.584	62	Mickey Tettleton	.543	99	Johnny Bench	.530	136	Harold Baines	.514
25	Willie McCovey	.583	63	Bob Allison	.543	100	Andre Thornton	.530	137	Howard Johnson	.514
26	Chuck Klein	.582	64	Gavvy Cravath	.543	101	Gus Zernial	.529	138	Honus Wagner	.514
27	Eddie Mathews	.580	65	Jackie Robinson	.543	102	Bob Meusel	.529	139	Ron Cey	.514
28	Ken Williams	.580	66	Billy Williams	.543	103	Wade Boggs	.529	140	Don Mattingly	.512
29	Willie Stargell	.578	67	Kent Hrbek	.543	104	Joe Gordon	.528	141	Vern Stephens	.512
30	Bob Johnson	.572	68	Charlie Gehringer	.542	105	Ron Santo	.528	142	Del Ennis	.512
31	Babe Herman	.572	69	Dwight Evans	.541	106	Jackie Jensen	.528	143	Gene Woodling	.512
32	Darryl Strawberry	.569	70	Jim Bottomley	.541	107	Joe Adcock	.528	144	Andre Dawson	.512
33	Harry Heilmann	.568	71	Fred Lynn	.541	108	Dale Murphy	.527	145	Heinie Manush	.511
34	Dolph Camilli	.568	72	Jim Rice	.540	109	Cliff Johnson	.527	146	Tony Oliva	.511
35	Hal Trosky	.567	73	Gabby Hartnett	.539	110	Paul Waner	.527	147	Wally Moon	.510
36	Jose Canseco	.567	74	Rafael Palmeiro	.538	111	Dave Winfield	.527	148	Tony Perez	.510
37	Al Simmons	.565	75	Al Kaline	.538	112	Yogi Berra	.526	149	Ken Boyer	.509
38	Danny Tartabull	.565							150	Ferris Fain	.509

Earned-Base Average Relative Scale

1	Babe Ruth	1.73	39	Jack Fournier	1.30	76	Bobby Bonds	1.24	113	Cliff Johnson	1.19
2	Ted Williams	1.60	40	Norm Cash	1.30	77	Rudy York	1.24	114	Kent Hrbek	1.19
3	Lou Gehrig	1.55	41	Babe Herman	1.30	78	Hank Sauer	1.24	115	Eddie Murray	1.19
4	Jimmie Foxx	1.47	42	Reggie Smith	1.29	79	Jim Wynn	1.24	116	Ron Cey	1.19
5	Mickey Mantle	1.46	43	Frank Howard	1.29	80	Roy Campanella	1.23	117	Roger Bresnahan	1.19
6	Hank Greenberg	1.45	44	Wally Berger	1.29	81	Gabby Hartnett	1.23	118	Zack Wheat	1.19
7	Rogers Hornsby	1.45	45	Jack Clark	1.29	82	Roy Cullenbine	1.23	119	Joe Cronin	1.19
8	Joe Jackson	1.45	46	Bob Johnson	1.28	83	Joe Morgan	1.23	120	Mickey Tettleton	1.19
9	Gavvy Cravath	1.42	47	Will Clark	1.27	84	Bobby Bonilla	1.23	121	Larry Doyle	1.19
10	John Mize	1.41	48	Chick Hafey	1.27	85	Gil Hodges	1.23	122	Tony Perez	1.19
11	Mel Ott	1.40	49	Rocky Colavito	1.27	86	Frank Baker	1.23	123	Gus Zernial	1.19
12	Mike Schmidt	1.40	50	Jeff Heath	1.27	87	Ernie Banks	1.23	124	Yogi Berra	1.19
13	Barry Bonds	1.40	51	Earl Averill	1.27	88	Dale Murphy	1.23	125	Andre Thornton	1.19
14	Willie Mays	1.40	52	Nap Lajoie	1.27	89	George Foster	1.22	126	Darrell Evans	1.19
15	Dick Allen	1.40	53	Billy Williams	1.27	90	Arky Vaughan	1.22	127	Ted Kluszewski	1.19
16	Stan Musial	1.40	54	Al Rosen	1.26	91	Eddie Collins	1.22	128	Charlie Gehringer	1.19
17	Ralph Kiner	1.39	55	Larry Doby	1.26	92	Paul Waner	1.22	129	Joe Gordon	1.19
18	Ty Cobb	1.39	56	Reggie Jackson	1.26	93	Don Mincher	1.22	130	Jackie Jensen	1.19
19	Hank Aaron	1.38	57	Bob Allison	1.26	94	Dwight Evans	1.22	131	Ken Singleton	1.18
20	Frank Robinson	1.38	58	Will Clark	1.25	95	Sid Gordon	1.22	132	Bill Dickey	1.18
21	Joe Dimaggio	1.38	59	Hal Trosky	1.25	96	Roy Sievers	1.21	133	Vern Stephens	1.18
22	Charlie Keller	1.37	60	Johnny Bench	1.25	97	Rick Monday	1.21	134	Richie Zisk	1.18
23	Tris Speaker	1.37	61	Sherry Magee	1.25	98	Fred Lynn	1.21	135	Riggs Stephenson	1.18
24	Hack Wilson	1.36	62	Joe Medwick	1.25	99	Jim Bottomley	1.21	136	Keith Hernandez	1.18
25	Willie McCovey	1.36	63	Fred Clarke	1.25	100	Jim Rice	1.21	137	Kiki Cuyler	1.18
26	Willie Stargell	1.36	64	Gene Tenace	1.25	101	Dave Kingman	1.21	138	Dave Winfield	1.18
27	Chuck Klein	1.35	65	Al Simmons	1.25	102	Mickey Cochrane	1.20	139	Carl Yastrzemski	1.18
28	Dolph Camilli	1.35	66	Al Kaline	1.24	103	Rico Carty	1.20	140	Enos Slaughter	1.18
29	Fred McGriff	1.34	67	Boog Powell	1.24	104	Tony Oliva	1.20	141	Joe Adcock	1.18
30	Ken Williams	1.34	68	Pedro Guerrero	1.24	105	Jackie Robinson	1.20	142	Minnie Minoso	1.17
31	Honus Wagner	1.34	69	Orlando Cepeda	1.24	106	George Brett	1.20	143	Joe Torre	1.17
32	Duke Snider	1.33	70	Jose Canseco	1.24	107	Goose Goslin	1.20	144	Bobby Murcer	1.17
33	Eddie Mathews	1.32	71	Greg Luzinski	1.24	108	Vic Wertz	1.20	145	Andre Dawson	1.17
34	Sam Crawford	1.31	72	Roger Maris	1.24	109	Ross Youngs	1.20	146	Sixto Lezcano	1.17
35	Harry Heilmann	1.31	73	Ron Santo	1.24	110	John Mayberry	1.20	147	Ernie Lombardi	1.17
36	Elmer Flick	1.31	74	Danny Tartabull	1.24	111	Rafael Palmeiro	1.20	148	Tony Lazzeri	1.17
37	Darryl Strawberry	1.30	75	Tommy Henrich	1.24	112	Jason Thompson	1.20	149	Ken Boyer	1.17
38	Harmon Killebrew	1.30							150	Bobby Veach	1.17

The Season Cycle

Only two players have achieved one

Madison McEntire

While studying the 1993 major league statistics looking for oddities, committing my favorite players' stats to memory, and making my personal judgement for MVP, the Cy Young Award, etc., I noticed one player who had managed only four hits for the season yet had one of each kind (single, double, triple, and home run). I suspected that this was a very rare occurrence and decided to discover if any other players had achieved a "season cycle." Using *Total Baseball* as my source, I found only one other player who achieved this feat. Since 1900 nearly two hundred players have hit for the cycle in the traditional manner but the only two players to have a season cycle are Fred Manrique with the Montreal Expos in 1985 and Curtis Pride, also with Montreal, in 1993.

Fred Manrique—After brief stints with the Toronto Blue Jays in 1981 and 1984 which resulted in only seven singles in 37 at bats, Fred Manrique was sold to the Montreal Expos on April 7, 1985. Playing for Indianapolis, Montreal's AAA club, Manrique batted only .240 with 8 home runs and 37 RBI yet earned a September visit to The Show. On September 15, during Montreal's 6-2 home loss to New York, the 23-year-old Manrique collected his first hit of the 1985 season. Pinch-hitting for Expo pitcher Bert Roberge, he singled against Met pitcher Ron Darling

Madison McEntire is a civil engineer who lives in Maumelle, Arkansas, with his wife, Crissy. He follows the Cubs and Braves on cable and opposes interleague play, wild card teams, and the DH. This is his first published article.

to lead off the bottom of the eighth. It was his eighth career hit, all singles. Batting for Montreal hurler David Palmer on September 23 at Wrigley Field, Manrique collected his first career extra-base hit by tripling off Steve Trout to lead off the bottom of the top of the seventh as the Expos beat the Cubs, 9-8. Manrique failed to collect another hit until October 3. Starting the game at second base, he belted his first big league home run when he lead off the bottom of the first against Philadelphia Phillies' lefthander Shane Rawley. In the fifth, with Rawley still on the mound, Manrique doubled to complete his season cycle. Despite Manrique's most productive day as a major leaguer, the Expos lost at home to the Phillies, 9-8.

Before the 1986 season, Montreal traded Manrique to St. Louis. During the next five seasons he was traded from St. Louis to Chicago (AL) to Texas and finally Minnesota, which released him following the 1990 season. Manrique managed to hook on with the Oakland A's in 1991 and appeared in nine games.

Fred Manrique's major league statistics :

G	AB	BA	H	R	2B	3B	HR	RBI	SB
498	1337	.254	340	151	59	11	20	151	18

Curtis Pride—This is the more interesting of the two. The four hits he gathered during the 1993 season were the first four hits of his career, each came as a pinch-hitter, and he collected the extra-base hits before he singled. The 24-year-old Pride earned a

September call-up with the Expos after compiling 21 HR, 61 RBI, 50 SB and a .324 average while splitting time between the Class AA Harrisburg Senators and the Class AAA Ottawa Lynx. He made his major league debut as a late-inning defensive replacement in left field and flied out to St. Louis center fielder Mark Whiten on the first pitch from reliever Todd Burns in the ninth inning of Montreal's 12-9 win at St. Louis on September 14. Batting for the second time in his brief major league career, Pride collected his first hit against Philadelphia on September 17 at Olympic Stadium. Pinch-hitting for Expo pitcher Chris Nabholz, Pride doubled in the seventh inning off Philadelphia pitcher Bobby Thigpen driving in teammates Randy Ready and Sean Berry, and later scoring his first run as a big leaguer as Montreal beat the Phillies, 8-7, in twelve innings.

During a 6-3 home loss to Atlanta on September 23, Pride (hitting for pitcher Butch Henry) ripped a ninth inning, two-out, RBI triple off Braves pitcher Greg McMichael.

Florida Marlins' pitcher Richie Lewis served up Curtis Pride's first major league home run on September 30 at Joe Robbie Stadium. Batting for pitcher Jeff Shaw, Pride hammered a two-run homer with two outs in the top of the ninth inning and provided the margin of victory in the Expos' 5-3 win over Florida.

With the extra-base hits taken care of, Pride completed his season cycle during the seventh inning of Montreal's 6-3 home win over Pittsburgh on October 1. Pinch-hitting for pitcher Brian Barnes, Pride singled to center against Pirates' pitcher Danny Miceli, stole second base (the first steal of his career), and later scored on Marquis Grissom's double. Pride did not appear on the Expos roster during the 1994 season, but did appear in forty-eight games for Montreal in 1995 and now plays for the Tigers.

Curtis Pride is with Detroit half-way through the 1996 season. His major league statistics through 1995:

G	AB	BA	H	R	2B	3B	HR	RBI	SB
58	72	.208	15	13	2	1	1	7	4

Close calls—From my research I found that while only Manrique and Pride have achieved season cycles dozens of players came close. Except for one glaring exception, these players were either rookies or journeymen struggling to hang on. Two other 1993 rookies came close to duplicating the feats of Manrique and Pride. San Francisco Giants first baseman J.R. Phillips and Atlanta Braves catcher Javy Lopez each collected one double, one triple and one home run. However, Phillips managed two singles, giving him five hits for the season, and Lopez collected three singles bringing his hit total to six. Ken Hubbs, the 1962 National League Rookie of the Year, collected five hits with the Cubs in 1961—two singles, double, triple, and home run. Ron Henry of the 1964 Minnesota Twins collected a single, double, triple, but belted two home runs. Rich Reese did collect a season cycle playing for the 1973 Twins, but he had fourteen hits with Detroit before he was traded to Minnesota late in the 1973 season.

Most players who came close to a season cycle collected three of the hits but could not come up with the fourth, usually the triple or home run. The most famous of these is Bill Dickey, who singled, doubled, and tripled in fifteen at-bats with the New York Yankees in 1928. Frank Howard, during his brief stint with the 1959 Dodgers, managed to single, triple, and homer but could not double in any of his other eighteen at bats.

Lack of speed may have kept several players from a season cycle. For example, Ernie Whitt, playing for Boston before being drafted by Toronto in the expansion draft, managed four hits in 1976—a single, two doubles, and a home run. If Whitt had just been able to take an extra base while running out one of his doubles, he would have had his season cycle. The glaring exception mentioned earlier is the legendary Ted Williams, who came close to a season cycle in his Korean War-shortened 1952 season. If the Boston Red Sox slugger had stretched a single into a double he would certainly have become the most unlikely hitter to have a season cycle. (Who would ever expect Ted to have only four hits in a season?) Instead he settled for two singles, a triple and a home run in only ten at bats.

Bunts, Flies, and Grounders

A history of the sacrifice

Bill Winans

The sacrifice in its different forms—bunts, fly balls, or grounders to advance runners—has been part of baseball for many years, but is scored in different ways for different reasons. This study will review the development of the sacrifice and its impact on the game, and will consider changes in its scoring.

The Sacrifice Bunt—The sacrifice bunt originated in the 1860s or 1870s, though its exact origin may be forever obscured. Nichols (1939) states that information about baseball is difficult to find before about 1880, when it began to be featured in the sports pages regularly and journalists devoted considerable time and space to it.

Dickson (1989) identifies Brooklyn shortstop Dickey Pearce as the first to lay down a bunt in 1866, creating a new offensive tool, though effective use of the weapon was not made for several years. McBride (1980) also credits Pearce with inventing the bunt in 1866, crediting this information to Hugh Fullerton (1912). Seymour (1960) and James (1986) credit Pearce as the first to bunt, and to beat out a bunt, but date the event sometime in the 1870's. Dickson identifies Boston's slick-fielding first baseman Tim Murnane as the man who popularized the practice, beginning in 1876. He quotes Couzens (1980) stating the bunt was still a freak play in 1888 which did not gain strategic importance until years later. Seymour concurs.

Fullerton (1912a) discusses bunting and sacrifice strategy in detail, not only in the majors, but also as used by college and Japanese teams, showing that this brand of "little ball" was popular, and had been used around the baseball world for some years before 1912.

The origin of the word bunt is as confusing as the origin of the act. The earliest use of the term in baseball was in 1891, and many believe the word is derived from "butt," as in butting heads. Webster's Dictionary, however, defines "bunt" as an obscure alternative form of "butt," dating back to 1582. Dickson says the word may also have originated from a railroad term for moving a car onto a side track, or nudging an uncoupled freight car to get it moving.

Fullerton indicates bunting began with a different method of laying the ball down than is practiced today. "Batters formerly turned their bats quickly and struck the ball with the small end, dropping it to the ground. Later many held their bats loosely in the hands and merely let the ball hit it and fall. The faster ball now in use compelled a change and now most of them push or hook the ball with their bats...." (McBride p. 38, Fullerton p. 200), Fullerton also comments on how the lively ball, adopted late in the 1910 season, had changed bunting; he saw many bunts that would have been successful sacrifices the previous season turned into double plays. Advertisements in *Spalding's Official Baseball Guide* from this period offer both the lively and dead balls for sale.

Murnane did much to develop the use of the bunt in baseball, even designing a special bat for the pur-

---

Bill Winans, a baseball fan since 1963, is a doctoral student in marketing.

pose (Dickson). More like a paddle than a bat, it allowed the batter to make contact with the ball, but could not be used to hit the ball sharply. McBride explains that Murnane whittled one side of his bat flat to better "butt" the ball. Like other experiments with the bat, such as a square barrel (four sided) bat that was supposed to increase the production of extra-base hits (Bryson 1990 p. 131), it was quickly abandoned.

The term sacrifice bunt or sacrifice hit was first used in 1880 (Nichols), as a noun in the June 29, 1880 Chicago *Inter Ocean* and the August 27, 1880 Brooklyn *Daily Eagle*, but not as a verb until 1905, with the September 2 *Sporting Life*. Seymour indicates that the sacrifice was first recognized in box scores in 1889, but the batter was charged with a time at bat even with a successful sacrifice. Spalding's *Guide*, edited by Henry Chadwick, who occasionally took it upon himself to announce rule changes that were never put into effect, first recognizes the sacrifice in 1889: "...sacrifice hits, which shall be credited to the Batsman who, when but one man is out, advances a runner on a fly to the outfield or a ground ball...." (p. 121). Despite this statement I find no evidence of flies or grounders scored as sacrifices. *Spalding* (1898) recognizes only bunts as sacrifices, and calls this "...an injustice to team-worker at bat" (p. 248).

Not until the 1890's, when legendary manager Ned Hanlon popularized the bunt, was the concept of a sacrifice, and the rules associated with it, recognized. Hanlon, called the best manager of the nineteenth century by Connie Mack, and the dirtiest ballplayer and manager in the country by others, always looked for a way, any way, to beat the other team. He believed in a strong bench and initiated spring training in Georgia for his team. He worked with John McGraw, Wee Willie Keeler, and others as they developed the hit-and-run play (Danzig and Reichner 1959).

In 1894 the batter of a successful sacrifice was officially credited with a sacrifice and no at bat. The practice actually started in 1893, before it became official, and was not universally recognized until 1897. In 1894 a batter bunting a ball foul was charged with a strike, in an era when a swinging foul was not.

The sacrifice had long been an uncredited, unrecognized part of the game. Dickson quotes *Sporting Life*, March 3, 1886: "Alike in the field and at bat, a man may do the most effective work in that branch of baseball technically called a 'sacrifice play' and not receive a word of credit for it at the hands of the reporters." Even today, *The Baseball Encyclopedia* makes no mention of sacrifices either in individual records, or all time leaders.

The Sacrifice Fly—Unlike the sacrifice bunt, the sacrifice fly has a clear origin and history. In 1908 the batter was first credited with a sacrifice fly, and not charged with an at bat if the runner scored on the play. In 1926 the rule was expanded to include any runner advancing after the catch, whether he scored or not. In 1931 the sacrifice fly rule was removed, and except for the 1939 season was not brought back until 1954, when a sacrifice fly was credited if a run scored. Supposedly, the reason for introducing the sacrifice fly was to increase batting averages, particularly the averages of sluggers, who often have a number of sacrifice flies in a season and would benefit most from the rule. Many batters have had their averages, season or lifetime, improved by this rule. Maracin (1991) identifies five .400 seasons that would not have been if not for the sacrifice fly rule:

Player	Year	#SF's	BA	BA w/o SF's
Ty Cobb	1922	3	.401	.3988657
Rogers Hornsby	1922	4	.401	.398724
Harry Heilmann	1923	6	.403	.3981132
Rogers Hornsby	1925	4	.403	.3996062
Bill Terry	1930	4	.401	.3987441

Hornsby's 1922 season is the majors' only 40 – .400 season, 40 home runs with an over .400 average. Had the sacrifice fly rule not existed, there would be no such season.

But there is another side to it. The drama of Ted Williams achieving his .400 average in 1941 would have been largely eliminated if the rule had existed then. Research by Maracin shows that Williams had six at bats that today would be scored as sacrifice flies. If no at bat had been charged for these, his average would have been .411, not .406. There would have been no final-game drama. Ted would have had it made.

The Sacrifice Grounder—Some today suggest that a new type of sacrifice be added, the sacrifice grounder. The most common forms would be a grounder to the right side that advances a runner from second to third, or scoring a runner from third. In the past few years the former has been recognized in box scores as advancing a runner, but a time at bat is charged. The logic is that a batter gives up his time at bat to advance the runner, as in other sacrifices, and should be charged with something other than a time at bat.

The other side of the argument is that the batter is trying for a hit. The batter hopes the ball will go through the infielders, and score the runner from second or third when it does. If he fails to get a hit, however, the runner will advance, and a purpose is accomplished. If the batter is really trying for a hit, then scoring a sacrifice is not appropriate.

Suggestions—What rules pertaining to the sacrifice that baseball accepts depends upon the purpose of those responsible for the scoring rules. If they want to increase batting averages, one set of changes could be made. If they want to accurately reflect the efforts of a batter to get a hit or to advance a runner, then other rule changes best suit the purpose.

For example, to accurately reflect a batter's intention, both successful and unsuccessful sacrifice bunt attempts should be scored. Under current rules, a batter who attempts to sacrifice but fails is charged with a time at bat. A new statistic, a failed sacrifice (FS) could be charged, and counted as not an official at bat. Scoring successful and unsuccessful sacrifices would also give a measure of a batter's ability to sacrifice successfully.

The sacrifice fly and sacrifice grounder are more complicated problems. Neither is an obvious attempt to sacrifice. A failed attempt to sacrifice here could not be scored. Box scores indicate runners advanced on grounders, perhaps this is sufficient recognition of the effort for both grounders and flies.

Further research could evaluate the effect on batting average of the failed sacrifice and the sacrifice grounder. Would they have any significant effect on batting averages or on the playing of the game? Would they influence strategy, either of the team at bat or the team in the field?

Sources:

Baseball Encyclopedia (1990), Macmillan Publishing Company, New York.

Bryson, Michael G. (1990), *The Twenty-Four Inch Home Run*, p. 131, Contemporary Books, Chicago.

Couzens, Gerald Secor (1980), *A Baseball Album*, Lippincott and Crowell, New York.

Danzig, Allison and Joe Reichler (1959), *The History of Baseball*, Prentice Hall, Inc., Englewood Cliffs, New Jersey.

Dickson, Paul (1989), *The Dickson Baseball Dictionary*, Facts on File, New York.

Fullerton, Hugh S. (1912), "The Baseball Primer," in *American Magazine*, June, 199-205.

Fullerton, Hugh S. (1912), "How to Win Games," in *American Magazine*, July, 298-306.

James, Bill (1986), *The Bill James Historical Baseball Abstract*, Villiard Books, New York.

Maracin, Paul R., "Ted Williams: Even Better than the Record Shows," in *Grand Stand Baseball Annual 1991*, Joseph W. Wayman, editor.

McBride, Joseph (1980), *High and Inside, The Complete Guide to Baseball Slang*, Warner Books, New York

Nichols, Edward J. (1939), *An Historical Dictionary of Baseball Terminology*, Pennsylvania State College.

Seymour, Harold (1960), *Baseball —The Early Years*, Oxford University Press, New York.

Spalding, A. G. (1889), *Spalding's Official Baseball Guide*, American Sports Publishing Company, New York.

Better than Best

MVP winners who improved the following season—and weren't MVP

Ed Menta

There have been three players who, after receiving the Most Valuable Player award one year, improved their overall offensive performance the following season—and yet didn't become the MVP again for their efforts. We're excluding consecutive MVP winners, such as Cincinnati's Joe Morgan, NL winner in 1975-76, or Barry Bonds, who won in 1992 for the Pittsburgh Pirates and in 1993 for the San Francisco Giants. Both improved their performances after their first MVP season, but both were recognized as Most Valuable the following season.

DiMaggio—Our first example is Joe DiMaggio. "Joltin' Joe" won his third MVP in 1947, despite being overshadowed by Triple Crown winner Ted Williams in every major offensive category. In 1948, DiMaggio improved in almost every category, as a quick glance at the accompanying chart shows. He raised his batting average from .315 to .320, belted a league-leading 39 homers (up from a modest 20 the year before), slugged .598 (up from .522 in '47), and, topping it off, led the league in RBIs with 155 as opposed to 97 in 1947. The only category in which he did not improve was doubles (26 in 1948, 31 in 1947). Yet who won the 1948 American League MVP? Lou Boudreau of the Cleveland Indians, who not only hit .355 while playing a brilliant shortstop, but also managed the Indians to a pennant.

In his autobiography, *My Turn at Bat*, Ted Williams, who won the batting title that year at .369, rates Boudreau's season as one of the greatest in the history of the American League; so DiMaggio wasn't robbed, despite his vastly improved performance.

Berra—Up next for consideration is another Yankee three-time MVP winner—Yogi Berra. Yogi copped the award in 1951, '54, and '55. But in 1956, Yogi improved his previous season's award winning performance in almost every way. He hit .298 to .272, slugged for an average of .534 to .470, and smashed 30 homers to 27. Yogi also upped his totals in hits, doubles, and runs scored. Only in RBIs (105 to 108) and triples (2 to 3) did he fail to improve. But perhaps the reason he didn't win the MVP award was also the reason he "dipped" in RBIs. In 1956 he hit behind Mickey Mantle's Triple Crown winning performance of 52 homers, 130 RBIs, and .353 average. Mickey probably often cleared the bases for his teammate, and despite Berra's improvement over the previous season, Mantle deserved to win the 1956 award.

Robinson—Our last candidate for this unusual club is our lone National League entry—Frank Robinson. In 1966, Robinson won his second MVP award by leading the American League with a Triple Crown campaign as a member of the Baltimore Orioles, thereby becoming the only man to win the MVP in both leagues. But five years earlier, Robinson led the Cincinnati Reds to their first NL pennant in twenty-

---

Ed Menta is an associate professor of theater at Kalamazoo College in Michigan, where he also teaches "Baseball in American Culture."

Transcendental Graphics

Yogi Berra

one years with an outstanding season. Yet, as spectacular as Robby was in 1961, he was better in '62. He batted .342 in '62 as opposed to .323 the year before, slugged .624 to .611 (leading the league both seasons), drove in 134 runs to 124, and smashed a league-leading 51 doubles over 32 in '61. Also, Robinson improved in homers, hits and runs scored in 1962. Only in triples (2 to 7) did Robinson not increase his 1961 totals. But 1962 was the year Maury Wills broke Ty Cobb's single-season stolen base record. Wills stole 104 bases, the most ever in the major leagues up until that time. His historic achievement rightly earned him the MVP.

There have been a few others who almost matched

this unusual feat of DiMaggio, Berra, and Robinson, most notably Thurman Munson for his 1976-77 seasons, Hal Newhouser in 1945-46, Mickey Cochrane in 1934-35, Don Mattingly in 1985-86, Marty Marion in 1944-45, Willie Mays in 1954-55, Roberto Clemente in 1966-67, and Mike Schmidt in 1986-87. But while these players all had seasons that either matched their previous year or came close to exceeding it, only DiMaggio, Berra, and Robinson all clearly surpassed their MVP seasons the following year—and did not win the award.

These three players all won MVP awards in seasons that were not, for them, "career years." This in itself attests to their greatness.

THE BASEBALL RESEARCH JOURNAL

Frank Robinson

Transcendental Graphics

Player	Year	G	AB	R	H	2b	3b	HR	RBI	BA	SA	MVP Voting
DiMaggio	1947	141	534	97	168	31	10	20	97	.315	.522	1st
	1948	153	594	110	190	26	11	39	155	.320	.598	2nd
Berra	1955	147	541	84	147	20	3	27	108	.272	.470	1st
	1956	140	521	93	155	29	2	30	105	.298	.534	2nd
Robinson	1961	153	545	117	176	32	7	37	124	.323	.611	1st
	1962	162	609	134	208	51	2	39	136	.342	.624	4th

Best Offensive Statistical Years

Closing in on all-time records in a single season

Bill Szepanski

Any baseball player can only dream of a season with these numbers: 61 home runs, 190 RBIs, a batting average of .426, and stealing 130 bases. Each of these is an all-time record, but each was accomplished by a different player. I thought it would be interesting to see how close an individual player got in a single year to these twentieth century records:

1.	Runs scored:	Babe Ruth	1921	177
2.	Hits:	George Sisler	1920	257
3.	Doubles:	Earl Webb	1931	67
4.	Triples:	Chief Wilson	1912	36
5.	Home Runs:	Roger Maris	1961	61
6.	Runs Batted In:	Hack Wilson	1930	190
7.	Walks:	Babe Ruth	1923	170
8.	Batting Average:	Nap Lajoie	1901	.426
9.	On Base Pct.:	Ted Williams	1941	.551
10.	Slugging Average:	Babe Ruth	1920	.847
11.	Stolen Bases:	Rickey Henderson	1982	130

I converted statistics in each category to a percentage of the record. For example, 143 runs is 81 percent of 177, so I assign that accomplishment 81 points. If a single player in a single year set the all-time record in each of the eleven categories, he would have 1100 points.

Of course, by its very nature, this system deals only with simple, year-end statistics. It does not take into account any of the relative statistics that have been developed over recent years. Using these parameters, the thirty offensive years that are closest to baseball perfection are shown below.

Top thirty statistical years

	Year	R	H	2B	3B	HR	RBI	BB	BA	OBP	SLG	SB	Total
1. Ruth	1921	177	204	44	16	59	171	144	.378	512	846	17	
pts.		100	79	66	44	97	90	85	89	93	100	13	856
2. Gehrig	1927	149	218	52	18	47	175	109	.373	474	765	10	
pts.		84	85	78	50	77	92	64	88	86	90	8	802
3. Ruth	1923	151	205	45	13	41	131	170	.393	545	764	17	
pts.		85	80	67	36	67	69	100	92	99	90	13	798

Bill Szepanski *is a retired high school math teacher from Juneau, Alaska. He believes that with the trend toward high scoring games many all-time records are in jeopardy.*

4. Ruth	1920	158	172	36	9	54	137	148	.376	530	847	14	
pts.		89	67	54	25	89	72	87	88	96	100	11	778
5. Gehrig	1930	143	220	42	17	41	174	101	.379	473	721	12	
pts.		81	86	63	47	67	92	59	89	86	85	9	764
6. Ruth	1927	158	192	29	8	60	164	138	.356	487	772	7	
pts.		89	75	43	22	98	86	81	84	88	91	5	762
7. Gehrig	1931	163	211	31	15	46	184	117	.341	446	662	17	
pts.		92	82	46	42	75	97	69	80	81	78	13	755
8. Foxx	1932	151	213	33	9	58	169	116	.364	469	749	3	
pts.		85	83	49	25	95	89	68	85	85	88	2	754
9. Hornsby	1922	141	250	46	14	42	152	65	.401	459	722	17	
pts.		80	97	69	39	69	80	38	94	83	85	13	747
10. Cobb	1911	147	248	47	24	8	127	44	.420	467	621	83	
pts.		83	96	70	67	13	67	26	99	85	73	64	743
11. Wilson	1930	146	208	35	6	56	190	105	.356	454	723	3	
pts.		82	81	52	17	92	100	62	84	82	85	2	739
12. Gehrig	1936	167	205	37	7	49	152	130	.354	478	696	3	
pts.		94	80	55	19	80	80	76	83	87	82	2	738
13. Klein	1930	158	250	59	8	40	170	54	.386	436	687	4	
pts.		89	97	88	22	66	89	32	91	79	81	3	737
14. Ruth	1924	143	200	39	7	46	121	142	.378	513	739	9	
pts.		81	78	58	19	75	64	84	89	93	87	7	735
15. Greenberg	1937	137	200	49	14	40	183	102	..337	436	668	8	
pts.		77	78	73	39	66	96	60	79	79	79	6	732
16. Ruth	1930	150	186	28	9	49	153	136	.359	493	732	10	
pts.		85	72	42	25	80	81	80	84	89	86	8	732
17. Foxx	1938	139	197	33	9	50	175	119	.349	462	704	5	
pts.		79	77	49	25	82	92	70	82	84	83	4	727
18. Ruth	1926	139	184	30	5	47	146	144	.372	516	737	11	
pts.		79	72	45	14	77	77	85	87	94	87	8	725
19. Williams	1949	150	194	39	3	43	159	162	.343	490	650	1	
pts.		85	75	58	8	70	84	95	81	89	77	1	723
20. Gehrig	1934	128	210	40	6	49	165	109	.363	465	706	9	
pts.		72	82	60	17	80	87	64	85	84	83	7	721
21. Musial	1948	135	230	46	18	39	131	79	.376	450	702	7	
pts.		76	89	69	50	64	69	46	88	82	83	5	721
22. Ruth	1931	149	199	31	3	46	163	128	.373	495	700	5	
pts.		84	77	46	8	75	86	75	88	90	83	4	716
23. Hornsby	1929	156	229	47	8	39	149	87	.380	459	679	2	
pts.		88	89	70	22	64	78	51	89	83	80	2	716
24. Ruth	1928	163	173	29	8	54	142	135	.323	461	709	4	
pts.		92	67	43	22	89	75	79	76	84	84	3	714
25. Hornsby	1925	133	203	41	10	39	143	83	.403	489	756	5	
pts.		75	79	61	28	64	75	49	95	89	89	4	708
26. Klein	1932	152	226	50	15	38	137	60	.348	404	646	20	
pts.		86	88	75	42	62	72	35	82	73	76	15	706
27. Sisler	1920	137	257	49	18	19	122	46	.407	449	632	42	
pts.		77	100	73	50	31	64	27	96	81	75	32	706
28. Gehrig	1937	138	200	37	9	37	159	127	.351	473	643	4	
pts.		78	78	55	25	61	84	75	82	86	76	3	703

29. DiMaggio	1937	151	215	35	15	46	167	64	.346	412	673	3	
pts.		85	84	52	42	75	88	38	81	75	79	2	701
30. Foxx	1933	125	204	37	9	48	163	96	.356	449	703	2	
pts.		71	79	55	25	79	86	56	84	81	83	2	701

Best years by other players

Aaron, H.	1959	638		Kluszewski, T.	1954	609
Appling, L.	1936	579		Lajoie, N.	1901	661
Averill, E.	1936	661		Mantle, M.	1956	673
*Bagwell, J.	1994	604		Maris, R.	1961	606
Banks, E.	1958	598		Mathews, E.	1953	624
Bench, J.	1970	578		Mattingly, D.	1986	608
Berra, Y.	1950	558		Mays, W.	1955	645
Bottomley, J.	1928	657		McCovey, W.	1969	611
Brett, G.	1980	592		Medwick, J.	1937	665
Burkett, J.	1901	579		Mize, J.	1939	635
Campanella, R.	1953	569		O'Doul, L.	1929	667
Canseco, J.	1988	614		Olerud, J.	1993	632
Carew, R.	1977	639		Ott, M.	1929	661
Cash, N.	1961	666		Rice, J.	1978	630
Cepeda, O.	1961	576		Robinson, F.	1962	665
Clemente, R.	1967	555		Robinson, J.	1949	628
Colavito, R.	1961	615		Rosen, A.	1953	627
Collins, E.	1914	578		Schmidt, M.	1980	594
Collins, Rip	1934	619		Simmons, A.	1930	699
Crawford, S.	1911	605		Snider, D.	1954	652
Cronin, J.	1930	598		Speaker, T.	1923	682
Cuyler, K.	1930	687		Stargell, W.	1973	593
Foster, G.	1977	622		Terry, B.	1930	673
Frisch, F.	1930	571		Thomas, F.	1993	610
Gehringer, C.	1936	657		Trosky, H.	1936	652
Griffey Jr., K.	1993	620		Vaughan, A.	1935	609
Heilmann, H.	1923	646		Wagner, H.	1900	615
Herman, Billy	1935	545		Waner, P.	1928	633
Jackson, J.	1911	653		Williams, B.	1970	619
Jackson, R.	1969	616		Yastrzemski, C.	1970	628
Kaline, A.	1955	576				
Killebrew, H.	1969	613				
Kiner, R.	1951	635				

* Jeff Bagwell's total for 1994 converts to 719 points for a 154 game schedule.

Big Win-Small Loss Pitching Records

Remarkable twentieth century performances

Scott Nelson

The remarkable winning percentages of Atlanta's Greg Maddux (19-2) and Seattle's Randy Johnson (18-2) in 1995 highlight a listing of big win-small loss pitching records since 1900.

Maddux and Johnson became the first moundsmen in major league history to post .900 percentages with at least 20 decisions. And they did it in a season shortened by 18 games due to the strike and late start.

Still, possibly the most noteworthy entry in the following rundown is Lefty Grove's 59-9 record for the 1930 (28-5) and 1931 (31-4) seasons with the Philadelphia A's.

The focus here is on big win-small loss numbers in three categories: (1) a pitcher's record in a single season, (2) teammates' combined marks in a single season, and (3) a pitcher's numbers in two consecutive seasons. Some related figures deal with consecutive pitching victories.

Most wins without a loss

Pitcher	Team	Year	W-L
Tom Zachary	New York (AL)	1929	12-0 (AL Record)
Dennis Lamp	Toronto (Relief)	1985	11-0
Howie Krist	St. Louis (NL)	1941	10-0 (NL Record)
Joe Pate	Phil. (AL) (Relief)	1926	9-0
Ken Holtzman	Chicago (NL)	1967	9-0
Frank DiPino	St. Louis (NL) (Relief)	1989	9-0

Most consecutive wins, career

NL—24—Carl Hubbell, New York, July 17, 1936 through May 27, 1937

      (16 in 1936, 8 in 1937)

AL—17—Johnny Allen, Cleveland, Sept. 10, 1936 through Sept. 30, 1937

      (2 in 1936, 15 in 1937)

    —Dave McNally, Baltimore, Sept. 22, 1968 through July 30, 1969

      (2 in 1968, 15 in 1969)

Scott Nelson is retired after eleven years as sports editor of the Mankato (Minnesota) Free Press and twenty-six years of teaching high school English and Journalism and advising student publications. He and his wife Marge recently celebrated their fortieth wedding anniversary. Scott's chief claim to fame is that he was born on September 30, 1927, the day Babe Ruth hit his sixtieth home run of the season.

Most consecutive wins, season

NL—19—Rube Marquard, New York, April 11 through July 3, 1912

      (Went 7-11 rest of season to finish 26-11)

AL—16—Walter Johnson, Washington, July 3, (second game), through Aug. 23, 1912 (first game).

    —Joe Wood, Boston, July 8 through Sept. 19, 1931.

    —Lefty Grove, Philadelphia, June 8 through Aug. 19, 1931.

    —Schoolboy Rowe, Detroit, June 15 through Aug. 25, 1934.

Fourteen or more wins with one loss

Roy Face	Pittsburgh (Relief)	1959	18-1 (NL Record)
Rick Sutcliffe	Chicago (NL)	1984	16-1*
Johnny Allen	Cleveland	1937	15-1** (AL Record)
Phil Regan	Los Angeles (Relief)	1966-2	14-1

*Sutcliffe was 4-5 with Cleveland before being traded during season. Was awarded NL best pct. record for season.

**Allen won his first 15 decisions before losing on last day of season.

Fourteen or more wins with two losses

Greg Maddux	Atlanta	1995-1	19-2* (NL record)
Randy Johnson	Seattle	1995	18-2* (AL Record)
Fred Fitzsimmons	Brooklyn (NL)	1940	16-2

Transcendental Graphics

Whitey Ford

Bob Stanley	Boston (AL) (Relief)	1978	15-2
Tom Seaver	Cincinnati	1981**	14-2
Ron Davis	NY (AL) (Relief)	1979	14-2
Deacon Phillippe	Pittsburgh	1910	14-2

*Maddux's .905 pct. and Johnson's .900 are best in major league history for pitchers with 20 or more decisions.

** 1981 was a strike-shortened season.

Fifteen or more wins with three losses

Ron Guidry	New York (AL)	1978-1	25-3 (AL Record)
Preacher Roe	Brooklyn	1951	22-3 (NL Record)
David Cone	New York (NL)	1988	20-3
Orel Hershiser	Los Angeles	1985	19-3
Chief Bender	Philadelphia (AL)	1914-2	17-3
Tom Hughes	Boston (NL)	1916	16-3
Emil Yde	Pittsburgh	1924	16-3
Schoolboy Rowe	Detroit	1940-2	16-3
Sandy Consuegra	Chicago (AL)	1954	16-3
Ralph Terry	New York (AL)	1961-1	16-3
Ron Perranoski	Los Angeles (Relief)	1963-1	16-3
Hoyt Wilhelm	New York (NL)(Relief)	1952	15-3

Sixteen or more wins with four losses

Lefty Grove	Philadelphia (AL)	1931-2	31-4 (AL Record)
Bill Donovan	Detroit	1907-2	25-4
Whitey Ford	New York (AL)	1961-1	25-4
Dwight Gooden	New York (NL)	1985	24-4 (NL Record)
Roger Clemens	Boston (AL)	1986-2	24-4
King Cole	Chicago (NL)	1910-2	20-4

Spud Chandler	New York (AL)	1943-1	20-4
Ed Reulbach	Chicago (NL)	1906-2	19-4
Elmer Riddle	Cincinnati	1941	19-4
Sal Maglie	New York (NL)	1950	18-4
Mark Portugal	Houston	1993	18-4
Ed Reulbach	Chicago (NL)	1907-1	17-4
Doc Crandall	New York (NL)	1910	17-4
Johnny Allen	New York (AL)	1932-1	17-4
Ted Wilks	St. Louis (NL)	1944-1	17-4
Phil Niekro	Atlanta	1982	17-4
Jimmy Key	New York (AL)	1994	17-4
Ed Doheny	Pittsburgh	1902-*	16-4
Bert Humphries	Chicago (NL)	1913	16-4
Firpo Marberry	Washington	1931	16-4
Ed Lopat	New York (AL)	1953-1	16-4
Jim Palmer	Baltimore	1969-2	16-4
Larry Gura	Kansas City	1978	16-4
Tommy Greene	Philadelphia (NL)	1993-2	16-4

Nineteen or more wins with five losses

Joe Wood	Boston (AL)	1912-1	34-5 (AL Record)
Lefty Grove	Philadelphia (AL)	1930-1	28-5
Lefty Gomez	New York (AL)	1934	26-5
Sandy Koufax	Los Angeles	1963-1	25-5 (NL Record)
Chief Bender	Philadelphia (AL)	1910-1	23-5
Bob Purkey	Cincinnati	1962	23-5
Alvin Crowder	St. Louis (AL)	1928	21-5
Bobo Newsom	Detroit	1940-2	21-5

Tiny Bonham	New York (AL)	1942-2	21-5
Larry Jansen	New York (NL)	1947	21-5
Dave McNally	Baltimore	1971-2	21-5
Catfish Hunter	Oakland	1973-1	21-5
Sam Leever	Pittsburgh	1905	20-5
Stan Coveleski	Washington	1925-2	20-5
Don Newcombe	Brooklyn	1955-1	20-5
John Candelaria	Pittsburgh	1977	20-5
Dutch Leonard	Boston (AL)	1914	19-5
Sandy Koufax	Los Angeles	1964	19-5
Wally Bunker	Baltimore	1964	19-5

Twenty-two or more wins with six losses

Denny McLain	Detroit	1968-1	31-6 (AL Record)
Jack Chesbro	Pittsburgh	*1902	28-6 (NL Record)
Dazzy Vance	Brooklyn	1924	28-6
Bob Welch	Oakland	1990-2	27-6
Mordecai Brown	Chicago (NL)	1906-2	26-6
Russ Ford	New York (AL)	1910	26-6
Eddie Plank	Philadelphia (AL)	1912	26-6
Carl Hubbell	New York (NL)	1936-2	26-6
C. Mathewson	New York (NL)	1909	25-6
Howie Camnitz	Pittsburgh	1909-1	25-6
Dave Ferris	Boston (AL)	1946-2	25-6
Juan Marichal	San Francisco	1966	25-6
Ellis Kinder	Boston (AL)	1949	23-6
Sal Maglie	New York (NL)	1951-2	23-6
Bret Saberhagen	Kansas City	1989	23-6
Lon Warneke	Chicago (NL)	1932-2	22-6
Tex Hughson	Boston (AL)	1942	22-6
Ron Guidry	New York (AL)	1985	22-6
Doug Drabek	Pittsburgh	1990	22-6
Tom Glavine	Atlanta	1993	22-6

Twenty-five or more wins with seven losses

Walter Johnson	Washington	1913	36-7 (AL Record)
Dizzy Dean	St. Louis (NL)	1934-1	30-7 (NL Record)
Ed Cicotte	Chicago (AL)	1919-2	29-7
Robin Roberts	Philadelphia (NL)	1952	28-7
Don Newcombe	Brooklyn	1956-2	27-7
Bill James	Boston (NL)	1914-1	26-7
Joe Bush	New York (AL)	1922-2	26-7
Sam Leever	Pittsburgh	1903-2	25-7
Paul Derringer	Cincinnati	1939-2	25-7
Mel Parnell	Boston (AL)	1949	25-7
Tom Seaver	New York (NL)	1969-1	25-7
Steve Stone	Baltimore	1980	25-7

Two big win–small loss pitchers on a team in a season (biggest winners with 40 or more total wins)

Forty or more wins and seven to eleven losses

Yr.	Team	Pitchers	W-L
1961-1	New York (AL)	Whitey Ford 25-4, Ralph Terry 16-3	41-7
1963-1	Los Angeles	Sandy Koufax 25-5, Ron Perranoski 16-3	41-8
1985	New York (NL)	Dwight Gooden 24-4, Ron Darling 16-6	40-10
1931-2	Phil. (AL)	Lefty Grove 31-4, G. Earnshaw 21-7	52-11

Forty or more wins with twelve losses

1902-*	Pittsburgh	Jack Chesbro 28-6, J. Tannehill 20-6	48-12
1978-1	New York (AL)	Ron Guidry 25-3, Ed Figueroa 20-9	45-12
1951	Brooklyn	Preacher Roe 22-3, D. Newcombe 20-9	42-12
1925-2	Washington	Stan Coveleski 20-5, W. Johnson 20-7	40-12
1956-2	Brooklyn	D. Newcombe 27-7, Sal Maglie 13-5	40-12
1993	Atlanta	Tom Glavine 22-6, S. Avery 18-6	40-12

Forty or more wins with thirteen losses

1949	Boston (AL)	Mel Parnell 25-7, Ellis Kinder 23-6	48-13
1910	New York (NL)	C. Mathewson 27-9, D. Crandall 17-4	44-13
1942-1	St. Louis (NL)	Mort Cooper 22-7, Johnny Beazley 21-6	43-13
1971-2	Baltimore	Dave McNally 21-5, Pat Dobson 20-8	41-13
1988	Cincinnati	D. Jackson 23-8, Tom Browning 18-5	41-13
1919	Cincinnati	Slim Sallee 21-7, Dutch Reuther 19-6	40-13

Forty or more wins with fourteen losses

1910-1	Phil. (AL)	J. Coombs 31-9, Chief Bender 23-5	54-14
1912-1	Boston (AL)	J. Wood 34-5, H. Bedient 20-9	54-14
1913	Washington	Walter Johnson 36-7, J. Boehling 17-7	53-14
1903-2	Pittsburgh	S. Leever 25-7, D. Phillippe 24-7	49-14
1906-2	Chicago (NL)	Mordecai Brown 26-6, J. Pfiester 20-8	46-14
1966	San Francisco	Juan Marichal 25-6, Gaylord Perry 21-8	46-14
1963-2	New York (AL)	Whitey Ford 24-7, Jim Bouton 21-7	45-14
1929-1	Phil. (AL)	G. Earnshaw 24-8, Lefty Grove 20-6	44-14
1907-1	Chicago (NL)	O. Overall 23-8, M. Brown 20-6	43-14
1932-1	New York (AL)	Lefty Gomez 24-7, Red Ruffing 18-7	42-14
1927-1	New York (AL)	Waite Hoyt 22-7, W. Moore 19-7	41-14
1923-1	New York (AL)	S. Jones 21-8, Herb Pennock 19-6	40-14
1986-2	Boston (AL)	R. Clemens 24-4, Oil Can Boyd 16-10	40-14

Pitchers with two consecutive big win–small loss seasons (forty or more total wins)

Forty or more wins with nine losses

Pitcher	Team	Years	Records	Total
Lefty Grove	Philadelphia (AL)	1-1930-31-2	28-5, 31-4	59-9

Forty or more wins with ten losses

Joe Wood	Boston (AL)	1-1912-13	34-5, 11-5	45-10
Sandy Koufax	Los Angeles	1-1963-64	25-5, 19-5	44-10
Sal Maglie	New York (NL)	2-1950-51	18-4, 23-6	41-10
Ron Guidry	New York (AL)	1-1977-78-1	16-7, 25-3	41-10
Dwight Gooden	New York (NL)	1985-86-1	24-4, 17-6	41-10
Chief Bender	Philadelphia (AL)	1-1910-11-1	23-5, 17-5	40-10

Forty or more wins with eleven losses

Lefty Grove	Philadelphia (AL)	2-1929-30-31	28-5	48-11
Bill Donovan	Detroit	2-1907-08-2	25-4, 18-7	43-11

Ed Reulbach	Chicago (NL)	1-1907-08-1	17-4, 24-7	41-11

Forty or more wins with twelve losses

Don Newcombe	Brooklyn	1-1955-56-2	20-5, 27-7	47-12
Mordecai Brown	Chicago (NL)	2-1906-07-1	26-6, 20-6	46-12
Sam Leever	Pittsburgh	1905-06	20-5, 22-7	42-12
Whitey Ford	New York (AL)	1-1961-62-1	25-4, 16-8	42-12
Catfish Hunter	Oakland	1-1972-73-1	21-7, 21-5	42-12

Forty or more wins with thirteen losses

Roger Clemens	Boston (AL)	2-1986-87	24-4, 20-9	44-13
Whitey Ford	New York (AL)	2-1963-64-2	24-7, 17-6	41-13

Forty or more wins with fourteen losses

Lefty Grove	Philadelphia (AL)	2-1931-32	31-4, 25-10	56-14
Eddie Plank	Philadelphia (AL)	1-1911-12	23-8, 26-6	49-14
Carl Hubbell	New York (NL)	2-1936-37-2	26-6, 22-8	48-14
Waite Hoyt	New York (AL)	1-1927-28-1	22-7, 23-7	45-14
Dave McNally	Baltimore	1-1970-71-2	24-9, 21-5	45-14
Lefty Grove	Philadelphia (AL)	1928-29-1	24-8, 20-6	44-14
Bob Welch	Oakland	1-1989-90-2	17-8, 27-6	44-14
Walter Johnson	Washington	1-1924-25-2	23-7, 20-7	43-14
Red Ruffing	New York (AL)	1-1938-39-1	21-7, 21-7	42-14
Tom Glavine	Atlanta	2-1992-93	20-8, 22-6	42-14
Preacher Roe	Brooklyn	1950-51	19-11, 22-3	41-14
Sam Leever	Pittsburgh	*1902-03-2	16-7, 25-7	41-14

What happens when teams claiming pitchers with remarkable marks meet each other in World Series competition?

While one might think their Series meetings would be close, half of the ten team confrontations resulted in 4-0 sweeps and the four of them went only five games.

The results of Fall Classics pitting teams with pitchers in our study—and their teammates with standout records—follow:

Yr.	Series Winner	Series Loser	W-L
1907	Chicago Cubs	Detroit Tigers	4-0
	Orvie Overall, 23-8	Bill Donovan, 25-4	
	Mordecai Brown, 20-6		
	Ed Reulbach, 17-4		
1908	Chicago Cubs	Detroit Tigers	4-1
	Ed Reulbach, 24-7	Bill Donovan, 18-7	
1910	Philadelphia A's	Chicago Cubs	4-1
	Jack Coombs, 31-9	King Cole, 20-4	
	Chief Bender, 23-5		
1914	Boston Braves	Philadelphia A's	4-0
	Bill James, 26-7	Chief Bender, 17-3	
	Dick Rudolph, 26-10	Eddie Plank, 15-7	
		Bob Shawkey, 16-8	
1932	New York Yankees	Chicago Cubs	4-0
	Lefty Gomez, 24-7	Lon Warneke, 22-6	
	Red Ruffing, 18-7		
	Johnny Allen, 17-4		
1939	New York Yankees	Cincinnati Reds	4-0
	Red Ruffing, 21-7	Paul Derringer, 25-7	
1942	St. Louis Cardinals	New York Yankees	4-1
	Mort Cooper, 22-7	Ernie Bonham, 21-5	
	Johnny Beazley, 21-6		
1963	Los Angeles Dodgers	New York Yankees	4-0
	Sandy Koufax, 25-5	Whitey Ford, 24-7	
	Ron Perranoski, 16-3	Jim Bouton, 21-7	
1969	New York Mets	Baltimore Orioles	4-1
	Tom Seaver, 25-7	Jim Palmer, 16-4	
1986	New York Mets	Boston Red Sox	4-3
	Dwight Gooden, 17-6	Roger Clemens, 24-4	
	Bob Ojeda, 18-6	Oil Can Boyd, 16-10	

Note: The number 1 before or after a date indicates the team won its league pennant and the World Series. The numeral 2 indicates the team won its league pennant but lost in the World Series. An asterisk (*) before the entry indicates there was no World Series (1902).

Hall of Fame pitchers in study

Chief Bender	Lefty Grove	Christy Mathewson
Mordecai Brown	Waite Hoyt	Herb Pennock
Jack Chesbro	Carl Hubbell	Eddie Plank
Stan Coveleski	Catfish Hunter	Robin Roberts
Dizzy Dean	Walter Johnson	Red Ruffing
Whitey Ford	Sandy Koufax	Dazzy Vance
Lefty Gomez	Juan Marichal	Hoyt Wilhelm

From a Researcher's Notebook

Al Kermisch

Milt Gaston—one of the Babe's favorites

Milton Gaston, who celebrated his 100th birthday last January 27, but who passed away three months later on April 26, pitched in the majors for eleven years. He won 97 games and lost 164, but most of the time he pitched for second division clubs. Gaston gave up 114 home runs in his career. He was one of Babe Ruth's favorite hurlers, giving up thirteen homers to the Bambino. He ranked third on the Babe's list, behind Rube Walberg with seventeen, George Dauss with fifteen, and tied for third place at thirteen with Walter Stewart. When Ruth hit his record 60 circuit clouts in 1927, Gaston tied with Walberg, each giving up four to the great slugger. Overall, Gaston gave up five home runs to Ruth while with the Browns, four with the Red Sox, and also four while pitching for the White Sox.

Gaston, who began his major league career with the Yankees in 1924, got a measure of revenge on his old mates in their great year of 1927. He prevented the Yanks from setting a major league record of winning all twenty-two games from one club in a season. After New York had defeated the Browns for the twenty-first consecutive time, Gaston broke the spell by downing the home club, 6-2, on five hits at Yankee Stadium on Sunday, September 11. One of the two runs he gave up was Ruth's fiftieth home run, a terrific drive into the rightfield bleachers.

An unusual triple steal for Orioles

On June 10, 1972, the Orioles pulled off an unusual triple steal against the Rangers in Texas. One would assume that the principals would include some of the speedier players on the Baltimore team, such as Mark Belanger, Paul Blair, Don Buford, Bobby Grich, and Don Baylor. But the shocker is that the trio included catcher Johnny Oates, current Texas manager; second baseman Dave Johnson, back with the Orioles this year as pilot; and Hall of Fame third baseman Brooks Robinson. Oates had five steals for the season, while Johnson and Robinson each posted his only stolen base of the campaign.

The triple steal, the first in modern Oriole history, was something of a fluke. It came in the sixth inning. Grich and Oates singled. Robinson doubled in Grich and Johnson was given an intentional pass. Pitcher Dave McNally attempted a suicide squeeze bunt but missed the ball, which wound up in the dirt and bounced away from catcher Dick Billings. Since all three runners were in motion at the time it was ruled a triple steal. The Orioles won the game 5-2.

Al Kermisch began researching baseball under the guidance of Ernest J. Lanigan, a great historian of the past.

Addie Joss held seven-year grudge against umpire

Hall of Famer Addie Joss pitched a perfect game for Cleveland against the White Sox on October 2, 1908, and after the game he stated it was time for him to forgive umpire Bob Caruthers. Joss had held a seven-year grudge against Caruthers, who umpired his first game in the majors against St. Louis on April 26, 1902. Despite the fact that Joss broke in with a 3-0 one-hitter against the Browns, he was peeved at two of the umpire's decisions, one of which he felt kept him from becoming the first American League pitcher to pitch a no-hitter—and in his first major league game. The other decision that irked Joss was a call which also deprived him of a home run in his first big league contest.

The only hit credited to St. Louis came in the fourth inning. Jesse Burkett hit a short fly to right field and "Zaza" Harvey came charging in and caught the ball several inches from the ground. Caruthers, however, called it a trapped ball. After the game even the St. Louis players admitted that Caruthers had made a mistake. Then when Joss hit a ball into the center field bleachers that bounced back onto the field after hitting the edge of one of the seats, Caruthers called it a double. After that Addie always had it in for Caruthers, but after the perfect game he said, "it's time to forgive him now." Just why did Joss hold the grudge so long? Until he pitched the perfect game his record did not include a no-hit game or a home run. After the perfect game Joss finally hit his only home run on September 7, 1909. He also pitched another no-hit game against the White Sox on April 20, 1910.

Pitcher could not resist throwing glove at ball

Cleveland southpaw Al Smith, who along with righthander Jim Bagby, Jr., stopped Joe DiMaggio's record 56-game batting streak, was with Buffalo in the International League before moving up to the Indians in 1940. Smith had a sensational year at Buffalo in 1939, winning sixteen and losing only two, including fifteen consecutive wins. But for a momentary lapse at Baltimore on the night of June 5, Smith might have been 17-1 with sixteen straight victories.

Smith was pitching well and went into the last half of the seventh inning with a 3-2 lead. Eddie Moore led off with a single and Bill Lillard bunted. The bunt was a little to the left of Smith and just out of the reach of the pitcher. In frustration Smith took off his glove and threw it at the ball, partly stopping it. Manager Rogers Hornsby, coaching at first base, immediately protested to umpire Lou Jorda, who had no choice under the rules but to wave Moore home and Lillard, who was credited with a triple, to third base. Completely unnerved, Smith gave up a single to pitcher Harry Matuzak and Lillard came in with what proved to be the winning run in a 5-3 victory. After the game Smith was asked why he threw his glove at the ball. He said that he always wanted to do it and just couldn't resist.

Nick Altrock's joke home run in 1918

In 1918, the major league season was curtailed because of World War I. The campaign in Washington ended on Monday, September 2, with a twin bill against the Philadelphia Athletics. After the A's won the first game, the Senators came back to win the nightcap, 8-3. During the teens manager Clark Griffith tried to put some humor in the final home game if it had no bearing in the standings. It was such a game in the season finale in Washington in 1913 that was termed one of the most farcical games ever played in the majors, and eventually cost Walter Johnson his record 1.09 ERA—the lowest ERA in a season. Many years after Johnson retired a game-to-game check of his record revealed that the two batters he had tossed up pitches to had scored and had to be charged as earned runs. It didn't mean anything until 1968, when Bob Gibson turned in a 1.12 ERA, thereby bettering the revised 1.14 Johnson ERA.

In the 1918 closing game, with the Senators holding a comfortable lead, coach and comedian Altrock was allowed to finish the game. In the bottom of the eighth inning Altrock came to bat. There were two outs and Wickey McAvoy, normally a catcher but playing first base, changed positions with pitcher Mule Watson. McAvoy did everything but hit the ball for Altrock. Nick fouled off two pitches and then hit one that didn't have enough speed to break a pane of glass. Watson made no effort to stop the ball and outfielder Charley Jamieson did a couple of somersaults before he retrieved the ball. He finally threw the ball to second and Nick neglected the formality of touching the base and also failed to touch third. Catcher Cy Perkins made no effort to take the throw at the plate and when umpire Billy Evans called Nick safe it went for a home run and sent the crowd of 10,000 into hysterics. It was the seventy-fourth home game for the Senators and Altrock's joke home run was the only one credited to a Washington player in its home park. After the game ended, General Peyton C. March threw out the last ball as it was called by announcer E. Lawrence Phillips "until we reach Berlin." The band played "Auld Lang Syne" and the crowd rose and sang.

Teammates Lajoie and Flick in fist fight in 1900

Hall of Famers Nap Lajoie and Elmer Flick were hard-hitters with the Philadelphia Phillies from 1898 through 1900. On May 31, 1900, Lajoie and Flick were missing from the Phils lineup and the club issued a statement that they were injured in morning practice. It finally came out that they had engaged in a fist fight and that Lajoie had broken his thumb and received a black eye. After the fight Flick left the clubhouse, vowing he would not play again with the team. Manager Bill Shettsline, in admitting the cause of the absence of the two star players, stated that Flick had changed his mind and would play in the game that day but that Lajoie, with a broken hand, would not be able to play for several weeks.

Long absence in majors no handicap to Gowdy

After a long playing career in the majors with New York and Boston in the National League from 1910 to 1925, Hank Gowdy came back to the Braves as a coach in 1929. On August 18 that year Hank was asked to go behind the bat in a regular league game against Cincinnati. Hank was just six days shy of his 40th birthday and had not taken part in a big league game for four years. Gowdy, who had led the Miracle Braves to a four-game World Series sweep over the Philadelphia Athletics in 1914 with a .545 batting average, and who was the first major league player to enlist in the army in World War I, played like he was still in his prime. He was 4 for 4 at bat with one RBI, and threw out the only runner to attempt to steal a base as the Braves outlasted the Reds, 10-9.

Satriano had to homer twice for first major hit

Tom Satriano joined the expansion Los Angeles Angels straight off the campus of the University of California in 1961. He played in 35 games and batted .198 with one home run in 96 times at bat. Satriano's first hit was a home run, but after hitting it in only his fourth time at bat in the majors he had to be very disappointed when the contest was called before being an official game. The game was played at Baltimore on Sunday, August 6, 1961. Satriano hit his home run off Dick Hall in the third inning, but the contest was rained out in the same frame. Six days later, at Cleveland, Satriano finally got credit for his first hit to go into the records and again it was a home run, this time off Jim (Mudcat) Grant.

Accepts raise reluctantly and has great year

Pitcher Jack Coombs won twelve games and lost eleven for the Philadelphia Athletics in 1909. He was given a raise for 1910 but declined it, saying that he did not think his record in 1909 entitled him to any raise. Club president Ben Shibe, however, insisted that Coombs accept the increase, but he must have been very surprised to learn of the pitcher's attitude. The Athletics certainly got the best of the deal as Coombs posted a sensational record for the 1910 American League pennant winners. He won thirty-one games against only nine defeats while setting a league record of thirteen shutouts. He went on to lead the A's to victory over the Chicago Cubs in the World Series, winning three complete games as the Athletics took four of the five games.

Baseball and the Law

Whereas baseball was and is intended for the enjoyment of all and,
Whereas Willie Mays thrilled millions with incontrovertible skills and,
Whereas runs and rallies render boredom "void on its face",
Be it resolved that baseball will never be devitalized.

Articles of Agreement:

3 strikes	9 frames
3 outs	0 clock
2 teams	1 affirmative decision
0 pepper	

Argue the truth? Argue the evidence!
The evidence: thousands attend per game from Boston to LA.
The experience: warm wind, a white sphere, a rounded bat.

500-foot homers	dubious
babies in mezzanine?	dormant
fan dissatisfaction?	inadmissable

In the World Series, Bronx, New York

In Re the Game of baseball: }
                                               }
Tony Kubek, ss   }
Bobby Richardson, 2b   }
Tom Tresh, of   }
Mickey Mantle, of   }
Roger Maris, of   }   October 2, 1963
                                               }
et al.   }
                                               }
-vs-   }
                                               }
Sandy Koufax, p   }

the people having heard the evidence and testimony of the parties (duly sworn and examined in open Stadium); and considering all the evidence and being fully advised in the premises,

FIND AS FOLLOWS

1. that the American people are now, and have been for more than 140 years, lovers of the game of baseball.
Batter up, and hold us all harmless!

witnesseth:

Edward R. Ward